The Westminster Pulpit

VOLUME I

THE Westminster Pulpit

VOLUME I

The Preaching of

G. CAMPBELL MORGAN

WIPF & STOCK · Eugene, Oregon

Wipf and Stock Publishers
199 W 8th Ave, Suite 3
Eugene, OR 97401

The Westminster Pulpit vol. I
The Preaching of G. Campbell Morgan
By Morgan, G. Campbell
Copyright©1954 by Morgan, G. Campbell
ISBN 13: 978-1-60899-304-8
Publication date 1/1/2012
Previously published by Fleming H. Revell, Co., 1954

CONTENTS

CHAPTER		PAGE
I	THE LIMITATIONS OF LIBERTY	13
II	CHRIST IN YOU THE HOPE OF GLORY	24
III	THE TERMS OF DISCIPLESHIP	33
IV	THE POTTER'S WORK ON THE WHEELS	46
V	DWELLERS IN FIRE	58
VI	THE AUTHORITY OF JESUS	71
VII	THE BURNING OF HEART	85
VIII	BACKSLIDING	97
IX	MY FRIEND	111
X	AMAZING LOVE	125
XI	IF CHRIST DID NOT RISE—WHAT THEN?	139
XII	THE SPIRIT'S TESTIMONY TO THE WORLD	153
XIII	THE FRUIT OF THE SPIRIT	166
XIV	THE SPIRIT OF LIFE	180
XV	THE SIFTING OF PETER	190
XVI	THE TURNING AGAIN OF PETER	204
XVII	LOVE'S PROOF AND PRIZE	218
XVIII	THE LACK OF THE SPIRIT	230
XIX	HIS WORKMANSHIP	242
XX	THE CHILDREN'S PLAYGROUND IN THE CITY OF GOD	256
XXI	A PROFOUND QUESTION	270
XXII	ABILITY FOR DISABILITY	284
XXIII	THE PURPOSE OF THE ADVENT:	
	1. TO DESTROY THE WORKS OF THE DEVIL	298

CHAPTER		PAGE
XXIV	THE PURPOSE OF THE ADVENT:	
	2. TO TAKE AWAY SINS	312
XXV	THE PURPOSE OF THE ADVENT:	
	3. TO REVEAL THE FATHER	326
XXVI	THE PURPOSE OF THE ADVENT:	
	4. TO PREPARE FOR A SECOND ADVENT	339

INTRODUCTION

FOR FORTY YEARS, BEGINNING IN THE FIRST DECADE OF OUR CENtury, the entire Christian world acknowledged that the greatest Biblical expositor known in the pulpits of both England and America was Dr. G. Campbell Morgan. As far back as 1896, when Dr. Morgan was only thirty-three years old, D. L. Moody, who knew most of the great preachers of the Western world, brought him to the Moody Bible Institute to lecture. In 1904, at the age of forty-one, Dr. Morgan went to London to begin the most epochal ministry of Biblical exposition, covering a thirteen-year period, that London had witnessed for a century. I am speaking here strictly of Biblical exposition, not simply preaching or Gospel preaching, though Dr. Morgan could preach the Gospel with tremendous power. I am fully aware that for many years Charles H. Spurgeon drew larger crowds and that Canon Liddon was recognized as the greatest preacher of London in his day (his ministry at St. Paul's having closed a few years before Dr. Morgan came) and that there was a certain brilliance about Joseph Parker (whose ministry at City Temple also closed just before Dr. Morgan came to Westminster Chapel); but I must say that for sheer Biblical exposition Dr. Morgan stood above all of his contemporaries.

It was not long before Westminster Chapel, seating some 2,500 persons, was filled to the second gallery. Soon after coming to London Dr. Morgan began his famous Friday night Bible class, probably the largest and most fruitful Bible class London had ever seen, when, week after week, with notebooks and Bibles, from 1,500 to 1,700 people moved across that great city to sit for an hour at the feet of this master teacher.

Dr. Morgan began to publish books as early as 1897, when thirty-four years of age, with his little book, *Discipleship*. In 1903 appeared what is probably his greatest work, *The Crises of the Christ*—a volume that every minister should read and study early in his life as a preacher. Altogether, more than seventy volumes came from his pen. The greatest series of pulpit messages for which he was responsible are those which appeared in what was entitled, "The Westminster Pulpit." These appeared annually for about forty Sundays each year from 1906 to 1916. Here are the foundations of many of Dr. Morgan's books. These volumes contain some of the greatest Biblical preaching of the twentieth century. Now they are exceedingly scarce. In twenty years I have known only one volume of the series to appear in any catalogue of secondhand books. The set just cannot be purchased. The Fleming H. Revell Company, therefore, deserves the deepest gratitude of all ministers of our generation for making these glorious messages available once again.

In rereading these messages and remembering the unique ministry of Dr. Morgan, one cannot help but ask, "What made G. Campbell Morgan the greatest Bible expositor of his day? Why was it that in his prime he could draw more people with sheer Biblical exposition than any other man in the Western world?" In the first place, he gave himself utterly to the Word of God day and night. He himself said in 1937, "I began to read and study the Bible in 1883, and I have been a student ever since, and I still am." Once he told a close friend that when he was asked by young ministers what was the secret of his success, he replied, "I always say to them the same thing—work, hard work, work." The title of one of his greatest books, *The Ministry of the Word*, might be taken as the clue to all he did.

I have always felt that of all the various gifts named in the New Testament Dr. Morgan possessed two: he was both teacher and prophet. In addition, there was something about his public ministry that we can only call magnetic, which Jill Morgan (Mrs. K. J. Morgan), in the truly great life of her father-in-law, *A Man of the Word*, refers to as "the intangible atmosphere of union between teacher and taught." Still vivid in my mind are those winter afternoons in Baltimore, now a quarter of a century past, when I heard Dr. Morgan unfold the opening chapters of Luke's Gospel: we felt a tenseness, a magnetic pull, a lift, an atmosphere saturated with terrific intensity; our souls were confronted with eternal and transforming truths that sent us out of that sanctuary cleansed, ennobled and determined to go back to the Book. I have been moved by others, in one way or another, but no Bible teacher in the world, in the twentieth century, could cast over his audience, without flash, without show, that mystic spell that Campbell Morgan cast when he was at his best. In reverence, I think it can be truly said that after attending one of Dr. Campbell Morgan's meetings, a most appropriate comment would have been to quote the words of the two disciples returning to Jerusalem from the walk to Emmaus with our Lord, "Did not our hearts burn within us while he talked with us by the way and while he opened to us the scriptures?"

This very day in which I am writing this introduction a letter came to my desk from a faithful Christian worker of years of service in our country who had gone to a Bible Conference for greatly needed spiritual refreshing, but had found only a deadness in the meetings and the poorest kind of spiritual food, which led this servant to ask, "What is happening in the Christian Church today?" How wonderful it would be if the republication of Campbell Morgan's masterly, moving, Biblical, passion-born messages should be used of God to lead hundreds of ministers into a new life of the study of the Word of God, if they could be led to say, with the Apostles of old, "We will give ourselves continually to prayer and to the ministry of the word."

Fuller Theological Seminary
Pasadena, California

WILBUR M. SMITH

THE
Westminster
Pulpit

VOLUME I

CHAPTER I

THE LIMITATIONS OF LIBERTY

All things are lawful for me; but not all things are expedient. All things are lawful for me; but I will not be brought under the power of any.
I CORINTHIANS 6:12.

All things are lawful; but not all things are expedient. All things are lawful; but not all things edify.
I CORINTHIANS 10:23.

THE APOSTLE PAUL WAS PRE-EMINENTLY THE APOLOGIST OF Christianity. His mind was naturally alive to all the thinking of his own age. Its Hebrew training made him familiar with the highest religious conceptions. Its Roman sympathy caused his vision of empire. Its Greek interest made him conscious of the philosophies of the intellectual world. Yet his relation to Christ affected, rather than was affected by, all these things. To him the essential in each was included in the Lordship of Jesus and thereby redeemed. His message, therefore, was perpetually paradoxical, as he admitted, and then denied the ideals of his own age. He was the uncompromising foe of the tyranny of the Hebrew priests, and yet he argued passionately for the priesthood of the saints. He most evidently admired the far-reaching splendor of the Roman Empire, but for him it needed correcting, until it should become a commonwealth, answering the law of One Head and feeling with the fervor of one heart. He was captivated by the analyses of life and the mysteries of the Greek philosophies, but for him the former needed restoration to naturalness, and the latter purification by light. In Christ this man found the truth lying at the base of all error, and his teaching was uniformly directed to the work of correcting error by the declaration of the truth. It is this method which obtains in the two verses which I have read as text. They occur in a letter written for the correction of the life of a Christian Church in a Greek city. This letter reflects as in a mirror the conditions obtaining in Corinth at the time. The false conditions in the Church were caused by the fact that the Church had passed under the influence of the city. In the divisions which had sprung out of discussions around the "wisdom of words" is seen the counterpart of the philosophic discussions then obtaining in Corinth. The lack of discipline which was cursing the Church was the reflex of the toleration of impurity in the life of the city. In the lawsuit which the Apostle condemned I see the shadow of the ceaseless litigation which had become almost a method of amusement in the Greek cities. The prevalent impurity within the Church which he so sternly denounced was possible in the atmosphere of the corrupt life of the city. The disorderly observance of the Lord's Supper by these Christians reflects the degradation of religious rite and ceremony in the Greek temples. In the violation of love against which he so strongly protested is manifest the selfishness prevalent among men outside. Finally, in the difficulties about the resurrection which he combatted in so stately and magnificent an argument, is discoverable the effect in the thinking of the Christian people, of the materialization of ideals which characterized Greek thought. The cause of these conditions of life was very largely the Greek conception that man was independent of all law external to himself. This was the Greek idea of liberty. It was expressed in a proverb which, being translated, runs: "Man is the measure of all things." Within the circumference of that conception men were living and claiming liberty, declaring all things were lawful unto them. It was a doctrine of liberty. Paul affirmed it, and corrected it. When the Greek philosopher declared all things were lawful, Paul answered, "All things are lawful for me; but—"

There are two matters for our consideration. First, the Christian affirmation of liberty—"All things are lawful." Secondly, the Christian description of limitation—"All things are lawful; but—" First, then, the Christian affirmation of liberty—"All things are lawful." Notice the inclusiveness of the affirmation. Here I must trespass on your patience while we look carefully at words, for if words be indeed the channels through which truth is conveyed, we need carefully to examine them, or we may miss the truth they are intended to convey. The Apostle made use of one word, *panta*. We must understand what it means if we are to perfectly realize the measurement of Christian liberty. It is the plural form of a Greek word which simply means "all." Theyer tells us that when the word stands in the plural without the article, it means all things of a certain definite totality, or the sum of things, the context showing what things are meant. In this Epistle the expression "all things" occurs no less than thirty times, and every time it is necessary, according to Theyer, to interpret the meaning by the context. I have been making a careful selection of the occasions in which the widest use is made of "all things," and I shall ask you to traverse the ground in order that we may know what the Apostle meant thereby.

First, let us remember that when the Greek used this phrase and declared "all things are lawful," he referred to the sum total of material things and moral values, and all the forces of life of which he was conscious. How, then, did Paul use the term "all things"? We are not left to speculation. In the third chapter is his own definition. "Wherefore let no man glory in men. For all things are yours," and then there is a parenthesis evident in the fact that the main argument is taken up at the twenty-third verse, so that if you read directly from that central word of the twenty-first verse to the end of the twenty-third verse, you will find the main statement, "All things are yours . . . and ye are Christ's; and Christ is God's." Between the first affirmation, "All things are yours," and the latter words there is Paul's exposition of his own use of the phrase, "all things" "whether Paul, or Apollos, or Cephas, or the world, or life, or death, or things present, or things to come." Not only, therefore, does the Apostle include all that the Greek philosopher included, but he sweeps out into a realm that far transcended anything that the Greek philosopher saw or understood. "All things are yours; whether Paul, or Apollos, or Cephas." The naming of these men is the naming of emphases of truth for which they stood. Every system of thought is yours. Again, "the world" is yours, with all its forces, and its movements. And "life," which you are perpetually attempting to analyze and account for; and "death," which to you is but a cessation of life, and a mystery, both are yours, that is "things present," an inclusive phrase which is the boundary of the thinking of the Greek philosopher; and things to come, which Greek philosophy denies, but which Paul includes in his "all things." Thus, when Paul wrote, "all things are lawful to me," he included all the schools of thought, and the world, and life, and death, and things present, and things to come. Then notice the claim in its nature as well as in its inclusiveness, "All things are lawful." Here, again, we take the word "lawful," and ask what its real meaning is. The root idea of the word is that of being out upon the public highway. It is the opposite of imprisoned. With regard to all things, I have liberty, I am not in prison, I am not shut away from any of them. I am on the great highway walking amidst them, and I am free. I have power and authority in respect to these things; they are permitted to me. He thus affirmed the freedom of the Christian man with regard to all things in the universe of God—material, moral, and spiritual. If we are to understand what the Apostle means there must be contextual exposition. You will find in the fifteenth verse of the second chapter a principle of discrimination. "He that is spiritual judgeth *all things*." The Christian man in the midst of things lawful to him does not take them promiscuously, but with discernment. He puts upon things lawful to him the measurement of the infinite. He that is spiritual judgeth or discerneth all things. Further on, we have a balance of relationship. "*All things are yours*" is not his last word, for he adds, "and ye are Christ's and Christ is God's." The final thing for the Christian man is not the all things which are lawful, but the Christ who reigns over him, and God Who is at the back of the Christ. It is a great cosmic conception which the Apostle gives us here. First, the infinite God, then Christ, then the Christian man, and, finally, all things stretching out beyond him, the man recognizing that he is crowned in the midst of all things, but never forgetting that he must exercise the principle of discrimination in dealing with them.

Then, in the eighth chapter at the sixth verse, is a great philosophy of the universe. "Yet to us there is one God, the Father, of whom are *all things*, and we unto Him." I go a little further, and I see this cosmic conception still dominating his thought, for in chapter nine and verse twenty-five I read, "And every man that striveth in the games is temperate in *all things*. Now they do it to receive a corruptible crown; but we an incorruptible." That defines the attitude of Christian endeavor in the midst of *all things*. In the tenth chapter at the thirty-first verse, "Whether therefore ye eat, or drink, or whatsoever ye do, do *all* to the glory of God." This is the law of action in the midst of the *all things* which are lawful. At last, in the twenty-seventh and twenty-eighth verses of chapter fifteen, I find Paul's vision of consummation. "He put *all things* in subjection under His feet. But when He saith, *All things* are put in subjection, it is evident that He is excepted who did subject *all things* unto Him. And when *all things* have been subjected unto Him, then shall the Son also Himself be subjected to Him that did subject *all things* unto Him, that God may be *all things* in *all things*." That is one of the most magnificent and stately passages in the whole of the Apostolic writings, and I can only hope that its majesty may break upon our consciousness as we read it. If we take these passages—and I am perfectly conscious that what I am saying is calculated rather to provoke thought, after the service, for I cannot cover all the ground tonight—we shall discover the Apostle's conception of *"all things."* It is as wide as the universe. It sets the horizon far back and widens the outlook, making the magnificence of Greek philosophy appear poor in comparison with the tremendous sweep of the Christian conception. Standing related to all, he says, "All things are lawful for me." There is nothing essential to the universe that I have not liberty to use. By hint and suggestion, he shows the relationship existing in the universe—God, Christ, the Christian man, and everything beyond him. He declares the direction that everything is taking in the universe, *all things* centering in the Christ, to be finally presented to the Father, until at last God shall be in all things, and all things shall find in God their perfect fruition. I interpret the Apostle's word only by his own writing; I would not have dared to say he meant so much if I had not taken all his argument and followed the movement of the phrase to this great consummation. The Christian man stands at the center of the universe, of the present and the coming things, known and unknown, material and moral and spiritual, and he is Christ's and Christ is God's.

Now notice the limitation of Christian liberty. It is threefold—

". . . But not all things are expedient."
". . . But I will not be brought under the power of any."
". . . But not all things build up."

This is the threefold test of how far I may use the things lawful. The test of personal progress—not all things are expedient. The test of authority—I will not be brought under the power of any. The test of social relationship—not all things build up.

First, the test of personal progress. Not all things are expedient. I think the word is almost unfortunate, not in its first meaning but in its present-day use. We have come to speak of a thing as being expedient when it is a thing that pays, without reference to principle. That is the degradation of the word. The word simply means foot free, set at liberty. The figurative idea of the word is that of freedom to make progress upon a pathway. The thing that is expedient is the thing that hastens the traveler upon his journey. The Greek word means "to carry together," that is, to co-operate, and the best translation you can possibly have of the word is "profitable." The profitableness is to be tested by the lawfulness already considered. Paul stands in the center of the universe, and he says all things are lawful to me. Art is lawful; also music, science, games, meats—all are lawful. But some of the things that are lawful are not expedient; they will not hasten the running; they will not minister to the progress; they will not make for development into perfect union with the cosmic order, which centers in Christ and God. That is the first principle as to the thing we may do, or may not do. There are a thousand things lawful to me in London that are not expedient, that will not help in my progress, that will not make me any stronger for the ultimate issue—things that will not minister to my strength for co-operation with Christ and God. All things are lawful, but not all things are expedient. Something is expedient for you that is not expedient for me; something is expedient for me that is not expedient for you. Every man stands alone in the great cosmic order, and every man must find his own relationship to lawful things, first by this principle: Is this something which ministers to my development so that I may fill my place in God's ultimate will and intention?

Secondly, there is the test of authority. "I will not be brought under the power of any." As a matter of fact, in the Greek there is here a distinct play on words which is not apparent in translation, nor is it possible to express it in English exactly. I may suggest it by saying, All things are in my *power*, but I will not be brought under the *power* of any, or perhaps by saying, All things are *permitted* me, but I will not ask *permission* of any. Here, again, is a great principle. The man submitted to Christ must submit to nothing else. The man under the authority of Christ must have no other authority over his life. Man must test relationship to all things by this principle, this thing is lawful but it must not master me. This thing comes within the scope of the universe, into which I am brought to have dominion over, never to be dominated by. Perhaps if I leave the principle there it is hardly helpful, so I take a simple illustration or two. What is the true relation of the Christian man to money? Money is lawful, but I will not be brought under the power of money. What is the relation of the Christian man to knowledge? Knowledge is lawful, but I will not be a slave of knowledge. What is the relation of the Christian man to love? Love is lawful to me, but I will not be brought under the power of love. The Christian man asserts his liberty by recognizing its limitations; his liberty to use anything perishes when the thing he uses becomes his master and he becomes its slave. This is a wonderfully searching principle if we will but have it so. This thing is lawful to me, but if this thing, habit or friendship, or manner of thinking, or passion of living, masters me, then have I not lost my liberty? And is not the fact that a man loses his liberty when he is brought under the power of anything a revelation of the necessity for the testing of liberty by this principle? I sometimes think I would have these words, "All things are lawful for me; but I will not be brought under the power of any," printed so that every young man could see them rather than any others. All things are yours, but ye are Christ's. Keep that balance of relationship and you are safe; change it and you are in peril. One is your Master, even Christ, and all things are lawful to you, but you must not let them master you; for if once the innocent, legitimate, proper thing becomes master it is no longer innocent, it is absolutely illegitimate, it is unutterably improper. Love, for father, mother, wife or child, becomes improper when a man is so brought under the power of it that he no longer yields first allegiance to the throne of the Christ and the throne of God.

One other test: "Not all things build up." That is the test of social relationship, and my reason for saying so is the context. "Let no man seek his own, but each his neighbor's good." Here, again, is a limit on my liberty. All things are mine, but there are some things which if I take and use I shall not build my neighbor up by so doing. Such things are not lawful. I beseech you notice carefully that this goes infinitely beyond what the Apostle has said in another letter, "Destroy not thy brother, for whom Christ died." This is more. He not merely says that the thing which is lawful to me becomes unlawful if it destroys my brother, but that the thing which is lawful to me becomes unlawful if it does not build up my brother. As a Christian man I am to recognize that over me are Christ and God, and under me all things—Paul, Apollos, Cephas, the world, and life and death, things present and things to come; but I am not to indulge in any of them save as I bear in mind that side by side with the necessity for my own advancement is the necessity for contributing to the building up of my brother's strength, and the thing that builds not up is not lawful to a Christian man.

This great affirmation of the Apostle makes it necessary for us as Christian men to assert our liberty, our possession of all things. That man is sadly mistaken who imagines that we as Christian men are excluded from anything that is essential to the universe of God. *All things are lawful.* We make a yet more terrible mistake if we imagine that we may exercise our liberty by indiscriminate use of the things that are lawful. The tender, strong love of God in Christ lays restrictions on our liberty; first, things lawful are to be exercised for our progress toward Christ's consummation; secondly, things lawful are to be kept under us while we are under Christ; and, finally, in the great, far-stretching universe, in which all things are lawful, we make illicit use of the lawful things if we ever forget for a passing moment that we cannot live alone, that our brother's life and our brother's edification are part of our responsibility. I thank God for the breadth and the narrowness of Christian liberty, and I pray that we may ever remember that there are limits to the liberty wherewith Christ has made us free, and that to keep within the limits is to live in spacious liberty.

CHAPTER II

CHRIST IN YOU, THE HOPE OF GLORY

. . . to whom God was pleased to make known what is the riches of the glory of this mystery among the Gentiles, which is Christ in you, the hope of glory . . .
COLOSSIANS 1:27.

THE TEXT IS PART OF A GREAT ARGUMENT. THE WORDS describe the central of three mysteries, which yet are not three but one. By way of introduction, let us notice the relation of these words to the context.

The Apostle in this epistle deals pre-eminently with the glories of Christ, and with these as at the disposal of the Church. The principal declarations of the epistle are, firstly, "It pleased the Father that in Him should all fulness dwell"; and, secondly, "Ye are complete in Him."

In the paragraph in which the text occurs the Apostle uses the word "mystery" three times. In verse 24, he says, "I rejoice in my sufferings for your sake, and fill up on my part that which is lacking of the afflictions of Christ in my flesh for His body's sake, which is the Church"; omitting verse 25, which as to argument is in parenthesis, we read again in verse 26, "Even the *mystery* which hath been hid from ages and generations." Then, in verse 27, the words of our text, "God was pleased to make known what is the riches of the glory of this *mystery* among the Gentiles, which is Christ in you, the hope of glory." Then, in the second chapter, and the second verse, "Unto all riches of the full assurance of understanding, that they may know the *mystery* of God, even Christ."

First, the Church, the *mystery* hid from the ages; secondly, this *mystery*, Christ in you, the hope of glory; finally, the *mystery* of God, even Christ. The word "mystery" has a uniform sense in the New Testament, and that sense has been most lucidly expressed by Dr. Handley Moule: "A mystery is a truth undiscoverable, except by revelation. Never necessarily, as our popular use of the word may suggest, a thing unintelligible or perplexing in itself. In Scripture a mystery may be a fact which, when revealed, we cannot understand in detail, though we can know it and act upon it. A mystery is a thing only to be known when revealed." If that definition of the use of the word "mystery" in the New Testament be accepted, the Apostle speaks of the Church as hidden in past ages, and never discovered until revealed.

He then passes behind the mystery of the Church and comes to the words of my text, "Christ in you, the hope of glory." The Church consists of souls in whom Christ has had a personal advent, and in whom He lives. This is another mystery, never to be explained by the unspiritual, never to be perfectly explained by the spiritual. The mystery of individual souls in whom Christ dwells lies at the back of the mystery of the Church.

Then, presently, he passes on, still following his argument, until he comes to the yet deeper mystery, the mystery of God, which is Christ. In order to see the connection let us take these in the other order. The first great mystery of God is Christ Himself. The central mystery of Christianity is that of Christ formed in individual souls. The final mystery is that of the Church of God fulfilling high and holy functions throughout all ages.

Now, out of the great sweep of that argument we take the central words, and turn from the things introducing, and the things issuing, that we may consider the central mystery of the Christian faith, which is thus expressed by the Apostle, "Christ in you, the hope of glory."

The first and second advents of our Lord initiate and perfect this mystery of the realization of Christ in the individual life of the trusting soul. In His first advent He came to atone, to make possible His entrance. At His second advent He will come to perfect His possession of individual life. I share in the atonement of the first advent and the perfecting of the second advent if he have His advent in my personal life.

Our rejoicing in His first advent, and our gladness in the hope of the second advent, are alike due to the mystery of His personal coming into our own life. Let us consider that central advent, first as to the fact suggested, then as to the experience resulting. First, "Christ in you"; and, secondly, "the hope of glory."

"Christ in you." It is significant that at this point the Apostle uses the title rather than the name of our Lord. This indicates the inclusion of the Person and His work. There is no one perfectly sure of Jesus Christ in history unless he is sure of Him in experience. No one can have a final demonstration of truth concerning the nature of Christ or His work save as he can say, I know Christ because He is in me. It may be said that this is mystical, and cannot be explained to the scientific age in which we live. That is perfectly true. That is what the Apostle says. It is a mystery; this presence in the individual life of Christ Himself in all the marvelous glory of His Person as Very God and Very Man. Human sympathy, human love, human purity, and human power, all surcharged with those infinite resources of God, which made Him as man perfect Victor, are present in all in whom He is formed, eventually and through processes, to make them equally victorious with Himself. It is a mystery, but if it be a mystery that cannot be explained to the scientific age it is a fact known in the lives of countless multitudes.

Christ in me—and I need hardly apologize for testimony at this point, for speaking rather as a witness than an advocate —Christ in me is the most certain thing in all my personal experience. He is present in my inner life, so that I have not to ascend to heaven to find Him or descend into the depths to bring Him up. Neither have I to go on long pilgrimages to reach Him. Amid the hurry and rush of the day, the Christ is within. He was not always there. He came by the act of the Spirit when I fulfilled the conditions of the Word, but His advent was positive, and His presence is as real as, and more real to me than, the advent long ago in the Judean country far away. The historic is proved by the experimental.

As I have already said, the use of the title suggests not merely the presence of the Person in the life, it suggests also the work of Christ in you. He was at once Prophet, Priest, and King. "Christ in you," the one Prophet and Teacher by whom the whole life is to be governed and ordered, whose philosophy is the only philosophy, whose teaching is the only teaching which the soul trusts. "Christ in you," also as Priest, the one perfect Saviour, operating in the inner shrine of the indivudual life on the altar, and by the way of sacrifice, so that through the intermediation, not of Christ far off, but in me, I have personal and immediate access to the Presence of God, which is both within and encompassing me. Then "Christ in you" also as King, ruling all the life, not by the law of carnal ordinances, written on tables of stone, but by the perpetual inspiration of His indwelling presence.

This is the essential, personal, individual miracle of Christianity. Christ within, the Prophet, teaching so that I need no man to teach me. Christ within, the Priest, so that I need no other priest and need take no pilgrimage to find a shrine of worship. It is in my own life, for He is there. Christ within, as King, so that I bow the knee to no scepter and no throne, except to such as He authorizes.

"Christ in you." That is the great miracle, the great mystery, the individual fact on which all the other facts of Christianity are based, and through which the other forces of Christianity become operative in the history of man. Christ in me—the Christ light—so that I see with His eyes. Christ in me—the Christ aspiration—so that I desire with His desire. Christ in me—the Christ impulse—so that I am driven as He was driven. Christ in me—the Christ consciousness—so that the world's sin burdens me in the same fashion as it burdened Him, and the world's agony hurts me as the world's agony hurt Him.

What is a Christian man? A "Christo-centric" man is a man in whom Christ is enthroned at the center of personality, not as a sentiment, but as a Person; not as an ideal without, but as a dynamic at work within.

What is the issue as to the Christ and as to myself? As to the Christ, He gains in every soul He indwells an inheritance. As to the indwelt soul, that soul gains in the Christ an inheritance. If that statement seems to be almost unbelievable it is but the teaching of the Word, and the experience of the soul answers it and seals it true. Is Christ formed in you? Hear me, for I speak with great reverence, and yet with all boldness—that Christ is richer for having you. That is the individual application of the magnificent argument of the Ephesian epistle in which Paul tells us plainly that God gains an inheritance in the saints. But what does Christ gain in you? He gains an instrument through which He can flash His light upon some other dark soul. He gains a medium through which He is able to touch with healing other wounded spirits. He gains a channel through which He is able to move out in the grace of healing to other wounded hearts. He gains whatever He comes to possess. By His advent nineteen hundred years ago He came to claim the wide world, and He will never cease to work until He has absolutely won it and subdued it. There may be other methods ahead. There may be other dispensations. But, believe me, He will not fail or be discouraged until He hath set His judgment in the earth, and answered the waiting isles with His own law. But if I am to be—oh, matchless miracle of grace—the means and medium of manifestation what do I gain? I gain all His resources, for I have fellowship with Him in all the larger purposes of His life.

Now let us turn to the experience resulting, "the hope of glory." The word "glory" here refers to the great consummation in which God's purposes are to be perfectly fulfilled; in which Christ, seeing the travail of His soul, is to be satisfied; in which the Church, with one voice of perfect song, will say, "Thou, O Christ, art all I want"; and in which the whole creation, which is still waiting in its groaning for the manifestation of the sons of God, will find its groaning cease, and join the chorus of praise to Him who sits upon the throne. God's glory consists in the realization of the purpose of His love in all that His hands have made. Christ in you is the hope of this glory. What is hope? I often wish we bore in mind more carefully the real significance of the good old Anglo-Saxon word "hope." It does not mean foundationless expectation, but rather confidence in something yet to be, with an accompanying endeavor to reach it.

Christ in you is the hope of glory. Christ in you creates the consciousness of the better thing to be. Christ in you drives you with perpetual passion towards its realization. Christ in you is the one unanswerable evidence of the ultimate victory. He is always singing the song of the future. He is also always energizing the effort of the present. Is there anything we need more today than to hear the anthem of the indwelling Christ telling us of the victory that is yet to be? It is a wonderful thing how in the history of the race, whenever men have really climbed the mountain heights and looked out, they have sung. Great dirges have been uttered, but always in the valleys, and they have their place. But all the seers, the prophets, and the psalmists in all human history and literature, when they have climbed have begun to sing. The dream of the golden age is part of humanity's inheritance from God, and, notwithstanding the fact of man's sin, has never been utterly obliterated. It has been caricatured, and men have drawn us the most curious pictures of the age to be, from Moore's *Utopia* to Bellamy's *Looking Back*. Yet underneath the mistaken interpretation is the passion for something better and the belief in its possibility. If Jesus Christ had not come into the world all these songs would have ceased long ago. They had well-nigh ceased when He came. The Hebrew nation had produced no prophet for four hundred years. They had been years of hopeless despair in Judaism, and the great thinkers and the great hopers of the world had lost hope. The Greek teachers had said, and it was their final word, We can only ask questions; we wait for another to answer them. So said Plato, and so said Socrates. But Jesus came to little Bethlehem, and angels brought the music again that men had lost, and it has continued through the centuries, permeating the literature of all civilized people. Men are singing of "a good time coming," of which they would not have dreamed if our Christ had not come to start them singing again. He has started the music, and all the world hears it, and yet it never becomes perfectly articulate, perfectly harmonious, until He sings it in the individual life. Thank

God for the company in whose lives Christ is singing the anthem of His coming victory. We are in the midst of the smoke and din of battle. There are days when we sit and fold our hands and say, "Where is the promise of His coming?" No Christian man has ever wailed that out but that presently there came singing back through his soul the answer of the Christ. When I face human agony, and am appalled by the suffering of humanity, the Christ in me says, "I know all the pain better than thou. I have trodden the *via dolorosa* alone, and as out of My cross and suffering there sprang the light and glory of the first resurrection morning, so through the suffering and sorrow of humanity at last I will lead them into the light." Then I go back and pick up my piece of work again. Christ in me is the hope of glory; the anthem of the ultimate in my soul is perpetually the inspiration of the present.

But "Christ in you, the hope of glory" means a great deal more than that He sings an anthem of the future. That would be a poor thing by comparison. That in some senses is what other men did in other ages of the world's history. But the great value of my text is that Christ is in me as hope; not merely in the sense of expectation, but in the sense of endeavor, Christ energizes the present.

He who gives us a vision of the ultimate as He sings the anthem of it in our heart is present to deal with all the forces which oppose. When I say to men, "God loves you," I say it, first of all, because He sings it in my heart, but I say it knowing that when I say it He will clothe my poor word with the power of God, and men will know it is true because He says it through me.

If there be a larger outlook and application than this, and surely there is—if the hope of glory means that at last the wrongs will be righted, and the tyrannies broken, the despotisms spoiled, and humanity delivered, then remember that Christ in me means power in me to help to bring it to pass. I am renegade if I sit still and listen to His singing and do not co-operate in His effort.

The song of the coming victory is the call to present battle, but it is, moreover, power for the fray, ability to accomplish. So the real optimist is the man in whom Christ is singing and Christ is driving. He is not a superficial optimist. He does not shut his eyes to evil and say there is none, but he looks through it. Take up your letter to the Romans, and there is not a more optimistic book in the whole Bible. Its grand song is "rejoicing in hope of the glory." The man who wrote Romans was not a man who shut his eyes to existing evils and said things were better and there was nothing to trouble about. If you want to know what evil is at its worst read the first chapter. The Christian man is the man in whom Christ dwells, and who, therefore, has Christ's vision; and Christ was the Man who said to His own generation, "Ye are an evil generation," and yet who died to master the evil and redeem the generations and set up the city of God. So if the great untold mystery of God in Christ has become the personal mystery of Christ in me, then what? Then I see with His eyes all the evil, and evil is never so devilish to the conscience as when eyes anointed with Christ's life look out on it. But that is not the ultimate thing. What is the ultimate thing? It is that He who came to destroy the works of the devil will destroy them in me. He who came to destroy them throughout all the round world until His kingdom is established cannot fail.

His victory is assured. The song of it is in our hearts. God help us to answer the call of the song and hasten the triumph.

CHAPTER III

THE TERMS OF DISCIPLESHIP

If any man would come after Me, let him deny himself, and take up his cross, and follow Me.
MATTHEW 16:24.

So therefore whosoever he be of you that renounceth not all that he hath, he cannot be My disciple.
LUKE 14:33.

IN THE WORDS OF JESUS, PRESERVED FOR US IN THE RECORDS, there are two elements perpetually noticeable. There is that with which, perhaps, we are most familiar—the element of tenderness, of gentleness, or, as it has been very often recently described, the wooing note. But there is also manifest another element—that of severity, the element which sometimes seems almost to amount to harshness of expression, or, in contrast with the phrase already referred to, the element which may be described as the warning note.

These are also to be found in the story of the influence He exerted upon His own age, and in the influence He has exerted on every successive age, as well as in the influence which He is exerting today.

Jesus was and is the most attractive personality that the world has ever known. Yet, both when He was in our world in earthly form, and by His spiritual presence in every successive century, He has repelled the men He attracted—whispering, on the one hand, to the sorrow-burdened heart of humanity words so full of mother love and father love as to make men crowd and press round Him, and then, on the other hand, suddenly speaking words that flash and scorch and burn until men draw back in astonishment.

Let us think of this apparent contradiction a little more closely. The fact of the attractiveness of Jesus needs no argument today. The story of the life of Jesus as set forth in the four Gospels is the story of One Who was constantly drawing men to Him. I do not say for the moment with what issue; neither do I now deal with the motive which prompted the men that came. It was not always the same so far as their consciousness was concerned. I simply insist upon the fact that He drew men to Him. I think that perhaps the whole story may best be told in the somewhat rough and ready way of saying that the one thing the men of his age could not do with Jesus was to let Him alone. There was a strange attractiveness about Him in the early years. Luke has opened for us one or two windows through which we may see some of the facts about those hidden years. Among those windows there is one through which I love to look. It is the statement which Luke makes that He went down to His own home and that there "He grew in favor with God and man." Taking only one half of that double window, we have a declaration that Jesus as a boy, youth, and young man, grew in favor with men. May I not be allowed to put that in another form and say that Jesus, the boy, the youth, the young man, was a favorite in Nazareth. I am not sure that this is not almost startling put in this form. We have, somehow, come to imagine that real Christian character is not popular among men. We have come to imagine that some of the traits of Christianity are awkwardness, and such peculiarity as repels men. It was not so in the case of Jesus. He was a favorite in Nazareth, that little town far up from the great high roads of the nations, one of those little towns where everyone knew everyone; there the boy was known, the young man was known and loved, and was a favorite. That is one of the windows looking through which a man is tempted to let his imagination run away with him. I think Jesus the carpenter was such a carpenter that children went to see Him, and took their broken toys to Him, and He mended them. If you do not understand that sentiment be sorry for yourself. Some of you are men whom no child would bring its toy to and ask to have it mended. I think young men loved to crowd to Him and talk to Him, this sweet, strong carpenter, about their difficulties and problems. I am not sure that the old men did not love to gather around the door of the carpenter's shop and listen to Him and talk with him about the Father's house of many mansions, and the rest that followed the turmoil and strife. Be that as it may, "He grew in favor"—they loved Him, they believed in Him in Nazareth. I know perfectly well that presently they tried to murder Him, that the day came when they took Him to the brow of the hill and fain would have cast Him down headlong. That was the effect of His teaching, the result of His having to rebuke their sin; but while He was living His quiet, strong, heroic life in the midst of them, He was a favorite. And when He turned His back upon the workshop and came into public life, how men pressed after Him wherever He went! I need not repeat it, you know your New Testament. "Much people . . . much people . . . much people." You cannot read the Gospels without feeling that you have been in the midst of the crowds. There are great, solemn, silent moments, midnight moments, but most of the time you are in the midst of the multitude, and men of all classes and castes are crowding after Him. I read that "the common people heard Him gladly"—which does not mean the poor people. The phrase translated "common people" is the identical phrase elsewhere translated "much people." So far from meaning people of the lower order, it means all sorts of people, rulers and ruled, learned and illiterate, rich and poor, privileged and oppressed.

In the early part of His ministry, the rulers were deeply interested in Him, and, more than interested, they hoped that they might have made something out of Him. They even went to the length of asking Him to dinner, and I never read the story of His going but I worship His strength, for more prophets have been spoiled by dining out than in any other way. This Man was able to sit at the table with the rulers, and with fine courtesy tell them the truth which scorched them. And the people followed Him out of the villages and cities. How many days' work were lost in following Him who can ever tell? How many long, dusty pilgrimages were undertaken, who can imagine? One day, tired of the throng, He entered into a boat and put across to the other shore, and then I have this wonderful declaration: when the boat had kissed its way across the water and arrived at the other side, all the multitudes were waiting for Him, for they had outrun the boat round the shore in their anxiety to be near Him. That is the first fact about the days of His ministry in the world.

Set over against it this other fact. He was constantly warning men as they came. There was the moment when they came to Him and would have made Him King, but He slipped away and hid Himself, and would not so be made King. There were moments such as those of which we read in Luke's gospel when the multitudes were following, and even His own disciples fondly believed the opportunity was at hand when He should exert His power, and by popular acclaim become King, when He suddenly said, Unless you hate your father, mother, brother, sister, you cannot be My disciple.

When you read those words after nineteen centuries is it not true you are afraid? I am. Is it not true that even now in the heart of most of us there is something of questioning rebellion? What does He mean? What are those strange, severe things by which He repels the very crowds He gathers? Instead of attempting to cover all the ground, I read these two incidents because they are typical. The words I read in Matthew 16 were not spoken primarily to the crowds, but to His own disciples. It was at Cæsarea Philippi, at the parting of the ways, after He had fulfilled the first part of His ministry, and one soul at least had seen and known Him for what He really was, the Christ of God. There He began to unfold the mystery of His method, to tell them the story of His cross and His suffering and resurrection, and there and then the whole company of His disciples fell back, and they never came into close fellowship again until He was dead, buried, risen, ascended, and the Holy Ghost was poured upon them. They shunned the cross. Do not be angry with them—we are shunning it still, many of us, and we have more light than they. While He talked of the keys, their faces were radiant and their following was faithful; but when He talked of the cross, their faces were shadowed and their following faltered. Then it was that, looking at the little group of men, He said: "If any man would come after me, let him deny himself, and take up his cross, and follow me." And they dared not do it, and if we watch the story carefully from the beginning of His ministry to Cæsarea Philippi, we see men perpetually leaving Him—rulers, scribes, Pharisees—until this little group is left alone. If you follow the story after Cæsarea Philippi, you will reach its tragic last chapter and find it written in these few burning words: "They"—all the disciples—"forsook Him and fled." So that at the end I see the most attractive personality in human history absolutely alone, no one by

His side, no sympathy in His dying. It is a strange story. It is a contradiction that needs careful examination. Why this repelling method of Jesus in the presence of His attractiveness?

Having asked that question, it is our business to answer it, not speculatively, but in the light of the Scriptures we read, in the light of the teaching they contain. I have read these two Scriptures because I think we have the one answer delivered in two sets of circumstances—first to the disciples, in Matthew 16, and then to the crowds, in Luke 14. Let us begin with the story of Luke. Why is it that Jesus upon such an occasion should say such strangely severe things? Mark the occasion. There went with Him great multitudes, and He turned and said—and you know the words. If you follow on you will find that He explains their meaning. "For which of *you* desiring to build a tower, doth not first sit down and count the cost . . . ? Or *what* king . . . will not sit down first and take counsel whether he is able with ten thousand to meet him that cometh against him with twenty thousand? . . . So *therefore* whosoever he be of you that renounceth not all that he hath, he cannot be my disciple."

Here, for a moment, I must crave your very close attention and patience, because I want, if I may, to rescue this passage from popular misinterpretation. It is almost always read as though Jesus meant to say, "You must hate father, mother, wife, children, brethren and sisters, because if you are going to build a tower you must count the cost; if you are going to war you must see whether you are able to meet twenty thousand with ten thousand." One little word in the Authorized Version has given color to this interpretation. In verse 33 we read, "So likewise," but in the Revised Version we have an entirely new meaning suggested by the words, "So therefore." The difference is that, according to this rendering, what our Lord meant to say was this: You ask in your heart why I insist upon such severe terms, why I hold men away from me in this manner. And this is His answer. Which of *you* going to build a tower will not first count the cost, or going to battle is not careful about the quality of the men who will serve under you. So therefore, because my work is the work of building and of battle, I am bound to be careful about the men that I choose to follow me; because I am not merely asking men to come after me in order to save them, but in order to help me and help God and humanity. My business is to build—that is constructive. My business is to conduct a war, a battle—that is destructive, and I must have men I know where to find. Which of *you* going to build a tower doth not first count the cost, or *what* king going to war does not take account of the quality of the men?

Let us leave Luke for a moment and go back to Matthew and see what our Lord said there, and inquire if we find anything like the same explanation. Here the same two figures occur in the Lord's description of His work. Peter had confessed Him, and immediately He named something in the economy of His work which had never been named before. He said, "Blessed art thou, Simon Bar-Jonah: for flesh and blood hath not revealed it unto thee, but my Father who is in heaven. And I also say unto thee, that thou art Peter, and upon this rock I will build My Church; and the gates of Hades shall not prevail against it." In that statement about the Church you have Christ's revelation of the nature of His work.

First, "I will build"; secondly, "The gates of Hades shall not prevail against it." Our Lord did not here state the same thing concerning the Church in two ways. He did not mean, "I will build the Church here, on this rock foundation, and when Hades comes against it it shall not prevail." When an enemy attacks a city, it does not take its gates with it. What Christ here meant is, My Church is, first of all, my building, and consequently impregnable; but my Church is also to be an aggressive force, which I shall lead to battle against all foes of God and humanity; and then, with the far vision of a great Conqueror, He sees the last enemy, death, the gates of Hades, the last citadel which His Church will storm, and sweeping over the intervening foes, He says: "The gates of Hades shall not prevail against it." Here, then, as in Luke, there are two things—building and battle. "I will build My Church"—"Which of you going to build a tower doth not first count the cost?" "The gates of Hades shall not prevail against it"—"What king going to make war doth not count the cost?"

Thus we find the answer to our question as to the severity of Jesus. Because He is committed to the building of the Church, and is committed to battle against all the forces that are against man and God, He must have those associated with Him on whom He can depend. He not merely seeks to save individuals, but also to gather about Him men and women on whom He can depend for co-operation in building and comradeship in battle. That is why He is so severe in His terms. That is why, when multitudes gathered about Him, He seems to have been sifting them.

Behold the crowds, oh, Jesus, the day of Thy crowning is coming. In a few moments they will put the crown upon Thy brow! No, I must build and fight! If any man will come after me, if there is one man among the crowd that really will follow, let him deny himself and take up his cross. Not by popular acclaim, but by solid building and hard fighting is my victory to be won. Who is coming with me?

> The Son of God goes forth to war,
> A kingly crown to gain.

His blood-red banner streams afar;
Who follows in His train?

Who best can drink His cup of woe,
Triumphant over pain,
Who patient bears his cross below,
He follows in His train.

Quality is always more than quantity. We are a little slow to believe it, but we all know it. We do not like the sifting process when Christ confronts us and sends back the multitudes that we fain would keep, but we know He is right. It is in the Old Testament as well as in the New. We read that thirty-two thousand men came up to fight the battle of the Lord, but Jehovah said, They are too many, sift them; and within a few moments twenty-two thousand men tramped home. Sing the Doxology!—we are stronger the moment they are gone. But still the people are too many—test them by the water brooks, and the men who take unnecessary time over necessary things are to go home. Nine thousand seven hundred of them went away, leaving only three hundred, but infinitely mightier the three hundred than the thirty-two thousand.

Not by popular vote, or acclaim, but by souls who can suffer and dare and die He builds the tower and fights the foe. Our Lord has not altered His method, and yet—here let me speak with great carefulness—there is not one in all this house that He does not want. There is no one that He will not enroll among His soldiers and employ in His great building enterprise—that is, if we are prepared to fulfill His conditions.

I am making my appeal tonight from perhaps a slightly different standpoint from the usual one. I am not speaking to you of the fact that you need personal salvation. In my heart is this great thought, that Jesus has need of you, not merely for your sake, but for His sake. He has not built His Church yet; He is building it, and will never finish until the top stone is brought on with shouting of, "Grace, grace unto it." He had not ended the battle yet. He has fought the Armageddon, the greatest battle is over; but battles are fought all along the line, and He it is who leads the hosts of God. He is building God's city, and He wants you if you are such a man as He can depend on. Jesus Christ in London today wants really faithful, consecrated souls far more than patronizing multitudes.

Christ confronts us all and says, "If any man would come after Me let him deny himself, and take up his cross, and follow Me." Who follows? You can applaud without following. You can admire without helping. You can be near enough to touch His sacred garment in a crowd, and never lay a brick in God's city, or strike a blow for God's victory. I dare believe there are young hearts everywhere that are sighing to help Him. Oh, young man, young woman, was there ever such a King, such a Leader, such an enterprise? Was there ever anything dreamed of by angels or men so calculated to stir the pulse and drive the heart as the King's building of the city, the King's battle for the victory? Will you come after Him?

Let us hear His terms, and God help us to hear them solemnly. "If any man will come after Me, let him deny himself, and take up his cross, and follow Me." Three things, and yet only one. The essential is the last-named, the first two are preliminary. They are necessary; you cannot reach the third save through them, but the third is the final, the essential, "Follow Me." I have been interested anew in Christ's use of the word, and have taken these Gospel stories, and have been surprised how often He said, "Follow Me." The call is so simple that any little child will tell you what it means. It is so sublime that no Christian philosopher has ever exhausted the infinite meaning of the word. If we are to help Him in His building and battle we must follow Him. What is it to follow? Two very simple things are included; to follow is, first, to trust, and, secondly, it is to obey. I cannot follow unless I trust; but I can trust in a general sense and never follow. There are many who believe Him to be the one and only King and Saviour of men, who never take His name in vain, and would not allow anyone to speak disrespectfully of Him; but they are not following Him.

"If any man will come after Me, let him deny himself, and take up his cross." Denial of self is the hidden and internal process, the taking up of the cross is the outward and external manifestation. If I may adapt and use in this connection old and familiar words, I would say that the taking up of the cross is the outward and visible sign of the inward and spiritual grace of self-denial. What is self-denial? Jesus says everything when He speaks, and there is nothing more to be said; our danger is that we minimize when we explain. To deny self is to say no to every wish that comes out of the personal life. To deny self is radical; it goes down to the roots of things. A man may practice self-denial all his life and never deny himself. A man may practice self-denial in this and that respect, and all the while his self-centeredness is strengthened. Jesus did not say, Exercise self-denial in externalities. He said, Deny self. Have done with choosing, wishing, planning, arranging for self. Choose no more; will no more, except to will that God shall will.

> Our wills are ours we know not how,
> Our wills are ours to make them Thine.

I deny self when I hand over the keys of the citadel to the King and say, Enter and reign in every chamber of the being, in all the possibilities of the soul.

Is this easy? How is it to be expressed? Take up thy cross. What is that? I do not know for you, my brother. I do not know for myself tomorrow. The cross in its practice changes perpetually, in its principle it abides. The cross is the one thing that intrudes itself upon your vision at the moment of your denial of self. I am increasingly impressed with the fact that whenever a soul comes to Christ the last battle is fought out over one thing. I do not know what it is in your case, but you know exactly what you have to do if you are to follow this Christ, to build and to battle—the thing that must be set right, the friendship that must be dropped, the habit that must be abandoned, the restitution that has to be made, pride that has to be humbled, prejudice that has to be crucified. God tells us what it is, and we know. Oh for one five minutes of soul honesty! Do not indulge in subterfuges. You are asked to be true about the thing that you know is between your soul and God. For some of you it will mean a hasty return home to find the woman you insulted ere you left. For some it will mean going home and telling your children that you were wrong in your treatment of them. For some it will mean asking for the money back that you put on the plate to make restitution. It is a real cross when you begin to follow Jesus. They are Christ's terms. Nothing I have said is quite so hard as the words He uttered. Unless you hate father, mother, wife, children, brethren, sisters; unless you put every other love, every other interest in the background and Christ in the foreground, you cannot be His disciple. So help me God, I will not tone down my Master's message. I will not make this thing for my heart and yours one bit smoother than He made it. Take up *your* cross

—not Christ's. You cannot take up Christ's cross. He took it up alone, and in the mystery of it made it possible for you to take yours and find the virtue of His; but you must take up your own.

There is one other thing I would say. If you stand where I stand you are appalled at the tremendous claim of Jesus. How can I ever deny myself and take up my cross? I come from the negative to the positive, and say to you that the only way in which you will ever be able to deny yourself and take up your cross is by fixing your eye upon Him and crowning Him. If I must stretch out my hands to the rugged cross in order to get to Him I can do it in only one way, that is by seeing Him and doing it for His sake. If I do it for my own sake, or for the sake of men, I shall fail, for I am such a coward; but if I may but look at His face as I come to my dying, I can say, "I am crucified with Christ, but nevertheless I live."

> From the ground there blossoms red
> Life that shall endless be.

The cross is but the prelude to resurrection. How often shall we say it! Let us come, those of us who will, and say to Him, Christ, Thou hast drawn us irresistibly. We are here to see Thee, to hear Thee. Thou has frightened us with Thy terms, but we also would help Thee in Thy building and in Thy battle, and we will deny self and take up the cross with our eyes fixed upon Thee. And by the way of the cross we enter the army, and enter upon the enterprise, and if we suffer with Him we shall also reign with Him. May God grant that there may be many who will join Him in His building and His battle by denying self and taking up the cross and following Him!

CHAPTER IV

THE POTTER'S WORK ON THE WHEELS

Then I went down to the potter's house, and, behold, he wrought his work on the wheels.
JEREMIAH 18:3.

THE FIGURE OF THE POTTER AND THE CLAY IS PERENNIALLY attractive. Perhaps it has not been so popular in recent years as formerly. There is a note of severity about it, of which our softer age has been afraid. In every age characterized by strength the figure of the potter has been one of those most often used by the prophets and messengers of God. It is interesting to notice that in the Bible it is used by the men mightiest in their personal thinking and in the influence they exerted on their age. Four Bible writers use it, perhaps borrowing it from each other. Whether that be so or not, they are men of peculiar strength: Isaiah, a man of clear vision of God's uplifted throne; Jeremiah, a man of deep understanding of God's heart of love; Zechariah, a man who saw further than any Old Testament prophet, and whose book is a veritable apocalypse not yet fulfilled; and Paul, the man of massive thinking and keen penetration to the heart of the philosophy of the Christian religion.

This figure contains a deeper note than that of its severity, which, when discovered, explains and justifies that severity of which some of us have been afraid, and in the presence of which we still tremble. To refer again to the men to whom I have made reference, it will be seen that while they were men of a severe note, yet to speak of severity as their final note would be to misinterpret them altogether. The thunder of Isaiah perpetually merged into the plaintive wail of his tender love as he expressed the thought of God concerning the sinning people; Jeremiah's deepest and profoundest note was reached when he cried: "Oh that my head were waters"; Zechariah looks on to great consummations, to the outworking of the infinite love and pity; and although Paul, with pitiless scorn and sarcasm, tracks sin until we see it in its deepest and inner meaning, he is also the man who says: "I call God to witness I could be accursed from Christ for my brethren's sake." Wherever you find a man of strong outlook and severe note you find him using the figure of the potter sooner or later, but you also find him melting into tears, a man moved with compassion.

I want tonight, as God shall help me, to bring you back to this old and familiar figure, that we may consider its application to personal life. In the passage which I read to you from Jeremiah the figure is used in relation to national affairs. It is almost invariably so used in the Old Testament. We are perfectly justified in arguing from the nation, which is composed of individuals, to the individual lives, which constitute the nation. There are national applications even today of this great message, upon which I do not propose to touch. I desire to take the principle here revealed and apply it to our individual and personal life.

In the passage from which my text is taken the picture of the potter is given in all simplicity and clearness of outline. Jeremiah is seen going down to the house of the potter, and in imagination we accompany him. If we have ever been to the house of the potter we have been in very close comradeship with Jeremiah, for among all the changes that have taken place in manufacture the house of the potter is almost exactly today as it was in the olden days. There have been some small changes in the matter of the wheel, but practically no change in essential things, the potter and the clay. So we may imagine we are standing with Jeremiah in that actual house, and seeing exactly what he saw.

Let us look at these things in all their simplicity, without any reference for the moment to the teaching suggested. What did Jeremiah see? He saw the potter, the wheel, and the clay. In the potter he saw an intelligent and capable worker; in the wheel an instrument by which the worker accomplished a definite purpose in the clay; and in the clay a capable material, something with which it was possible for the potter to accomplish his purpose. These facts constitute the essential revelations of the potter's house for all time concerning the relationship which exists between God and man.

The potter speaks first of God's authority, and we are afraid of the figure because we stay there. That is not all, the potter speaks also of God's interest and God's perpetual attention, and finally of God's absolute power. Looking at the potter as he sits at the wheel and places his hand upon the clay, I am conscious of his right and authority over the clay, but if I watch him more closely, I also see his keen interest as the clay changes its form under his fingers. If I watch yet more carefully I see his close and unvarying attention to his work; his eye is never lifted from the clay while the wheel revolves and his hand is molding. Having started with his authority and observed his interest and unvarying attention, I also recognize his power. Those hands which press so gently, or so heavily, are hands of power, infinite so far as that clay is concerned.

Turning from the potter, I look at the wheels upon which the clay is turned, and they speak to me of all the circumstances in the midst of which I find myself. I think that perhaps the truth concerning these wheels can be told most expressively in the words of Browning:

> . . . this dance,
> Of plastic circumstance,
> This Present, thou, forsooth, wouldst fain arrest:
> Machinery just meant
> To give thy soul its ben',
> Try thee and turn thee forth, sufficiently impressed.

The wheel is incidental, necessary but transitory, to be flung aside when the potter remains and the clay has found its final form and shape. The things of supreme moment are the potter and the clay.

The clay speaks of man's capacity and relation to God. It is of plastic nature; it can be molded. There are other forms of matter which you never find upon the wheel of the potter. There is never any attempt on the part of the potter to mold steel filings into form for beauty or for use. Clay is material which will take the impress of the potter's fingers.

These are the simplest lessons of the potter's house. There I see God and myself and all the circumstances of my life: the intelligent Master Workman, with the thought in His mind which no one has ever seen; myself of such a nature as to be able to express that thought for others to see it; and all the circumstances of my life, turning wheels, so swiftly turning oftentimes as to make me afraid, presently to be set aside when the vessel is fashioned. So in the potter's house, the simplest of all manufacturing centers and yet the sublimest, for here art and artifice meet, I learn the profoundest lessons of what man's relationships to God really are.

I shall ask you, then, to follow me as I attempt to lead you, first, to the discovery of the principle taught; secondly, to the recognition of purpose suggested; and, finally, to the knowledge of the Person who chooses to stand revealed in this ancient figure as the Potter. Unless these three things are recognized we shall surely rebel against the whole conception. If we simply discover the principle of this figure we shall be afraid. We must also find the Person of the Potter. It is this last quantity which we have too often missed in our consideration of this wonderful figure. We have too often preached the principle of submission to God's absolute sovereignty without reference to the character of God. I shall never submit myself to the principle, so frail and weak and afraid am I, until I see the Potter. If I can but see Him, and know Him, then as plastic clay I shall yield myself to His hand, knowing that in this figure, severe and strenuous, there is the music of infinite tenderness, and patience, and love.

On the other hand, if a man know the Person, and refuse to obey the principle, or accept the purpose, he will fail. The principle taught is that of the absolute sovereignty of God and the necessity for the submission of man thereto. The potter has a right which is absolute over the clay. It cannot resist his hand finally. It has no right to suggest to him what form or fashion it shall take. We hear much today of the rights of man. The first truth which the potter's house teaches is that of the rights of God. Our fathers expressed the truth in a way which we would never care to use, and yet it is sometimes well to go back and listen to the tremendous and overwhelming emphasis which they laid upon it. It is told of a pastor of one of the New England churches in the olden days that he almost invariably asked candidates for membership, "Are you perfectly willing to submit yourself to God whatever His will concerning you may be? Are you willing, if you knew it would be for His glory, to be eternally shut out from His presence?" That question is entirely out of place, since God has said that He willeth not the death of any sinner; and yet at the back of it there is a tremendous truth, of which we are in danger of losing sight—the truth that no man would have any right to complain, whatever God decided to do with him. We know what God would do, He willeth that all should come to Him and live. That is the purpose of God for all, but, knowing that, we must not minimize this other tremendous truth of God's sovereignty. Shall man challenge God? God has a right to take this whole world and annihilate it and sweep out the race that has condemned His law and turned its back on all His infinite love.

Therefore, man's right in the presence of God is that he should have no wish, no claim, no desire of his own, save only to discover the wish, the claim, the desire, the right of God.

But I can quite imagine that someone is stating a difficulty. The clay has no will, and I have will. The clay has no power to choose, and I have power to choose. I was created by this selfsame God with will and the power to choose. Therein lies disparity, and the figure is spoiled by the disparity. Not at all. The distance between God and man is greater than the distance between the potter and the clay. The distance between the infinite will and the finite will is far greater than the distance between the finite will and the thing that lacks will. When you are working out your ratios of comparison you must be very careful to remember that when you compare the infinite with the finite in any form you have a greater distance to bridge than between the finite and finite in any form. What is will? The power to choose within limitation. Will answers a governing principle. It never acts, save with something at the back of it that drives it. Consequently, the highest exercise of will is the choice of the governing principle, the choice of that which shall be master. When God gave man will, He did so that man might choose his master, that he might either submit himself to the one eternal throne of God, which, in turn, is dominated by righteousness and love, or submit himself only to himself, to his own ruin. So far, man has will. Every man and woman, youth and maiden, and child will choose for himself his master, his ruling principle, and so his destiny. God allows man to make his choice, but when he chooses he is still acting under the government of God, and he cannot finally escape therefrom. He will choose truly if he does so by the principle revealed in the house of the potter, saying as he chooses: "Our wills are ours . . . to make them Thine." Any other exercise of the will is prostitution of the power bestowed, and must issue in the ruin of the one who makes such use of it. So that while there is a difference between the potter and the clay, on the one hand, and God and man on the other, the distance between potter and clay and the distance between God and man are not equal. If the finite man has a right to complete authority over clay, which is finite matter, much more have the infinite and eternal mind and will of God the right to claim absolute authority over the finite mind and will of man. Thus, the teaching of this picture as to principle is the sovereignty of God, and the fact that man's wisdom lies in unconditional and uncompromising surrender to that will of God, of which man's will is but the spark and offspring.

But there is purpose manifest as well as principle. "Behold, *he* wrought *his* work on the wheels." The potter has a thought in his mind for the clay, and he alone can transfer that thought to the clay. The clay is necessarily ignorant of the thought in the potter's mind, but can find that thought, and realize and manifest it by quiet submission to the hand of the potter. My brethren, when I pass from this great principle, which I confess taken alone fills me with fear, to notice that there is a purpose, my heart begins to find comfort. The potter, as the wheel revolves, is not dealing capriciously with the clay; his fingers are not working aimlessly. As I watch him in the beginning of the work I cannot see what he means, but *he* knows what he means, and as his hands rest upon the clay he is translating into the outward and manifest the thought of beauty and use which is in his own mind and heart. The clay gains in the potter; the potter gains in the clay. The clay is shapeless as clay, but the clay plus the potter becomes a thing of beauty and of use. The potter has in his mind a thought of beauty, which none but himself can see apart from the clay, but the potter plus the clay can express his thought so that others may see it. Here I think we touch one of the deepest mysteries of human life. Man is created that God may have a medium through which He can manifest the things in His own mind. Man is fashioned in His likeness, in His image, that those who cannot see the essential and eternal Spirit may yet see the things of the essential and eternal Spirit in man. How man has missed his mark, and yet by the redemption of Jesus Christ this great purpose is fulfilled. Paul declared: "We are His workmanship." What Paul really writes is, "We are His poetry," not that the Apostle meant we are His poetry, but His work of art, that through which He gives others to see the things of beauty resident in His own infinite mind. This same truth is expressed in Peter's words: "Ye are an elect race, a royal priesthood, a holy nation, a people for God's own possession, that ye may shew forth the excellencies of Him who called you out of darkness into His marvellous light." God gains in men that through which He can reveal Himself as the potter gains in the clay the medium through which he can express his thought. But the other side is also true. See what the clay has gained. It was but a shapeless thing, lacking beauty, lacking expression of anything that has refinement in it, lacking utility; but it gains from the hand of the potter form and shape and usefulness. Man alone is as the clay, lacking beauty, lacking true utility, making shipwreck of his own personality; but let man find God's throne and yield to it, submit his whole life to the hands of the great Master Potter, and he finds the poor clay of his life made into something fair and beautiful and full of use to God and to man. You came into this house tonight saying, My life is purposeless. Give it to God, and it will be purposeful. You said, These years have gone from me, twenty, thirty, forty, and I have done nothing. Yield to God and the Potter's hand will be upon you to mold and to make. It may be that the molding and making will not yet be recognized by your fellow men. That matters nothing. It may be that the molding and making will be that of a thing of use rather than of beauty. It may be that He will mold you to some service that men count menial. There is no menial service which the King appoints. There must be yielding to the Potter, but then, oh, soul of mine, when thou art so yielded purpose is the story of thy life.

We go yet one step further in this study. The thought of sovereignty is terrible, and the principle is enough to affright the heart of man. So also is the purpose unless I know the Person. Tyranny may have purpose, but I am afraid of purpose if you only speak of it. Tyranny may demand submission, but I am afraid of submission if you only speak of it. If you bring me to the potter's house and say to me, See the potter and his authority, and yield; see the potter and his purpose, and yield, I will not speak for anyone else, but I am afraid. I know there must be some authority, but I am afraid when I am asked to yield to this infinite authority, although I know there ought to be some purpose. But what is the purpose?

The figure of the potter's house is never perfect until you

have passed beyond the principle and the purpose to the Person. Who is the potter? That is the final question before I can yield. There need be no argument, for the answer has been given by revelation in a Person. God is the Potter. Who is God? There is only one answer: "God is love." I might have given a hundred answers. I might have said God is righteousness, is holiness, is beneficence, but I want to gather up all the possessions and express them at once; and when I want to gather up all the characteristics and write them as character there is only one answer: "God is love."

I can submit to love. Now I am not afraid of the purpose. This is the quantity we have too often lost sight of when we have preached about the potter's house. Suffering one, how those hands of God have pressed some days upon the clay, and this clay is feeling, thinking, suffering clay. Oh, how these hands have pressed, but they are the hands of God, and God is love. That great truth is established. I am not going to insult God by arguing it. We know it. The thought of the Potter is love as He molds the clay upon the wheels, and remember He governs the wheels as well as the clay. There ought to be comfort in that for someone. He comes, not only with a thought of love, but with such a nature of love that all the process is a process of love, and if He break by the pressure of His hands it is but to make; if He crush, it is but to create.

I bring you to the principle taught in the potter's house and tell you that until you have learned it, until you submit to it, your life is failure. I bring you to the fact of purpose taught in the potter's house, and tell you, here is infinite comfort if you will but have it so; your life may be purposeful. If I leave you there I leave you afraid, so I bring you finally to the Person. Would we know what the heart of the Potter is we must see it transfixed with wounds upon the brutal cross. Would we know the real meaning of the Potter's hands we must see them with wound prints in them. Would we know the deep truth both as to principle and purpose we must lay our weary heads upon the bosom of God, and feel the beating of the infinite Heart. When I feel that, then I can trust, then I can submit to the principle, then I can consent to the purpose.

My last word to every man and woman, Christian or not, is this: to revel is to take the clay out of the Potter's hands and to render it purposeless and useless—waste—in the economy of the universe. Oh, the wrecks in the potter's field! Vessels half formed, and marred and flung away. The potter's field is full of wreckage, lives that might have been fashioned to forms of beauty, but that they would not yield to the hands of the Potter.

I cannot leave my story with that solemn word of warning. I am perfectly willing that you should charge me with fanciful interpretation, but the potter's field is last mentioned in Scripture in strange company. They bought the potter's field with the price of Him Whom they priced, and they called it, little thinking how deep the significance of their calling might be, the field of blood. Are there some wrecks in the potter's field in this house tonight, men and women who are saying, I have been spoiled and flung away. I am waste in God's universe. The potter's field has been purchased with blood. I come back to Jeremiah, and I read that when the vessel was marred in the hands of the potter he made it again another vessel. Blessed be God, He came to the potter's field, and He gathered up the wrecks to make them again. There is another chance for you, my brother. By the mystery of His betrayal, by the mystery of His denial, by the mystery of His being sold for the price of a slave, the potter's field is bought, and though you have missed your purpose by disobeying your principle, the Person, the Potter Himself, has come down to the midst of the wreckage, and by the price of His own mysterious life has bought it, and the wreck can be remade. But you must begin with the Person and submit to the principle, and find the purpose. May God help us all to do so.

CHAPTER V

DWELLERS IN FIRE

The sinners in Zion are afraid; trembling hath seized the godless ones: who among us can dwell with the devouring fire? Who among us can dwell with everlasting burnings?

ISAIAH 33:14.

THIS CHAPTER IS A GRAPHIC DESCRIPTION OF DIVINE DELIVERance wrought, and the text reveals the effect produced upon some in the delivered city as they gazed with wonder and astonishment at the judgment of that God who was their King. The hosts of Assyria had melted away, and yet of these hosts they had been afraid. It must have seemed to those within the city as though they would be utterly overcome by the great armies that lay encamped about the walls. It was of this occasion that Byron sang:

> The Assyrian came down like a wolf on the fold,
> And his cohorts were gleaming in purple and gold;
> And the sheen of their spears was like stars on the sea;
> When the blue wave rolls nightly on deep Galilee.

And yet, though Judah had struck no blow, but through her King and her prophet had waited upon God only, the vast hosts had been driven back, many of them escaping to Nineveh, many of them being left dead upon the field. As the men of Zion looked out at this wonderful work of God, and became conscious of how God wrought without human instrumentality when it so pleased Him, the sinners in Zion were afraid, and the godless inside the delivered city trembled and cried out in their anguish, "Who among us can dwell with the devouring fire? Who among us can dwell with everlasting burnings?" They had seen the fire at its work. They had seen the age-abiding burnings take hold of the enemies of God, until they became weak and were driven and consumed. Isaiah had perpetually taught the truth of the presence of God as righteousness and as fire amongst men. That truth was demonstrated in the destruction of the hosts of Sennacherib. When in answer to prayer God delivered them they were impressed, not so much with the deliverance as with the method. As it proceeded in fiery judgment upon the foes outside, and the consciousness of God as fire came home to those within, they cried out in trembling and anguish: "Who among us can dwell with the devouring fire? Who among us can dwell with everlasting burnings?" Are *we* safe? May not that fire burn *us* ere the night fall upon us? May not that age-abiding burning scorch *us* at it has scorched the men outside? The question is a revelation of the dawning upon the consciousness of these men of the truth which Isaiah had attempted to teach them, that of the presence of God as devouring fire and as age-abiding burnings. This consciousness raised in their case, as it must ever raise in the case of men who arrive at it, an inquiry of the utmost importance. How can man live in fire without being burned or scorched?

Turning from the local coloring, coming at once from Jerusalem to London, from the bygone age to the age that now is, I propose to ask you first to consider with me in the light of the inquiry of the men of old the fact of the presence of God in human life as fire; and, secondly, I shall invite you to make the inquiry they made, "Who among us can dwell with the devouring fire?" and then to listen to the answer of the prophet which immediately follows.

First, let me speak to you of this vision of God as fire. I have already said that this was the burden of Isaiah's message. Certainly the great burden of his message was the immanence of God, the nearness of God. Isaiah, perhaps the mightiest of all the Hebrew prophets, the man of largest outlook and keenest insight, came to an age characterized by its practical godlessness. We know the history of Israel and Judah, and how terrible had been the forgetfulness of God. To these people Isaiah came, saying in effect, You forget God, but you do not escape God; though you put Him out of your thinking, and make no calculation upon His presence and will, He wraps you round about in every hour of your life. This man of far-seeing vision, as he looked on to consummation and deliverance and salvation, expressed the whole of it by one word—Emmanuel, God with us. He taught constantly the presence of God in human affairs, and that in the processes of the method of God there would be a mysterious moment in human history when God would be present in the form of a child. Whether he saw clearly all the issue of his teaching I am not prepared to say, but this was the underlying truth, the nearness of God and the impossibility of human escape from that nearness. Isaiah taught, moreover, the righteous character of God, and insisted that the uplifted throne was based upon righteousness and holiness and equity. He declared with scorching and biting scorn that their religious observances were of no value in the sight of heaven if in their own life they were not true and upright and righteous. He insisted first upon the immanance of God, and, secondly, upon His righteousness and His righteous requirements. Then he perpetually used fire as a symbol of the

Divine presence and method. Go back to the opening of the prophecy, to chapter 6, in which he describes the wonderful way in which he was called to the work, when he saw the Lord high and lifted up, and His train filling the temple, and when there came out of his own anguish the cry that told of his sin and of the people's sin, "Woe is me! for I am undone; because I am a man of unclean lips, and I dwell in the midst of a people of unclean lips." How was he prepared for his work? "Then flew one of the seraphim unto me, having a live coal in his hand . . . from off the altar; and he touched my mouth with it, and said, Lo, this hath touched thy lips; and thine iniquity is taken away and thy sin forgiven." God came to him as fire for purification, according to the figurative language of that chapter. Then coming to the end of the prophecy, in chapter 66, speaking of the coming of God in punishment, he says: "For behold, Jehovah will come with fire, and His chariots shall be like the whirlwind; to render His anger with fierceness, and His rebuke with flames of fire. For by fire will Jehovah execute judgment, and by His sword, upon all flesh." It is not Isaiah only who uses this figure of fire. All Scripture brings us back again and again to this symbolism. From beginning to end you will find that the presence of God is suggested under the figure of fire. When from the Garden of Eden man was excluded from intimate communion with God it was a flaming sword which was the symbol of that exclusion and of God's holiness. When God would reveal Himself to a man for the making of a nation it was in a bush which burned with fire and was not consumed. Then in the New Testament all truth about God is expressed in one remarkable sentence in the Epistle to the Hebrews: "Our God is a consuming fire." Or, if I think of Christ, the last prophecy foretelling His coming declared that "He is like a refiner's fire." Christ Himself used the same figure: "I have come to cast fire upon the earth." In the final book of the Bible, John, describing the glorious vision of this selfsame Christ, said: "His eyes were as a flame of fire." Or, if I come to the Holy Spirit of God, omitting all the incidental words concerning Him in the old economy, and taking up the simple story of His coming to initiate the era in the midst of which we live today, what was the symbol of His coming? Tongues of fire that sat upon the heads of the assembled company. I have but gathered these things together to show that this figure runs through the Word of God, teaching us certain truths concerning God Himself.

What, then, are we intended to learn by its use? What is fire? Fire is the evolution of light and heat by combustion. Those of you who perfectly understand what that means are welcome to the definition. I think I see enough of what it means to understand the use of this marvelous figure in the Word of God. In the New Testament, which is the final revelation, we have three definitions of God, which it is well to put together. "God is love." "God is light." "God is a consuming fire." The greatest of the three is not the first, nor the second, but the last, because it includes the other two. God is love and light, and therefore He is fire. The evolution of light and heat is fire. The combination in one mysterious personality of light and love is fire. Love is heat, passion. Light is illumination, principle. Combine the two and you have fire. "Our God is a consuming fire." Omit if you will the distinguishing word "consuming." It is used there because it is needed in the connection, but the great word stands, "God is fire." Whether He be consuming or not depends entirely upon the condition of that which comes into contact with Him. Whether He be a devouring fire or an age-abiding burning depends entirely upon the condition of the person who comes into contact with Him. To put the whole thing superlatively, whether when a man is wrapped about with God he be in hell or heaven depends upon what the man is in himself. No man escapes God in hell. I need not say that no man escapes God in heaven. It is the One Presence which makes heaven and hell the presence of the God of fire, who is to certain people a devouring fire and to others an age-abiding burning. It is this combination in a personality of passion and principle acting upon each other, holding each other in true proportion, which blazes out into fire. If there were nothing but principle it would petrify itself into stone. Where there is principle—light, and passion—love, principle is suffused with passion and passion is held in check by principle, and there is fire. Not fire that needs feeding with any earthly fuel or else it die, but the eternal fire, the age-abiding fire, which fire is God Himself.

Take this symbolism of fire a little further. What shall we say of the presence of fire? It is everywhere. Scientists make use of the word "eremacausis," and believing with John Ruskin that it is well to translate such words into simpler words, I find that eremacausis means a slowly burning fire. There is in nature everywhere a slowly burning fire. There is fire in everything, there is no escape from it. We do not always see its flame, but it is always burning, and it is most beneficent. Without it nature could not renew itself, nature would be halted in its procession from season to season, and in its unfolding of new glory and beauty. Sometimes we speak of this in other words as the process of oxidation going forward everywhere. I pick up a piece of metal from the highway. It is rust covered. What is rust? Fire. I stand in autumn looking at the hillside clothed with trees, and I admire the beauty of the tints. But what is this? Fire. This is not poetry. This is not imagination. This is cold, scientific fact. The fires in nature flame out in autumn time. What

CHAPTER V

SIN

Sin is lawlessness.
                                            I JOHN 3:4.
Lust when it hath conceived beareth sin.
                                            JAMES 1:15.

IN THESE TWO BRIEF PASSAGES WE HAVE INCLUSIVE STATEments of the nature and the genesis of sin. I am proposing to consider this subject in the most personal and immediate way, desiring to discuss the question of sin in the individual life, as to what it really is, and as to how it comes about.

What is sin? "Sin is lawlessness." How does a man sin? "Lust when it hath conceived beareth sin." We exclude from our consideration, first, the question of sin among the unenlightened peoples; and, second, the question of racial inheritance. Concerning those who have never heard the Evangel there is but one thing to be said, that the Judge of all the earth will do right. Concerning the subject of racial inheritance, or, if you will, the subject of heredity, I am not proposing to speak, save to say that while it is perfectly true that very many of us may have inherited tendencies from our fathers, it is equally true that we all have another inheritance, mightier than the inheritance of evil. The mightier inheritance is our inheritance in God, both by creation and redemption. We are living in the midst of the sanctions of the

Christian ideal. Wherever the ideal came from, the common consent of enlightened humanity agrees that it is right. There is no man in this house but that in the deepest of him consents to the standard of life revealed in the ethical teaching of Jesus. The standard of right and wrong for us is necessarily the Christian standard. We are all living in the light of that conception of life which has come to us through Christ, and we are all, in the deepest of us, consenting to the beauty of that conception.

Moreover, we are all conscious, however much we may debate it philosophically, of our power of choice. The man who, today, or yesterday, or the day before, committed sin, knows full well he need not have done so. I grant that there may have been unnatural predisposition to sin; I grant that the surroundings may have been very difficult; yet if a man be perfectly honest he will confess that he never yet committed an act of sin but by the choice of his own will. If the act of sin was not by the choice of his own will, then it was not sin. If you can conceive of circumstances in which a man is compelled by physical force to the doing of a thing which his conscience does not approve, circumstances in which a man has no choice left, under such circumstances he does not sin. Sin is always in the realm of the will. I am not discussing evil. Evil is a larger subject. Evil is all that is hurtful and harmful, whether as to cause or effect, whether material, mental, or moral. I am discussing sin.

Let us first, then, consider John's definition, "Sin is lawlessness." In order to understand this, we must take time to look at these two words, "sin" and "lawlessness," and see what they really mean.

"Sin." The word translated "sin" here is one of doubtful origin. From the philological standpoint, there is doubt as to its derivation. We are in no doubt, however, when we trace presence. Draw me what graphic picture you will of the condition of the lost, it may be lurid, it may be medieval, according to the fastidiousness of this age, out of date, but no picture of the Middle Ages is half so dreadful as the fact of the soul abiding in God yet out of harmony with Him—destroyed by the fire that ought to have made it, because of deliberate and final choice on the part of that soul. Hell is begun here as heaven is begun here. I am not foolish enough to tell you that hell ends here any more than I am foolish enough to tell you that heaven ends here. Some men tell me that heaven is beyond but that hell is all here. Hell begins here; some of you are in it. Heaven begins here; some of us are in it. When we have done with this material frame we shall be where we choose here and now. Whether in hell or heaven, we shall have our being in God, and in God as fire. Whether to feel forevermore the eating and devouring of that fire upon the thing that is unworthy, or to feel forevermore the burning of that fire to high and noble purpose and permanence, depends entirely upon what we are ourselves. How often this text has been preached from as though it refers to hell. So it does, but it also refers to heaven. The deepest thing in it is not a description of hell, but a tremendous announcement that God is fire. It is the cry of a heart conscious of sin, Who can dwell in this? Who can dwell in such burnings as this?

Now we turn to that inquiry. Take the simple word used in both cases. Who can *dwell* in the fire. Who can *dwell* in the burnings? You will find that the word "dwell" is used four times in this chapter. Twice in the chapter of my text, in verse 16: "He shall dwell on high," and in verse 24, "The people that dwell therein." The Hebrew word is not the same. There are here three Hebrew words with different shades of meaning. In verse 24 is a word which suggests sitting down in perfect rest in a certain place. In verse 16 the word signifies being at home. In my text it signifies to sojourn as a guest. The word used in the text itself has three distinct significations: to sojourn as a guest, to fly away, and sometimes conflict. I am by no means perfectly sure what these men meant when they used it. I am not sure that the use of this many-sided word is not indicative of the trembling fear in which they asked the question, as though they had said: See that fire outside, how it has destroyed the Assyrians. Who of us dare visit it, dare flee it, dare fight it? There is evidence of a lurking subconsciousness that that fire is where they are also, and a desire to be out of it. Who are the men who ask the question? Sinners, ungodly ones, and they say, Who can be the guest of fire and not be burned or scorched by the flame? What flame is it, O men of Jerusalem? Of what are you speaking? And I think I hear their answer. There has been a scorching fire; behold the Assyrians dead about our city. We are delivered, but, oh, what a blast has burned Assyria! Who of us can live in it? Whether they were consciously in it is not definitely told by the word they used, but they were conscious of its nearness. They felt the hot blast of the fire sweeping toward them and said, Who among us can dwell there? If there had been nothing but the question we should have gone away feeling that the symbolism of the test was that of judgment only. How wonderful is the answer of the prophet: "He that walketh righteously and speaketh uprightly." That is, he whose attitude toward God is what it ought to be. It is as though the prophet had said: I have told you that God is righteous, God is upright, God is fire. But you need not be afraid of the fire if you have God's character: "He that walketh righteously and speaketh uprightly." How shall I know whether that is my condition or not? And the prophet turns from the relationship to God to the relationship to man. "He that despiseth the gain of oppressions, that shaketh his hands from taking a bribe, that stoppeth his ears from hearing of blood, and shutteth his eyes from looking upon evil: he shall dwell on high." Isaiah uses a stronger word than they used. He says, If you are right with God you can be *at home* in fire. Then follows the most marvelous description of the absolute safety of the soul that is right with God. He gives the position, "he shall dwell on high"; and the defense, "his place of defense shall be munitions of rocks"; his sustenance, "his bread shall be given him; his waters shall be sure"; his hope, "thine eyes shall see the King in his beauty."

May I venture to translate this message of Isaiah into other words? Oh, soul of mine, art thou afraid in the presence of the truth that God is fire? If thou art afraid it is because of what thou art in thyself. God's fires never harm God's children. The man who partakes of God's character can live in God's fire. You may well fear fire if you are a sinner. You may well fear the burnings if your hands are full of bribes and there is blood in your garments. You may well fear the fire if you are unholy, unrighteous, but not if you are right with God. To use the magnificent and daring word of Peter, the man who himself partakes of "the Divine nature" can live in the fire of the Divine nature. Hell and heaven are one in atmosphere, and the atmosphere is a burning, blistering pain, or a shining, beauteous glory, according to what I am in myself. Nothing can live in fire but that which is of the nature of fire. Nothing can live in fire but that which will take hold of the fire and be unweakened thereby. Who is it that can dwell in everlasting burnings and be unafraid? He that walketh righteously and speaketh uprightly. He can dwell in the fire.

This is the great rock upon which faith fastens in the midst of toil. I may be speaking to some tonight who are greatly overburdened in their toil for God. Perhaps there are some worshiping with us who have come from the country, and down there in your village or town it seems as though God was being beaten, it looks as though the Assyrian must triumph over Judah. It is not so. God is in this age burning, burning, burning, and only that can remain which partakes of the fire nature, which answers the call of righteousness and becomes righteous. The mightiest foe cannot abide, God will burn it to destruction. Assyria is very proud. She spoils, though none has spoiled her. She deals treacherously, though none has dealt treacherously with her. For a time evil has a glamour and apparent glory about it. Take heart, and be at rest, oh, warrior of the King! The one thing that evil cannot do is lock its door against God. He wraps it about in the flame of His own being, and there is no evil house in London, no evil man or movement that is not already in this all-embracing fire. I thank God that my heart knows it.

Then there is the other side of this great truth, which should give my heart pause tonight. Can *I* dwell with the fire? Can *I* dwell with the age-abiding burnings? Let me drop the figurative language of the prophet and ask, Am I right with God? That is the final question. If I am right with God then I can dwell with the fire. If not, I must still dwell in the fire, but the fire will blast me. Hell is an absolute necessity of morality. Deny me the fire of hell which burns the man who deliberately turns his back upon right, and by that denial you deny me the love of God, the love and light, from the commingling of which fire issues. Find me the man, the woman, the child, who is love-governed, and who walks in light, that is a son, a daughter of fire. Such can live in fire. Find me the man, the woman, hate-governed, and who loves darkness, such is stubble for burning. The very fire which purifies to perfection the son of fire consumes with age-abiding force the soul that is against God.

Oh, soul of mine, canst thou dwell in fire? I dare hardly ask *you*, so does the question press on *me*. Ask it of your own heart tonight. Having said with these men, *Who* can dwell in the fire? say, *I am* in the fire What will it do with me? Will this fire, from which I cannot escape, this fire so slowly burning that in my unutterable folly I think of it as some autumnal tint, when it is blasting devastation—will it finally devour or purify me?

> Eternal Light! Eternal Light!
> How pure the soul must be,
> When, placed within Thy searching sight,
> It shrinks not, but, with calm delight,
> Can live, and look on Thee!
>
> The spirits that surround Thy throne
> May bear the burning bliss;
> But that is surely theirs alone,
> Since they have never, never known
> A fallen world like this.
>
> There is a way for man to rise
> To that sublime abode;—
> An offering and a sacrifice,
> A Holy Spirit's energies,
> An Advocate with God.

CHAPTER VI

THE AUTHORITY OF JESUS

And it came to pass, when Jesus ended these words, the multitudes were astonished at His teaching: for He taught them as one having authority, and not as their scribes.
MATTHEW 7:28, 29.

THESE WORDS OCCUR AT THE CLOSE OF THE MANIFESTO OF THE King. They chronicle for us the fact of the impression produced upon multitudes who had been listening to His teaching of His followers. That which supremely arrested their attention was the note of authority. This becomes the more striking in view of the contrast suggested by the evangelist as he records the fact: "The multitudes were astonished at His teaching: for He taught them as having authority, and not as their scribes." Now, as a matter of fact, the most prominent note in the teaching of the scribes was that of authority. As revealed to us in the life of Jesus, these men were argumentative, dogmatic, critical, ready to ostracize and excommunicate all who did not receive their teaching. The people regarded them as the official interpreters of the law of Moses and the traditions of the fathers.

Yet, when the gathered multitudes had listened to Jesus unfolding the law of His Kingdom to His disciples, when they had heard Him pass from the winsome tenderness of the opening beatitudes to the solemn severity of the closing warnings, they were astonished at His authority as distinguished from that of their own teachers.

What, then, was the authority of the scribe? It was interpretative, dogmatic, official. None of these words is necessarily indicative of wrong condition. Interpretation is of infinite value; dogmatism has its place, and an official position is not necessarily false. To this kind of authority the people were perfectly accustomed, but having listened to Jesus, they said He taught as having authority, and yet they declared that it was not as their scribes.

His was not the authority of interpretation, although He was the great Interpreter. Neither was it that of dogmatic statement, although He taught without reference to other authorities and without apology. Neither was the sense of authority created in the mind of those who listened that of one who had a right to be heard because of some official position.

It was rather that of the self-evident truth of His teaching combined with a sense of His personality resulting therefrom. To put this in other words, men listened, and then said, "That is true." As they listened, moreover, they were conscious that this man was speaking not in the name of another. He was not exercising the authority of words already spoken. His was the authority of origination, of Kingship, of supremacy, the thrilling, awe-inspiring authority of the final voice.

We are not surprised to read the statement which immediately follows our text: "And when He was come down from the mountain, great multitudes followed Him." Authoritative speech is always attractive, because man everywhere is conscious of his need in this respect. The authority may be false, but nevertheless it is attractive. Dogmatism always draws. It has been demonstrated that a man may erect a great organization upon the basis of a lie if only he will utter it with authoritative emphasis. We have no right to be angry with people who follow a false authority, for it must be remembered that the desire for government is one of the essentials of human personality. Angry with the false leader we may be, but pity should fill our hearts for those who are deceived. The great cleavage in the Christian Church between Romanism and Protestantism has been created, not by a difference as to the need for authority, but concerning its true seat. The watchword of the Romanist is the authority of the Church. The watchword of the Protestant has been, and I pray it may remain so, the authority of the Scriptures. Man instinctively seeks for authority. This is especially true in the realm of spiritual things, in those matters which affect creed, and conduct, and character. Therefore it is not surprising that the authoritative note in the teachings of Jesus drew the multitudes after Him. What the issues of their following were is not the question under consideration. We must never forget that the element of will enters largely and finally into the question of issue. My ultimate relation is determined not by what is said to me, but by what I answer. For example, the claim of the Bishop of Rome to authority in matters of Christian doctrine does not constitute authority for me. I deny the claim, and therefore am not bound by it. If I am able to establish the claim that the authority of Christ is based on truth, even then how it affects any of us will depend upon one's answer. We may keep His sayings and so build upon the rock, or we may refuse them and erect the superstructure of character upon sand. In this lies the awful majesty of human life. The supreme and overwhelming dignity of human personality is that of will. The majority of the multitudes who were attracted by His authority did not crown Him.

This whole question is a most vital one. I do not desire to discuss it academically, but rather in its living relation to those choices by which character is built.

Thank God, we are emancipated very largely from the intervention of men in the realm of conscience, but we remain profoundly conscious of the need of authority. For the sake of illustration let me speak personally. I cannot allow any man to decide for me what line of action I am to pursue, or what is to be the creed upon which my life is based; yet I do need someone to direct me, someone who shall tell me what for me is really right or wrong. In hours when the consciousness of life's strength is strong upon us we imagine that we are masters of our own thinking, and are free to do exactly as we please. Sooner or later, however, there comes to every soul the crisis when the need is keenly felt for a voice of authority, for one who will lead us into the highest, and the best, and the noblest. In order to the perfecting of life we need guidance in the finer decisions and subtler choices of the will. Any authority, to be finally satisfactory, must satisfy the reason and move the heart, and so energize the will. It is only such authority that will enable us to make our decisions with a sense of perfect rest. The message I bring you is that this need is profoundly important and is met only by the One of Whom the multitudes of olden days declared that "He taught . . . as having authority." I affirm, therefore, at once, and shall attempt to prove my affirmation by argument and illustration, that there is but one voice which can perfectly answer the clamant cry of our souls. There is but one Lord and Master to Whom we may absolutely submit ourselves, and know that in such submission we tread the pathway leading to the highest realization of the possibilities of our own personality, and that one is Jesus.

So wide is the field of illustration that it will be better for

THE AUTHORITY OF JESUS 75

us to confine ourselves to one portion of survey. Therefore I shall draw my illustrations from that Manifesto, the uttering of which created the sense of authority in the minds of those who heard it. We shall follow two lines: first, that of the consideration of the authority of Jesus, and, secondly, that of our relationship thereto.

At first it might seem as though something in the manner of Jesus impressed the crowds with His authority. While admitting that almost certainly there were dignity and authority in the very way in which He spoke, there can be no doubt that this manner was associated in the closest sense with the matter of His speech. It is almost impossible to dissociate these two things in studying His Manifesto. To minimize the value of the teaching is to rob the personality of its dignity. On the other hand, to be convinced of the truth of the teaching is at the same moment to realize the Kingliness of the One Who speaks. We find ourselves constantly contemplating the Teacher as we listen to His teaching. As His words fasten upon my conscience, sometimes scorching, sometimes soothing, I find myself irresistibly appreciating the Kingliness of the Person. Each utterance of His convinces my reason, carries my heart, constrains my will, and I stand in the presence of the one and only royalty, the King of men. The manner and matter alike appeal. The "how" is born of the "what." The manner is created by the matter, and thus the great sense of Mastership breaks upon the soul. In attempting to see the Person through the teaching, nothing is further from my desire than to indulge in any merely imaginative speculation. I do not propose to attempt an ideal portrait of Jesus, but only to discover Him as He is revealed through His teaching. Taking for granted your familiarity with the general scheme of the Manifesto, I submit that it reveals One Who speaks with the authority of perfect knowledge, of pure emotion, of poised volition. His perfect knowledge is manifested in His clear conception concerning God, concerning man, and concerning their interrelationship. I do not mean to say that in this Manifesto final knowledge concerning God is given to us. Such knowledge is not possible to man. My argument is rather that the conceptions of God which underlie appeal to the deepest in man are absolutely true. As the unfolding of law proceeds, God is revealed to the mind as being essentially supreme, relatively interested, and actively reigning. There is no discussion by this Teacher as to the difference or agreement between the doctrines of the transcendence or immanence of God. He speaks familiarly rather than argumentatively. In the appeal it makes to the deepest in us every reference indicates His perfect knowledge. "Seek ye first the Kingdom of God," and in that word as in a flash of light I find that this Teacher places God in the position of absolute and final supremacy. "Be not anxious," "your . . . Father knoweth that ye have need of all these things." In that sentence, and in the paragraph of teaching connected with it, I learn His estimate of God's interest in all things which He has made. "Seek ye first His Kingdom . . . and all these things shall be added unto you." And in these words I discover His declaration of the active government of human affairs by God. Thus, listening to His teaching concerning God, I am constrained to say, "He speaks truth." Every view which He sets before me carries conviction to my reason, sways my heart, and woos my will into submission. According to Him, God is supreme, is interested, and reigns.

And yet again, while convinced that this man knows God, I ask, "Does He know man?" And I listen for His estimate of human life. First of all, I discover that He thinks of man as a being in whom the spiritual is supreme. According to Him, the measurements of life are not those of time but of eternity. The deepest consciousness of human nature is not that of the senses but that of the spirit. "Lay not up for yourselves treasures upon the earth, . . . but lay up for yourselves treasures in heaven." According to these words, man is able to possess things in the infinite life that lies beyond the present. Moreover, Jesus' view of man is that it is his nature to be anxious or to seek. Jesus recognizes the restlessness which is the inspiration of endeavor. No word of His treats this as wrong in itself. He corrects the method of its activity. There are things about which man should not be anxious. There are matters in which he may seek. Jesus deprecates the turning of this power to the issue of acquiring that which is sordid and material, and urges that it be exercised toward the realization of all the highest and abiding things. Moreover, He is evidently intimately acquainted with all the facts of human nature. Every beatitude suggests a common human capacity, and as we hear them falling from His lips we know that they make their appeal to the facts and forces which are part of our nature. Thus, by way of His teaching, I find myself in the presence of One who knows God and man.

Moreover, the Manifesto reveals to me His intimate knowledge of the true lines of relationship: the relationship of man to God, the relation of man to man, the relation of the things of time and sense to those of eternity and the spiritual world. Here is a Teacher Who is not an ascetic withdrawing Himself from the thousand and one matters which I must touch every day, but One Who understands me in all these, even to eating and raiment; One, moreover, Who understands the passion of my life for possession, and Who comes into the midst of everything with such light as enables me to see clearly all relationships. Thus I have found through this teaching a Person Whose knowledge is perfect

—knowledge of God, of myself, and of all the interests of my life.

But this Teacher is more than One of intellectual accuracy. He is also a Man of pure emotions. His sense of justice is of the keenest. His words are characterized by a fine scorn of imperfection, and yet they thrill with the tone of delicate and exquisite sympathy. He is not a mere man of tears, maudlin in His pity, and unable to help me. Neither is He merely an iron-handed administrator. He is both. The same lips said, "He that looketh on sin with desire hath committed it," and "Your Father knoweth." No tone of mine can give full expression to either of the things in these words. The first scorches and burns. The second has in it the infinite music of the love of God.

And yet once more, through this Manifesto, I discover a Person of perfectly poised volition. For Him it is evident there is one center for all life, and that is the throne of God. His conception of life in all its varied capacities and responsibilities is that it must maintain its relation to that throne. All His decisions are regulated by that central passion of His being.

"Having authority." And it is the authority of One who knows God, knows me, and knows the lines of relationship. It is the authority of pure emotion. I cannot fear and dread Him, though His sense of justice be of the keenest, though His scorn of imperfection be of the finest, for both are atmosphered in a sympathy which is exquisite in its tenderness. It is the authority of a will perfectly poised in the good, and perfect, and acceptable will of God. Standing in imagination among the multitudes of old, and listening to Him, I am constrained to say, "I have found my King."

And yet, again, let us think of the teaching, for it was this which led to the Person. As we attempt to review in general outline that teaching, let us ask ourselves the simple question, Are these things so? A survey of the Manifesto reveals certain estimates of Jesus. He first of all declares that character is supreme. That is the meaning of the opening of this discourse. He pronounces no blessing on having or doing, but all on being. This is certainly startling and remarkable. Men have never come into perfect agreement with this view—at least, in their active life. We still say, "Blessed is the man who has" money, property, position. We still say, "Blessed is the man who does." Jesus says, "Blessed is the man who is." According to His estimate, the great man is the man of character rather than the man of property or of activity. Now, whether in active life we yield to this conception or not, I affirm, without fear of contradiction, that we are all convinced that the estimate is true, that the great man is the one who is pure and strong and tender rather than the one who owns anything or even everything. In the presence of that fundamental estimate of the King the heart is convinced.

To take another emphasis, having declared the supremacy of character, Christ proceeded to declare to the men who by yielding to Him had accepted his view of the supremacy of character and of its nature, "Ye are the salt of the earth. . . . Ye are the light of the world." In these words He affirmed the importance of influence, and revealed His conception of the kind of influence which the world most needs. Salt is pungent and antiseptic, and not always pleasant in the vicinity of a wound, but it saves, it heals, it blesses. Light flashes and flames, and is not always welcome to the man hiding in darkness, but it will help him to find his way out if he desires to come.

Take another emphasis, that on the necessity of law, concerning which He said, "I came not to destroy, but to fulfill." Do any of us think that He was wrong in this? I will not stay to argue it. Every man's deepest conscience assents to His wisdom. Or, again, mark another emphasis, that which He laid on the matter of the true motive of righteousness of the scribes and Pharisees. The righteousness of the scribes and Pharisees consisted in doing right in order to be well thought of by their fellow men. The motive was bad, as it is not strong enough to ensure righteousness under all circumstances. The righteousness which exceeds is that which acts in response to the throne of God and for the glory of God. When I was a boy I remember writing in my copybook, "Honesty is the best policy." No one questions the truth of that, but the man who is honest only because it is the best policy is at heart a rogue. Again we are compelled to consent to His view as to the motive of righteousness.

Further, He recognizes that there is a place in human life for anxiety, and the recognition appeals to me. It is useless to tell me not to be anxious, that it is wrong to think, and plan, and arrange. The capacity for these things is in my very nature. This King does not forbid them, but brings them into highest use. He says in effect, "Take the capacity, which is restlessness to achieve, and use it, not finally to procure things which pass and perish, however necessary they may be, but rather to put the fire and passion of it into the business of seeking the Kingdom of God." Thus He places anxiety in its right relation to infinite things.

Or to refer again to things already dealt with, His emphasis on the care of God and the true responsibility of man appeals to the deepest within us.

Taking a still more general view of all, we find that this Teacher has a twofold intention. He is seeking by His enunciation of law to realize the glory of God, and this by securing the good of men. Now let us pause a moment and earnestly ask ourselves certain simple questions. Are these conceptions true? Has He said one false thing? Where do we differ from His positions? Where does our criticism commence?

I think I can answer the questions. We begin to criticize by saying, "It is too high. It cannot be obeyed." And at this point I will not argue. All I ask at the moment is, Is it high? Are we prepared to grant this?

Many years ago a man in Birmingham said to me, "My quarrel with your Christ is that He is not practical." And I said, "Give me an illustration." He replied, "Confucius said to his followers, 'Be just to your enemies.' Christ said, 'Love your enemies.' Confucius is practical. I can be just to my enemy, but I cannot love him." That was a criticism honest and straightforward. I said to my friend, "But suppose you could be brought to love your enemy, what then?" He answered, "Then you would solve all the problems of human nature." That is all I ask. Is this ideal high? Is it noble? Does it at least command your admiration? Do you recognize its tone of authority? The multitude of Jesus' own day passed from the mountain impressed with the authority of His teaching. "He taught as having authority, and not as their scribes." The scribes dogmatically interpret authority, but Jesus has authority.

Then it would seem as though there were no more for the preacher to say. The issue is so evident. Yet here begins his most solemn and tremendous work. What are we going to do? There is really only one thing to do, and that is to be true to conviction. There is only one honest attitude in the presence of established authority, and that is obedience. And yet, here is the realm of uncertainty. The relation between conviction and issue is dependent upon that most awe-inspiring power of human personality, the power of choice.

Therefore, in conclusion, let me say three things. First, a

word concerning the logical relation between conviction and conduct. That may be expressed in one word—submission. If there is authority in this teaching of Jesus, when the logical issue is that I submit. Submission may be explained simply as the crowning of the Person and consequent obedience to His teaching. But there is a possible alternative. This also may be stated in one word—rebellion. Rebellion against the truth of which the intellect is convinced—that, namely, of the authority of His teaching and the consequent supremacy of the Teacher—must mean submission to the base, surrender to the low, which, in turn, means ultimate degradation. Mark the fact carefully. This high truth stands before you, claiming the consent of your inner consciousness. That you have granted. You have said, "Yes, that is the ideal, that is the Teacher." Now, if, after having given such intellectual consent, you turn your back on Him and choose to disobey His teaching, by such action you submit yourself to that which is low, to that which is a lie, to that which will inevitably degrade. That is the appalling alternative. If we could but see this hour as God sees it, then we should see how, within the next few minutes, crowds of men and women, yea, all of us, will pass into close personal contact with the Teacher, and in that contact shall crown Him, and so find our feet set upon the highway which leads to the realization of life at its best; or, rejecting Him, shall hand over our lives with all their capacities to the low, the mean, the ignoble. There is no middle course for anyone who has stood in the presence of the King.

Let us follow this thought of the issue a little further. What follows submission? Inevitable conformity to the likeness of that to which we submit. Obey the truth and the truth will make you free. Crown the high ideal and it will transform you into its own nature. What is that? Heaven. Where?

Here, and forever. On the other hand, rebel against conviction, deliberately refuse to crown the Christ, decline to submit to the true. What then? Instead of conformity, disparity, difference. Instead of growing likeness to Him, increasing dissimilarity, drifting further and further from truth, and what is that? Hell. Where? Here, and forever. You make your own choice. God grant you may choose aright.

A final word. Someone in this audience is saying, "I will submit." Such decision immediately brings the one making it into a new consciousness of sin and failure, a consciousness more profound and overwhelming than it has ever been before. Consent to the truth of what Jesus utters and abandonment to its claims is always followed by a keen sense of past sin and present inability. I have often said, and sometimes have been misunderstood, that having been brought up in a godly home, and saved thereby from many of the vulgar forms of sin into which others who have lacked my privilege have fallen, I never trembled in the presence of Mount Sinai. I always feel the profoundest sympathy with the young man who looked into the face of Jesus, and said, "All these things have I kept from my youth up." But while the majestic mountain of the ancient law never filled me with trembling, when I came to the clear shining of the ethic of Jesus, and stood in the presence of the rare and radiant loveliness of His perfect humanity, then I cried, "I am unclean, a sinner before God." Such is the experience of any soul honestly submitting to Him. And more, sin is not merely a pollution, it is a paralysis. I am not only defiled, but weakened. It is not merely, and not principally, that I cannot wash out the stain; it is that "when I would do good, evil is present with me" as a poison, as a disability. In the presence of these things, what are we to do? The acceptation of the ideal of truth never enables a man to realize it in experience.

Thank God, when the King had ended His Manifesto He had not finished His work. He went forward until He hung on the cross, and in the stupendous and unfathomable mystery of that darkness bore our sins in His body on the tree. Yet more, He returned from among the dead, victorious over all the forces which are against us, and having won out of death a life which He communicates to all such as put their trust in Him.

Now, as I come to the wicket gate to enter the Kingdom in obedience to the call of the King's authoritative voice, He first gives me pardon for my sin upon the basis of infinite justice, but He gives me infinitely more. He gives me His own life as the dynamic which shall work to the realization of His ideal. Trust Him as the Saviour, crown Him as the King, and you will find, not only the quiet rest of the reign of truth, but the infinite ability of the communication of power.

CHAPTER VII

THE BURNING OF HEART

Was not our heart burning within us, while He spake to us in the way, while He opened to us the scriptures?
LUKE 24:32.

BURNING OF HEART. THAT, I TAKE IT, IS THE SUPREME NEED OF the Church today. We have principles, but we very largely lack passion. I believe that our understanding of Jesus Christ is more spacious and correct than ever before in the history of the Christian Church. I do not mean to say that we are not still making mistakes concerning Him, for let it be remembered that He can be appreciated only by that whole Church of the firstborn of which He is the Head. No man can ever know all there is to be known concerning Christ, and no age will ever be able perfectly to comprehend the height and breadth and length and depth of the riches of His grace and His glory.

Yet, in spite of all the failure of the Christian Church, there has been slow and sure progress in her understanding of Christ. I repeat, therefore, that we have more spacious and more correct comprehension of Him than ever before. Yet sometimes I am afraid that our sense of emotion and fire was never less. We are afraid of anything in the form of passionate enthusiasm, lest we should hear some cynical grumbler on the outside edge of the crowd murmur the dreaded word "fanaticism." I am sometimes inclined to think that the "Jesus,

Lover of my soul," of whom we so often sing, is standing in the midst of His people sighing after their lost first love. I am not pleading for anything like an attempt to manufacture passion which is not real. Painted fire never warms anyone. There may be a great deal of noise, which is not significant of power. There may be a great deal of protestation of love, while the overwhelming and majestic passion is absent. I am not suggesting that a single person in this audience should go away to talk more of love for Jesus Christ. I do say that the Church sadly lacks burning of heart, fire, fervor, passion, devotion.

The story which I read to you, and from the midst of which my text is taken, is most interesting, and I venture to think most suggestive in the light of these opening words. It is one of the post-resurrection stories, and we are still living in post-resurrection times. Christ as He appeared to these men was the same as before His crucifixion, and yet utterly and forever different. We are the followers of that selfsame Christ in the identity and disparity which characterized His relation to men after the cross. Such a story as this has a very great value for us, because these men were exactly in the condition which I have just described. They had lost their devotion—not their love altogether, not their faith, save in some senses, but their devotion—their passion, their fervor, and their fire.

I shall ask you to think with me first of what this story reveals to us of these two men as to their possession and their lack. I shall then ask you to look with me at the Christ, as to His quest, His method, and His victory, all of which is not merely that we may contemplate an old story, but that we may find its new, present, living application to our own souls.

Looking back, then, to the road that leads to Emmaus, and to the two men, one named Cleopas, the other a nameless disciple, I ask you carefully to observe what they still possessed. They still loved their Lord. They still believed in Him. Jesus had said to Peter not very long before His crucifixion, "Simon, Simon, behold, Satan asked to have you, that he might sift you as wheat"—that is, the whole of you, for there the pronoun is plural—"but I made supplication for thee,"—and though this pronoun is singular, no one imagines that all the rest were outside the prayer of Jesus—"that thy faith fail not." I am bold to say that that prayer of Jesus was answered. Peter's faith never failed. The faith of none of these men failed; I mean that peculiar quality of faith which saves a man. Their faith in Jesus did not fail. Their journey to Emmaus was not one of forgetfulness. They were still talking about Him and the things which had happened. Amid bitterness and disappointment, amid the darkness of disgrace, they still spoke a kind word for Him. When Jesus joined Himself to them they did not know Him, they did not suppose but that He was a stranger journeying the same way. He entered into conversation with them, and asked them what they were talking about, because they looked so sad; and they answered: "Dost thou alone sojourn in Jerusalem and not know the things which are come to pass there in these days?" And He said, with that fine art which characterized Him, in order to draw them out to confession, "What things?" Listen to their answer, "The things concerning Jesus of Nazareth, which was a prophet mighty in deed and word."

That is their testimony to Him. They had not lost their faith in Him. They had not lost their love for Him, and even though He had been beaten, crucified, and is dead, they loved Him. They loved His memory. They believed that He meant well, that He did good, that His ministry was a blessed ministry, and they were journeying toward Emmaus with faith in Him and love for Him still in their hearts.

Yet listen to them for another moment, and you will discover what they lacked. They had lost their hope, and they had lost their confidence in His ability to do what they thought He was going to do. Their attitude toward Jesus was the attitude of men who should say, "Oh, we believe in Him, we love Him, He meant well, but He has not succeeded." "We had *hoped* that it was He which should redeem Israel." I pray you mark carefully the past tense. Their hope was gone. He meant to redeem Israel. He meant well, but He has been defeated. He tried but He failed. The hope which had been burning like a beacon before them in the days when He was still amongst them had died out into gray ashes; but they will not say anything unkind about Him. They love Him still, and still speak a tender word for Him. "He had tried to do something He could not. He was a good man, a loving man. He was a prophet mighty in deed and word, but there were things to which He was not equal. We had hoped that He would break the chain of our oppression and lift us back, out of our ruin, and redeem Israel and set up the Kingdom. We hoped —but it is all gone. We have lost our hope."

Consequently, there was a cooling of enthusiasm, and instead of tarrying in Jerusalem they had started for Emmaus, and there was sadness upon their faces, a lack of gladness in their tone. The fire was burning low. There was no passion, no vision, no virtue, no victory, no force, no fervor.

That is the picture of these men as they set their faces toward Emmaus, and it is largely the position of the Church today, as it seems to me. Personal loyalty to Jesus Christ is undoubted. It is impossible to meet with assemblies of God's people, or to meet with individuals anywhere, without finding men who still believe in Him personally, and yet there is manifest a very widespread cooling of the Church's passion, and a dying down upon the altar of the fires which blaze in the day of the conflict which makes for victory. We are not quite confident in His ability to do what we thought He was going to do. The movement seems so slow. The chariot wheels are tarrying, and the victory does not come. We are inwardly, if not confessedly, pessimistic, and this pessimism manifests itself in the prevalent consent to compare Him with others. We hang his name on the wall beside the names of others. We put some picture of Him in our galleries beside the pictures of other men, and we say, "Of course, He was easily first. We love Him. We admire His ethic. We admire His ideal, but He was sadly mistaken, and He took His way in semidarkness toward failure." We are comparing Him with others. We are modifying our conceptions of His victories. We are even allowing ourselves to read and discuss magazine articles which suggest that perhaps, after all, the religion of Buddha is more suited to Eastern lands than the religion of Jesus Christ. We are discussing the possibility of His ultimate triumph, and are asking whether, after all, the victories in Japan recently did not prove that another and a finer ethic is finding its way into the thinking of our age. And all unconsciously the fire of the Church is cooling. She is not so passionate as she used to be in her endeavor. She does not break into song so often, or sob in tears in the presence of the world's agony.

This attitude is born, not of the fact that we are individually less loyal to Jesus Christ, but of the fact that we are not quite sure whether the ancient psalmists were right who sang of His Kingdom extending to the ends of the earth. We are not sure, and are not perfectly at rest. He is so near to us, and yet we do not see Him. He is walking with us along the shadowy pathway, but our eyes are holden. There is today an appalling lack of the clear vision of the Christ which makes the step elastic and the spirit buoyant, and the outlook spacious, and the heart burn with fire and fervor and passion.

How does Christ deal with these men? For, after all, I have said we shall have to reduce this to individual application. We go back again to our story. If I am surprised, looking back over these centuries, at the attitude of the men, I freely confess I am far more surprised at Jesus. I am surprised at the wonder of His coming to these men. I know my confession of surprise is a revelation of the fact that I have not perfectly learned the lesson of His love. I know it, and yet I am surprised. If I may turn aside from the main line of my argument I would like to say to you, Be very much afraid of yourself if Jesus Christ is ceasing to surprise you. If you are losing that sense of amazement that startled you in the olden days there is something wrong in your life. He is always surprising us if we will but follow Him simply. He surprises us now by the fact that He comes to these men. Listen to His own estimate of them, "O foolish men, and slow of heart to believe." That is not my criticism of them. That is His estimate of them, and He knew them. O foolish ones, and slow of heart to believe; and yet He comes to them and joins Himself to them, and walks at their side, and deals with their foolishness, and stirs up the slow heart until it burns and flames. That is the grace of God, and I am amazed. It is a radiant revelation of the tenderness of His heart and of the strength of His love for us.

Why does He come? He comes because He is seeking love. It is there in those doubt-shadowed hearts, and He knows it, and He will come and renew it. He always seeks the beautiful. Christ always sees the beautiful, and therefore seeks it where you and I would never look for it. There is an old legend about Jesus. I really do not know whether it is true. But suppose it is not true, still there is a principle involved which is true. They tell how that one day He was passing out through the gates of Jerusalem, and there lay on the roadway a dead dog, the horror of all the Hebrew people, to be held in supreme and bitter contempt. As one and another of the teachers and scribes and rabbis, and the ordinary people passed by, they but kicked it farther away with contempt. But Jesus, as He passed, stopped and looked down on it, and said, "Behold the pearly whiteness of its teeth." You are quite at liberty to reject that legend, but do not give away the truth which underlies it. Jesus can always see something of beauty and glory which other eyes cannot see. Perhaps a few of you do not know what I am driving at. Some do. I have lost the fire in my life, my passion and my fervor. I want to say here—out of place if you like—that Christ sees the little that remains, and will say to me today, "I have come to seek *that*. Strengthen the things that remain." In the case of these men He saw personal loyalty underneath the hope abandoned and the confidence shaken, and He went and joined Himself to them in order that He might fan to flame the fire which was dying out upon the altar of their hearts.

How did He do it? Mark His method. He made their hearts burn by giving them a new interpretation of familiar things. I would like so to say the next thing that you remember it if you forget everything else. In the memory of it you will have the very heart of the message I bring to you. He made their hearts burn by talking to them. Their hearts did not burn within them while they talked to him, or while they talked about him. Their hearts burned within them when He talked to them. That puts everything I want to say into a few words. Not in their questioning concerning Him was the fire rekindled. Not in their pouring out of complaint to Him did it burn, but when they had ceased talking to, or about Him;

when they were silent and listened, then the fire burned. "Was not our heart burning within us, *while He spake to us in the way?*"

What were the things that He said? Nothing new. I am increasingly impressed with this. He did not bring to them any new message. It was the old, so said as they had never heard it said before. "Beginning at Moses and all the prophets He interpreted to them in the scriptures the things concerning Himself." Have you not felt as I have, that you would have given almost everything to have walked to Emmaus and heard Him interpret the Scriptures? It did not take Him very long. It was not a long journey, and they had done a good deal of talking before He commenced. He talked of the Scriptures with which they were perfectly familiar, of Moses, of the ancient history and the law, of the prophetic writings in which they had been instructed from childhood, and tracked for them all the pathways that culminated in the Man Whose loss they were mourning, Who had been crucified. He showed them how all the prophets gave witness to Him, and all the symbols of the ancient ritual found their fulfillment in the work that He had done. They did not know the Man talking to them was the One of Whom He was talking. They did see a new meaning in their own Scriptures concerning their long-hoped-for Messiah and His relation to the cross. They began to see a new light and glory flashing back upon the cross where their hopes had been blighted, and the fire seemed to have been put out. He interpreted in all the Scriptures the things concerning Himself. I have often felt that it would have been worth a whole lifetime to have walked with Him and heard Him tell how the shadow of the Mosaic economy found its fulfillment in Him.

Then when He took their prophets one by one, how wonderful to hear Him explain, and how marvelous the rapture of their heart as they heard Him tell how all the prophets led up to the Messiah Who died just as they had seen that Man die, of Whom they had been speaking so kindly. As they listened to Him they would find out that He was David's King, "fairer than the children of men"; and in the days of Solomon's well-doing He it was that was "altogether lovely." He was Isaiah's child—king, with a shoulder strong enough to bear the government, and a name Emmanuel gathering within itself all excellencies. He was Jeremiah's "Branch of Righteousness, executing judgment and righteousness in the land"; Ezekiel's "Plant of renown," giving shade and shedding fragrance; Daniel's stone cut without hands, smiting the image, becoming a mountain, and filling the whole earth; the ideal Israel of Hosea "growing as the lily," "casting out his roots as Lebanon"; to Joel "the hope of His people and the strength of the children of Israel"; the usherer in of the great vision of Amos of "the plowman overtaking the reaper, and the treader of grapes him that soweth seed"; and of Obadiah the "deliverance upon Mount Zion and holiness"; the fulfillment of that of which Jonah was but a sign; the "turning again" of God of which Micah spoke; the One Whom Nahum saw upon the mountains publishing peace; the Anointed of Whom Habakkuk sang as "going forth for salvation"; He Who brought to the people the pure language of Zephaniah's message, the true Zerubbabel of Haggai's word rebuilding forever the house and the city of God; Himself the dawn of the day when "holiness unto the Lord shall be upon the bells of the horses" as Zechariah foretold; He the "refiner's fire," "the fuller's soap," "The Sun of righteousness" of Malachi's vision. All these things passed in rapid survey as He talked. He was taking their own prophets and unlocking them, flinging back the shutters and letting the light stream in. He talked to them, and they were silent; and there broke upon them a new vision of the truth, a new understanding of things with which they were perfectly familiar, and in this new vision they found new understanding of all the things which they long had known.

Their burning heart, what was it? The thrill of a new discovery of their Lord and the shame of the past failure to appreciate Him, and the passion of a new endeavor which should set their feet in the pathway which led to ultimate victory.

All this came when they listened, not when they spoke to Him, or of Him, but when He spoke to them. Here, then, as it seems to me, is the supreme need of the hour, that we should "strengthen the things that remain"—the doctrines which we hold as true, the ordnances of the Church which we observe with painful regularity lacking passion, the service to which our hands are placed, which so often becomes dull as mere routine duty. We need that these things should flame with a new meaning, that the doctrine that we hold as true, and about which sometimes we fight, should flame into passionate vision, driving us into actual service. A man may talk generalities for half an hour and get no further. What did I mean by the doctrine we hold as true, driving us? Let me give you one small quotation from Jesus' last words. He said, "Lo, I am with you alway, even unto the end of the age." We have recited it, we have sung it, and once or twice we have felt it burn; but in the majority of days we do not feel it burning, driving us. That declaration of Jesus that He was always with His disciples was made in connection with His command, "Go ye therefore and make disciples of all nations." If you want to know why we are not moved with the fire and fervor of the promise, it is because we have been attempting to appropriate the promise without fulfilling the condition, because we have not sat still and let Him tell us

His deepest meaning about this thing. If once we sit in His presence and listen quietly we shall feel moving in our heart His own great passion for the nations of the earth, and we shall hear His "Go," and then we shall know that the supreme thing to hear is, "Lo, I am with you alway." When He whispers it, it will be to us as the driving force of God sending us out upon the pathway. We have not listened. These things have become so familiar that we are not at all familiar with them in their actual power. The cooling of our passion is due to the fact that we have attempted to spell these things out for ourselves, to explain them by our own philosophy instead of sitting down while He talks to us.

What, then, is the message I bring to you today? It is this. In the midst of your discussion, I beseech you, at all cost, make time to sit still while He speaks to you. I think I am safe from the possibility of misunderstanding when I say we supremely need a little more sitting still, a little more silence, a little more time of listening to the voice of Jesus. I am speaking as much to my own heart as to the heart of anyone in this house. There is a terrible danger that in our attempt to discuss Jesus Christ, and in our attempt to serve Him, we should fail to remember that no discussion can ever place Him finally. He defies the grasp of the intellect merely as such. We may discuss Him in our colleges and theological halls, and all the while we discuss Him the fire burns low. That is the peril of the age in which we live. We may be so busy running on His errands and attempting to do His work as never to sit still and look into His face.

I do not want that application to evaporate as a mere generality. I pray you test it by any day in your life, and test it by asking yourself, How long have I taken today to listen to Him? Someone will ask, "Do you really mean this? Are you practical, or are you indulging in some kind of sentimental talk? Are we really to listen to Him, listen for Him? Men do not hear Him today as they did of old." Shall I make your statement from another standpoint. It is not true that men cannot hear Him as they did of old. Men do not wait to hear Him as they did of old. In this present age they do not listen enough. Listen in the morning, listen amid the babel of other voices, listen at eventide for Him. In the Scriptures, those selfsame Scriptures through which He spoke to men of old, listen for Him. The study of the Bible will curse us in the next ten years if we are not careful. Men will tabulate and analyze, and think they know everything. Man, listen, for, unless as a result of your study of the Bible you hear the imperial tone, the voice of the living Christ talking in your inmost soul, your Bible knowledge is a mere technique that will burn you and ruin you within the next ten years. Listen, listen for His voice. Cease petition sometimes, cease praise sometimes, cease your questioning every now and then, and listen. No man or woman, young man or young woman, youth or maiden, will cultivate the habit of waiting to listen for the direct message of the Christ and be disappointed. Then your Bible will be a new book. Then your organization will throb with the propulsion of a new power. Then the missionary fire will blaze and drive you out upon the path of service.

There must be more burning of heart. We are in danger of being overwhelmed with our principle and our machinery. My plea today is that we take time to listen, that by His interpretation of the meaning of the things we have, they may flame with light and with fire, and create in us that holy passion which sings and sobs, which serves and waits, which travails and makes His Kingdom come. May God give us all the opened ear that we may hear what He says to us, for His Name's sake.

CHAPTER VIII

BACKSLIDING

If from thence ye shall seek the Lord thy God, thou shalt find Him, if thou search after Him with all thy heart and with all thy soul.
DEUTERONOMY 4:29.

THIS BOOK OF DEUTERONOMY IS A SINGULARLY BEAUTIFUL ONE. It is not a history. Historically, it covers a period of a very few days, for in all probability these final discourses of Moses occupied only a brief time in delivery. The book is more than a code of laws. All it says had been said already by this self-same man. It consists of the last messages of Moses to the people of his heart. It is prophecy in the deepest and fullest meaning of that great word. It is the forthtelling of the word of God to listening men. It is a poem full of light and full of fire. Here again the words of law are uttered, but in reading one is conscious rather of the driving power of love's great reason than of the binding nature of law's requirement, not that the requirement of law is lowered in one single particular, but that love speaks with wooing winsomeness and tender constraint. It utters the same thunder, but always in the tone of infinite pity. One would be inclined to say that in Deuteronomy we hear the law from the lips of a man who after long years has found his way into intimate communion with the heart of God. It is the Evangel of law. In the pleading tones of the great leader of the people one discovers that the reason of law is love, and if I ever ventured to choose a motto from some uninspired writer to preface so great a book as that of Deuteronomy, I would write Browning's words:

> I report as a man may of God's work,
> All's love but all's law.

Law is here, but it is the law of love. The text on which I have chosen to speak to you is a supreme illustration of the consciousness of Moses of the tenderness of the heart of God. He had been supposing the possibility of backsliding on the part of the listening people. In the light of subsequent history his words are seen to have been prophetic.

After describing in detail the process of backsliding until the issue of it is revealed, he suddenly breaks out into these words: "If from thence thou shalt seek the Lord thy God, thou shalt find Him, if thou seek Him with all thy heart and with all thy soul."

My message tonight is to those who are conscious in their own lives of any measure of backsliding. To such persons as the Apostle would address in the words he used when writing to the churches of Galatia, "Ye were running well; who did hinder you?" to those persons to whom Jesus is saying tonight, through the language he used to the Church at Ephesus, "I have this against thee, that thou didst leave thy first love"; to men and women who, looking back on their past days, remember the thrill and passion of discipleship as the supreme consciousness of life, but who now are sighing, "Where is the blessedness I had when first I found the Lord?" to men and women who are conscious of backsliding from their loyalty to Christ and relationship to God.

I beseech you to remember that the distance between yourself and your Lord matters nothing. The first cooling of passion is the tragedy. The final corruption is but a sequence to be expected, and which cannot be avoided save as the first love is restored.

I am speaking tonight to some who have traveled a long distance from the Father's house, to some who seem as though they had lost track of the way that leads them home; or I may be speaking to many others who have just lost their first love, who are maintaining all the externalities of Christian relationship, but have lost the thrill, the fire, the passion, the devotion. Whether to those or to others upon the trackless burning desert of degradation my message is exactly the same.

What is my message? It is in my text. Would God I knew how to say it. "If from thence thou shalt seek the Lord thy God, thou shalt find Him, if thou seek Him with all thy heart and with all thy soul."

First, let us put our emphasis upon the word "thence," for to do so will be to be driven to inquire as to the process and issue of backsliding. "Thence." Whence? And we shall answer the question by reverting to Moses' description, which occupies the earlier verses. Secondly, we will lay our emphasis upon another word in the text, "if," for by so doing we shall see the conditions upon which a man may return. "If . . . ye shall seek the Lord thy God . . . if thou search after Him with all thy heart and with all thy soul." Finally, we will hear, as God shall help us, the great central song of the text, "Thou shalt find Him."

"If from thence." The ancient message contains striking illustration of the matters concerning which we desire to speak. We may forget all the local coloring and look through to the underlying principles, and in doing so we shall find that a master hand has sketched for us the whole story of backsliding in every successive age of the world's history. There is no man or woman, young man or young woman, away from the Master whom they once loved and served, be the distance great or small, but that the process described by Moses of old is the process through which they have passed to the place of degradation. The issues he describes are identical with those which always follow the path of backsliding.

What is this process? Mark three things: First, "When ye . . . shall corrupt yourselves." Second, "When ye . . . shall make a graven image." Third, "When ye . . . shall do that which is evil in the sight of the Lord."

The first is purely personal, perhaps hidden from men, corruption of self. The second is the sequel to self-corruption, the making of a graven image. Finally, the overt act of evil.

What is self-corruption? It is the devotion of the life to something lower than the highest. The first movement of backsliding may be accomplished without committing any sin which the age names vulgar. In the moment in which a man takes his eye from the highest and sets it upon something lower, be the distance apparently never so small, he has set himself upon the decline which ends in the desert and in the agony of rejection. Self-corruption is the first step in the backslider's pathway, the choice of something lower than the highest. What is the highest? The thing you have seen that is highest. That is the highest for you. To you it was the fair and radiant vision of the loveliness of the Christ in those days when you knew He was fairer than all the sons of men, more perfect in loveliness. You saw that, and you turned your eyes from it to something a little lower, to some ideal you built for yourself out of your own imagining. You corrupted yourself when you allowed the false ideal to intrude into the realm of your own thinking, your own desire, your own choosing. That was the beginning of the whole story. Following that is what always follows, the setting up of a graven image. You say, "Here your message breaks down. I have set up no graven image." Remember, the graven image is always the figure of that which lies behind it. When a man has corrupted himself, the issue is always that he thinks falsely of God. Man is so linked to deity in the very essential of his being that he will form his conception of God upon what he is in himself. There is a sense in which, try as he will, he cannot escape this. He is forevermore projecting his own personality into immensity, and calling that God. That is the whole history of idolatry through all the centuries. Man has flung the lines of his own personality into immensity, and called the result God. In proportion as his own personality has become corrupt and evil, he has projected corruption and evil into immensity, and made that his god. When a man corrupts himself, he corrupts the idea of God by putting something false in the place of God. In the old days it was a graven image, so that, as the prophet said, man took to himself a tree or a piece of stone, and carved out of it a semblance, a grotesque imitation of himself, and called it a god. So when a man has corrupted himself by accepting some ideal lower than the highest he immediately makes a god after the pattern of his own ideal, and descends a little lower on this course of backsliding, until swiftly and surely he descends to a course of evil which a little while ago he would have declared to have been impossible to himself. He does the evil thing who never intended to do it. He started by choosing the lower ideal. He proceeded, in the next place, to corrupt deity, by projecting into immensity the false lines of his own corrupt nature, and worshiping that. Suddenly the light that seemed to lure him fades, and the very ideal which he worshiped fails, and he finds himself doing things he never dreamed he could do.

I am trying, as God shall help me, to set the story of

your backsliding in relationship to the spiritual and infinite. Shall I put that story in slightly different language? You corrupted yourself in that hour when you ceased your devotion to the God of your mother, and ceased to hand over your life wholly and absolutely to Christ. Your backsliding proceeded when you put into the place of Christ something else. It may have been your business. It may have been your very passion for knowledge. It may have been a far more mean and paltry thing than either of these, your pursuit of pleasure. You put something where Christ used to be. You who once took of your talents, and time, and strength, and poured them out in sacrificial service in the cause of Christ have been worshiping with all the soul, with all the heart, and with all the mind, wealth, fame, pleasure, I know not what. You know. There is your graven image. The result has been that this week, in the prosecution of your business, in the pursuit of your pleasure, you have done things which, if you thought I could proclaim them in your name from this pulpit, would cause you to blush and hurry from the building. You did not begin here. You began with the lowered ideal. You continued with the false deity, and the hour has come in which your hands in the sanctuary are unclean with deeds of evil, and you know your very heart has become polluted. That is the process of backsliding.

I pray you mark the issue of backsliding as Moses describes it here: "I call heaven and earth to witness . . . ye shall soon perish utterly from off the land." That is the first thing. "The Lord shall scatter you among the peoples, and ye shall be left few in number among the nations, whither the Lord shall lead you away." It follows, finally, that "ye shall serve gods . . . wood and stone." I think there is a sacred, and holy, and tender, and burning satire in those words of Moses. "You," he says, "men of highest vision and noblest passion and fair ideals, men who have seen, but have turned your back upon the vision, you shall serve gods of wood and stone, which see not, hear not, smell not, eat not." That is the issue of backsliding. First, lack of possession. In the case of these people, possession of the land; in your case, possession of everything which you ought to possess. The man who turns his back upon Jesus Christ to possess anything inevitably loses it. Take one of the most burning and tragic illustrations in the whole of history, that of Judas. Judas let Jesus Christ go for thirty pieces of silver. Did you ever notice that he never spent one of them? Presently I see him hurrying back to the men who had bargained with him, and in a great intensity of agony I hear him say, "I have sinned in that I betrayed innocent blood." And the cruel mockery of hell is here in the answer of the men who say, "What is that to us? See thou to it," as though they had said, "You made your bargain, abide by it." And he flung down the thirty pieces of silver. They bought with them the potter's field. He never spent one of them. You turn your back upon the God of the land, and you lose the land when you lose the God of the land. You turn your back upon the God Who made you and put you with all the capacities of your personality into this world, and you lose the world into which He put you. I know that is a thing which can be said only by experimental knowledge. I pray that God's Holy Spirit may carry conviction to some man here tonight. You cannot see the flowers if your back is toward God. You can botanize, but you cannot see the flowers. The man who has turned his back upon God has lost his land. He may own it under the laws of his country. He may even shoot over it for two weeks in the year, but he has lost it. The man who has turned his back upon the highest ideal has lost every real thing that comes within his reach. There will be many a weary march, many a hot and eager rush over the desert to reach the blossom, the bloom, and the fruit, but when the hand touches it, it is an apple of Sodom. The man who turns his back upon God loses also his influence and his power. May I say a thing that may sound strange and startling, and ask you to think of it. I can imagine that a man who has never been a Christian can exert some kind of pure moral influence upon his fellow men, but the man who has been a Christian and has turned his back upon God cannot do it any longer. The world holds in supreme contempt the man who has turned his back on Jesus. You have cut the nerve of your influence, backsliding soul. You have become lonely and scattered, without power to help in the world, because you have turned your back upon your God. There is nothing more tragic in the whole wide world than the man who once ran well but has been hindered, and has gone back to the weak and beggarly elements of the world. Oh, the tragedy of it! Think of it. You serve the god you have made for yourself. Worship and service are linked. Service is the expression of worship. Worship is the method of service. There is no escape from this. You are serving your God. You turned your back upon the living God, and set up a god of wood or stone, a god of mist, of vapor, of your own imagination, a cloud that rose like smoke from the fires of your own evil doing. You serve it. The tragedy of this worship, of this false service, is here. Your god cannot see, cannot hear. It is an insensate deity. There is no answer from the thing you worship when you cry to it in the time of fear. There is no sympathy, no heart in idolatry. The god of wood or stone gives no answer to the agonized cry of man, and all the false deities of your rationalism never help you in the tragedy of your pain, never soothe or solace you in the agony of your loneliness. You serve a god that cannot see, cannot hear, cannot taste, cannot smell.

There is nothing so tragic in all London as the backsliding soul. Moreover, if that tragedy is more terrible in one place than another it is in the case of the man who is a backslider, and is attempting to go on with work for God. The backslider in the pulpit is the supreme agony and tragedy in human life. The backslider in the Sabbath school class, in office in the church, in the church membership, the man or woman who keeps up the external semblance when there is no fire burning upon the inner altar, who compels himself or herself to the deadly drudgery of worship when there is no voice of the Spirit in the soul—that man is more to be pitied than the man who has cut himself adrift from the church and gone out into the darkness. There is far more agony in the heart backsliding that lacks the courage to be out and open than in the heart of the backslider that passes outside. I sometimes am afraid that our churches today are crowded with backsliders. I remember Thomas Cook saying to me years ago, "It is almost refreshing to have to go in the inquiry room with a man who has never professed belief on Jesus Christ before." Oh, the tragedy of the men and women who keep up the external semblance of Christianity with no virtue, no dynamic, no passion, no fire!

Is not this the story of backsliding? Did not the agony and tragedy begin when you took that ideal lower than the highest, when in your folly you made your own god because you thought the God of your childhood was unnecessary? Is it not true today that, like Samson of old in his agony, you grind for the amusement of mocking Philistines? The god you have made has no heart, no power, no pity.

My message tonight is to be found in these words, "If from thence." Mark this "if," and see the conditions. "If thou shalt seek." Seek what? "The Lord thy God." The search to which a man is called if he would return from the desert of his backsliding agony is not geographical; it is not circumstantial. He is not called upon to search for lost conditions. Moses did not say, "If you will seek with all your heart the land you have lost you shall find it." That would be a hopeless thing. He did not say, "If you will seek to set up again for yourselves the conditions from which you have departed you will be able to do it." That would not be true in human experience. What, then, is man to seek for? The Lord. Seek for your God. Get back to the conditions by getting back to God. If you are at a distance from Him tonight, at a distance from the light and song and glory of bygone days, do not attempt to regain the light and the song and the glory. Do not waste your time dealing with effects which you cannot correct; deal with the cause. Seek the Lord your God. It was when you turned your back upon Him that you lost your land. It was when you turned your back upon Him that you lost your power. It was when you turned your back upon Him that you became the bondslave of the things which have no heart, no tears, no pity, no sympathy. Therefore, turn not back to the land. Turn not back to the hope of new influence. Turn back to God. "If from thence," from the lonely and distant place of disappointed hope and agony of spirit. "If from thence thou shalt seek the Lord thy God." How am I to seek? "If," says the servant of God, repeating his "if," and emphasizing its true meaning—"If thou search after Him with all thy heart and with all thy soul." That is, into this search after God, which is to be the way of restoration, man is to put his whole heart and soul. The man who has wandered far away is promised that he will find God, but the conditions are that he shall gather himself up for the business of finding, that he shall put into this search both passion and principle. My brother, are you waiting until some emotion created in a service or a mission, or by some preaching, shall surge upon you? You will wait long and hopelessly, and wait in vain. When you have done with your playing God is to be found. When you have done with your emotional fooling—and I am not proposing to alter that phrase, I am not proposing to take back either the adjective or the noun—when you have done with your emotional fooling, and will put the fiber of your being into the business of seeking God, He will break upon you in light and glory, but never till then. I am not here tonight to tell you that, having wandered away from God, the pathway back home is flowery, easy, or simple. I am not here to tell you that you must be carried to the skies on flowery beds of ease. If you are a man you would not thank me for lying to you, even in the name of hope. You must seek God with all your heart and all your soul.

Let us pass to the promise. "Thou shalt find Him." Hear me, and God help me to speak these last few words as I ought to speak them. He is as near to you as He was in the old bright days. It is you who have changed, not He. You turned your back upon Him. He never turned His back upon you. It has often been pointed out that the Scriptures never speak about God being reconciled to men, but always of men being reconciled to God, and the method of the statement is of absolute importance. The moment in which you with all your heart and soul set yourself to seek, you will find God close at hand.

What is this that Moses promises? "Thou shalt find Him!" To find Him is everything. As Philip said long ago, "Show us the Father, and it sufficeth us." Find God, and you have found all that your heart wants. You are crying, "Oh that I knew where I might find Him." You are quite right. If you can find Him there is nothing else. If you seek Him with all your heart and soul you will find Him. Find Him where? Just where you are. Will He come with flaming and flashing glory? In all probability, no. Will He come with some new sense of His coming, making you thrill in every fiber of your being? In all probability, no. It is far more likely that He will come with a still small voice. But you will find Him if you seek Him. To find Him is to find all that has been lost by the process of backsliding. Backsliding began with the corruption of self. The finding of God is the redemption of self. I find myself when I lose myself. There was infinite meaning in the word of Jesus when He said, "Whosoever would save his life shall lose it, and whosoever shall lose his life . . . shall find it." It is in that moment when I set myself to seek God as the first matter in my life, when I crucify myself with my affection and my desire, and will no longer ask whether this thing is for my pleasing, but will give myself to seeking God, that I find Him. To the man who finds the true God, God is enough. Dagon falls to be broken in pieces. The lost ideal and the lost joys are found. Instead of outward and external act of evil, the outward and external act of good becomes the habit of the life, but never until God is found.

The issues are changed. If you will find God you will find the flowers and the land, and the possibilities of your own being. All the gray sky will flash with the purple of morning if you will but find God. To find God is to find everything. Instead of serving insensate deities you will reign in life in fellowship with the living and eternal God.

Let me lay my final emphasis upon these words. "From thence." Are you away from God? And, of course, I take it for granted that every Christian in this house who is not away from God is in sympathy with me, and is praying for the man who is away from God. Are you away, just at the beginning of the backsliding process? Have you within the last few weeks or months turned your eyes from the highest to something a little lower, or are you far away from Him tonight, almost in despair? I want to crave the patience of this whole congregation while I speak to one man. I mean that very really. I do not know where he sits, but here is his letter. I do not know his name, and I do not ask to know it. I am perfectly willing to respect his expressed desire that I will not try to find him. Let me say to this man that this sermon was prepared before I got his letter. I say this for his comfort, for if ever God sent a message to one man by a messenger who did not know the man, it is so in this case. I am going to respect this man's confidence by not reading all his letter, but I am going to read a sentence or two, and I am sure he will let me do it, because, as he says in his closing words, there may be numbers here tonight like him. He is a young man, and tells me that he came to London thinking that religion was a prop for weak people, having his own ideal, which he attempted to follow. Then he tells the story of the loss of the land, the story of the loss of influence and power, the story of actual sin. Then he tells me how, not knowing why, he wandered into this building last Sunday morning, and heard me read about the risen Jesus, and he tells me how, in the light of that vision of Christ, he was conscious of his own degradation. Then he says: *"I crept home, broken down, broken-hearted. This is my tale. Surrounded by people yet utterly alone. There is no one to whom I can go, though my heart is aching and my mind is sick. Can you give me one word of sympathy, one word of hope, or, better still, one word of guidance? I shall be present at your service tomorrow night and all I ask is that you will say something which I can recognize and seize upon for myself. I do not want to be sought out in any way. Let me remain, as probably*

I am, the type of scores of unhappy men similarly situated." Can I give you one word of hope, my brother? Yes. If I could not, I would never preach again. What is my word of hope to you? This is it. "If from thence." God gave it to me before He gave me your letter. He knew you were going to write that letter. He led you here last Sunday morning, and brought you face to face with your lost Lord. He gave me that message for you: "If from thence." Just where you are tonight. How I know what it means, alone in the crowd! "If from thence ye shall seek the Lord thy God, thou shalt find Him, if thou search after Him with all thy heart and with all thy soul." "Oh that I knew where I might find Him." Are you saying that?

> Speak to Him, thou, for He hears, and spirit with spirit can meet—
> Closer is He than breathing, and nearer than hands and feet."

Man, I am your fellow man, a sinner like yourself. I cannot show you these things. See the vision of my text. Never mind my sermon. Seek Him, seek Him with all your heart and with all your soul. Trample your pride beneath your feet. Crucify your prejudice. Put the whole business of your life into this minute. Trust Him, and for you also, or I could never preach again if it were not true, the day will break, and "He will restore to you the years that the locust hath eaten." He will restore to you the land. He will put about you the arms of His love, and lift upon you the light of His face, and make you His own. But you must seek Him with all your heart and with all your strength. My brother, I will not attempt to drag you from your place of hiding until you want to come, but though my hand never rest in yours and my eye never look into yours, right there the Christ Whose purity your sin has insulted is waiting to take you back to His heart. Let Him do it. May God bless and help you.

CHAPTER IX

MY FRIEND

He that maketh many friends doeth it to his own destruction; but there is a friend that sticketh closer than a brother.
PROVERBS 18:24.

THOSE OF YOU WHO ARE FAMILIAR WITH THE RENDERING OF this text in the Authorized Version must notice the very striking change of the revision in the first part of the verse. In the King James Version it reads: "A man that hath friends must show himself friendly: and there is a friend that sticketh closer than a brother." There is no doubt that the rendering as we have it now is true to the original. The Authorized Version was due to a mistake made by confusing two words which are very nearly alike, and yet have totally different meanings. In the new rendering we see that which was most certainly in the mind of the Preacher. He is speaking to young people on the subject of friendship, and he warns them that the man of many acquaintances is in danger, but that there is a kind of friend that sticketh closer than a brother.

I am perfectly well aware that at the first my text has no application such as I propose to make of it this evening. You would at once be conscious when I read such a text that I am going to talk about my Friend, my one Friend. But when these words were written that Friend was not in view save as a great ideal. As a matter of fact, the Hebrew words used here for friend are quite distinct, and carry two meanings. The word translated "friends" in the first part of my text simply means associates or acquaintances. That translated "friend" is different, and may with all accuracy be translated "lover," and that conception harmonizes perfectly with an earlier proverb. "A friend loveth at all times, and a brother is born for adversity." The true quality of friendship is love, and the one expression of perfect friendship is that of adherence, loyalty, or, again in the somewhat rough and striking translation of both versions, a friend is one who *"sticketh closer* than a brother."

The heart of man is forever craving friendship. Let every man beware of the crowd of acquaintances. Let every man value at the very highest the friend who is a true lover. It is a little difficult in June days to distinguish between the acquaintance and the friend. We have to wait for November and December. It is not easy to know your friends when the sea is smooth and reflects heaven's blue. You will find them when the sky is overcast and Euroclydon beats the deep into fury, and you are in peril. It is not quite easy to distinguish between acquaintances and friends in your days of prosperity. "A brother is born for adversity." You discover him only then. Friendship is tested by tempest. May we not say that the difference between acquaintances and friends is the difference between the reeds that grow by the river side and the rough, gnarled old oak stick when you are contemplating climbing hills. If I have a rough hill to climb give me one rugged old oak stick to lean on rather than a hundred reeds that grow in perpetual green by the river bank. If I have difficulty to face and burdens to bear and tempests to weather, give me my friend—he may be very rough, quite a curious specimen of humanity, but he loves me, and he sticks—rather than a hundred butterflies who are round me while the sun shines and are gone when storms lower. That was the Preacher's meaning. It was a valuable meaning. It is a great philosophy of friendship, and we do well to consider it.

Interesting as the theme may be, I do not intend to discuss this subject of friendship on the level of the ordinary friendship of these passing days. When the Preacher said, "There is a lover that sticketh closer than a brother," he stated a high ideal of friendship, the very highest and the very best that his eyes had seen or his heart had conceived. In the process of the centuries He appeared, incarnate, the one true Friend of all men.

This evening I want to introduce you to my Friend. I have found this One of whom the Preacher spoke so long ago. I know Him personally, intimately, though not yet fully. I am not going to discuss the philosophy of friendship. I am not going to portray the ideal of friendship. I want to talk to you about my Friend, to tell you some things about Him, and then how you also, if you will, may come into the circle of His friendship, among those to whom He says in infinite tenderness and love, "No longer do I call you servants . . . I have called you friends."

Therefore, you will understand that I am speaking tonight, as I sometimes say, not as an advocate, but as a witness. With all reverent familiarity I want to tell you what I have found this Friend to be. You say, "Why do you come with this message?" This message, like those of recent Sunday evenings, has grown out of the necessity of the hour. I attempted to speak last Sunday night of the way in which men and women in conflict with evil may hope to be successful. I directed them to that philosophy of conflict contained in the words of James, "Submit to God; resist the devil." In the course of my message I referred to the loneliness of many in this great London, and once again I have been dealing all the week, by correspondence or in other way, with those who found that word touch a chord in their hearts. There are a great many lonely men and women in London. If before I turn to my real subject I say some word or two about them, I crave the patience of those who are not feeling lonely. There are so many lonely souls all about us. There are young people in business houses in this district who are awfully alone. Monday, Tuesday, Wednesday, nine in the morning till nine at night; Friday the same; Saturday, nine till eleven; Thursday, nine till five, and then— no friend! The home far away in some country place. The loved ones who understand best, not nigh at hand. It may be no home worth the name, no lovers, no friends who really care. I do not think I can say tonight all that ought to be said and all I want to say about such a condition of things. I think I shall have a good deal to say about it before long. I want to talk to those who are in such places. Perhaps there are some even more lonely. I have not described your situation, but you are awfully alone. Hundreds of people on the streets as you walk along, but no one who knows you. The most lonely moment I ever had in my life was in 1896, when I first landed in New York. I stepped from the great steamboat on to the wharf, and there were hundreds of people meeting friends, but no one meeting me. Not a voice I knew, not a face that was familiar, and I stood for a few moments feeling desolately lonely. I am never lonely now when I go there, but I was lonely for that first hour. And that was a mere nothing, because I could find my way to friends, and presently I did; but, oh, these men and women in London who are alone! I would like to say in passing that it is part of the work of Jesus Christ to see to it that such hours as I have named cease once and for all. Until that work is accomplished it is the work of Jesus Christ to find these lonely people and introduce them to a circle of living, warm, loverlike affection. God help us to do it. We are going to try.

There is something needed beyond anything we can do on such lines. For the rest of this evening I want to speak to the lonely hearts in this great crowd. All the rest of you be patient. Thank God if you are not alone, and pray that I may so speak of my Friend Who never leaves me utterly alone, that I may win these lonely hearts to Him, and introduce them to a comradeship absolute in its perfection.

My Friend is first of all a lover. He fulfills that fundamental condition of friendship which the Preacher of long ago described. To my unutterable surprise, He says He loves me. The Bible, treat it as you will, speak of it from whatever standpoint you will, have all the difficulties you may concerning its construction, is His love letter to me. And whereas it says many things I have not yet understood, the one message ringing through it from beginning to end is the message of love. The Friend Who drew near to men nineteen hundred years ago in such warm and tender nearness that they could touch and handle and see Him is the Eternal Friend of men, closer than breathing in spiritual presence forevermore, and always saying to me that He loves them. The one great message of this Letter is a love message. I take it up and read it, and the thing that comes home to my heart startling me, surprising me, is that the pure, white, holy God loves me notwithstanding my sin, notwithstanding my pollution and my failure. My Friend loves me in spite of all my degradation.

More than that, He has demonstrated His love so as to bring conviction to my heart. Whether I have responded or not is not the question for the moment. I simply state the fact. "God commendeth His own love toward us, in that, while we were yet sinners, Christ died for us." He explains that in His own words, for He rises to the highest conception possible to the mind of man when He says, "Greater love hath no man than this, that a man lay down his life for his friends." This is your greatest conception of love; you cannot climb higher than this. There is no supremer proof of love than that a man should lay down his life for his friends. But my Friend died for me while I was yet a sinner, while all the set of my life was against His true and holy purpose, while all the influences and forces of my being were running counter to the influences and forces of His holiness and tenderness. Even then my Friend died for me. He laid down His life for me. Not only is it true that my Friend tells me of His love. It is also true that He has demonstrated His love to my heart's deepest and profoundest conviction. My Friend is a lover. Out of that come all the other things. Because my Friend is a lover He is faithful. He is true. He is tender. He is strong.

He is faithful to me, never deserting, never tiring of me. It was Shakespeare who sang, "Love is not love that alters when it alteration finds." Like that of the Preacher of old, that high ideal has had its perfect fulfillment in the case of my Friend. One of the pictures which I think I love to dwell upon almost more than any other in this connection is the picture of Jesus standing upon the mountain and leaving His loved ones. He gives them their great commission, and tells them what they are to do. Then with hands stretched out in blessing He vanishes out of their sight and the heavens receive Him. The question that comes to me is this, Will He, having left the pathway of human sorrow and need, be unmindful of the men He has left behind, for this is how I have been disappointed in human friendships. The man that was my friend when we trod the same rough path together—or seemed to be my friend—when he escaped from the roughness, and found the place of ease, forgot the man with whom he tramped the rough pathway. There is a whole philosophy in a word of the Old Testament, "The butler forgat Joseph." As I once heard Thomas Champness say, "His name is not always Butler." This Man is going, will He forget them? The next thing that happens, to their unutterable surprise, is the coming out of the mystery of the all-encompassing heaven of God of two men in white, who stand by them and say, "Ye men of Galilee, why stand ye looking into heaven? This Jesus, which was received up from you into heaven, shall so come in like manner as ye beheld him going into heaven." I have not quoted that to discuss the meaning of what they said, but to bring you face to face with the fact of their coming. He loved them, this wondrous Man, this more than Man, this mystery of Being, so warm that they had touched Him, so distant that they had never comprehended Him. He has left them, and, call it imagination if you will, when He left them and the heavens enfolded Him, His first thought was for the men He had left behind Him. The glorified Man of Nazareth, even in heaven's own light, called two messengers, ministers of the presence of God, and said, "Go, comfort the men I have left, and tell them I am coming again." My Friend never forgets me, never deserts me. He does not find any in high heaven in whom He takes a greater interest than He takes in me.

His faithfulness is of another pattern also. He is my Advocate against slanderers. He stands forevermore pleading my cause in the presence of God against all the lies that can be invented against my soul.

My Friend is true as well as faithful. My Friend rebukes me. He tells me in my deepest heart when I am wrong. I do not always like His rebuke. I shrink from it and try to excuse the thing He rebukes; but He is persistent. Hear the paradox and know its truth. With pitiless pity He refuses to make peace with any evil thing in my nature, in my habit, in my life. My Friend is true to me. When He sees that my thinking and acting are likely to lead me astray from the path that leads to ultimate victory He rebukes me, and His rebuke is severe. If you would know how severe, listen to His answer when one of His friends said to Him in seeming pity about the cross, "Be it far from thee, Lord: this shall never be unto Thee." Jesus, looking into the face of Peter, said, "Get thee behind me, Satan." It was harsh, but it was very tender. It seemed unkind, but it was real friendship.

> Do you think He ne'er reproves me? What a false Friend He would be
> If He never, never told me of the sins which He must see.

It is also true that He praises me. It is a great proof of friendship to be able to do that. I have known people in this world who have come to me and said, "I am your friend, and now I am going to be faithful to you." I always try to escape. That may be a confession of weakness, but it is true. The true friend will rebuke, but he will also praise. Some people seem to think that my Friend will never say, "Well done," until we stand before His throne. It is a mistake. At the risk of being misunderstood, I tell you this, He often says, "Well done," even now. At eventide, when the shadows are lengthening and the day's work is over, and the heart is sore and sad that it has done so ill, in quiet communion He comes and says, "Well done." I am always surprised when He says it, but He says it. He does not postpone His tender caresses to the moment when the infinite light shall be about us. He comes with me all the way, and I am often surprised to hear the accents of His voice saying, "Well done." You know it is true. There are more than a thousand witnesses in this house upon whom I could call, and they would tell you it is true. Yesterday I was tempted. I resisted, almost to blood, and I won, although I was wounded in the winning, and I heard Him in my deepest heart say, "Well done." He is a true friend. He rebukes me for my wandering. He praises me for every victory. He knows how to save me by the severity of His reproof, and how to help me by the tender faithfulness of His praise.

This Friend is tender beyond all telling, in my sorrows always sympathetic. We have all had, or shall have, some sorrows into which our nearest and dearest earthly friend cannot come. I have never yet had a day of sorrow in which I did not find my Friend at hand. Sometimes He is quite silent, never a word, nor a touch of His hand, and I have thought I was alone; but in the moment when my heart has said, Where is my Friend?—not perhaps by word, but by a sudden mystic consciousness of His love—I have known He was there, silent, and in the silence gathering into His own dear heart of infinite love all my sorrow. He is, moreover, gentle with all my weakness. Two or three years ago I found what gentleness is, and that in a definition. It is not often we learn things from a definition, but George Matheson defined gentleness for me, and now I know what it is. He said, "Gentleness is strength held in check." I cannot quote his actual words here, but only his thought. One speaks of the gentleness of the brook. There is no gentleness in the brook. It rushes and presses, laughs and roars, and does all it can with its puny strength. There is no gentleness there. But if you will stand by the mighty ocean when there is such a tide as "moving seems asleep," and the great waters kiss the shore, and your little one paddles upon its edge, and is kissed by the crest of the wave, that is gentleness. With one great uprising the sea might engulf the child, but its strength is held in check. My Friend is so gentle. He might crush me even by the inflow of His strength. He might blind me by the very vision of His glory, but He does not. He bends over me and says, "I have yet many things to say unto you, but ye cannot bear them now." He is waiting for me. He has been waiting all my life to say some things, but He has not said them yet, because I cannot bear them. My Friend is tender with a great gentleness that waits for my weakness.

Yet my Friend is strong, so strong that He can overcome sin, and Satan, and self. Sin overcomes me even yet. Satan overcomes me yet. Self-uprising blots the sun out of the heavens for me even yet, but it is always because I try my strength against sin, or Satan, or self, and forget my Friend. I never hand self over to Him but that He puts His cooling hand on the pulses of desire, and self is conquered. I never remit to Him the conflict with the foe but that the Lion of Judah overcomes the Lion who roars, seeking to destroy. I never hand over sin to Him in any of its hundred forms but that "He breaks the power of canceled sin and sets the prisoner free." My Friend is strong on my behalf against all the foes that oppose themselves, and He is strong in my weakness. If He is gentle with my weakness He is also strong. To that wicket gate somewhere in the castle of Mansoul that I do not know how to guard, and in trying to guard which I have failed, and the enemy has broken in, my Friend will come and make it the mightiest in all the castle. That is but another way of saying what Paul said. I repeat it, out of an experience far off from his it may be, yet real to me, "He hath said unto me . . . My power is made perfect in weakness . . . when I am weak, then am I strong."

Then my Friend is rich. He owns the whole earth. All the keys hang at His girdle. When in resurrection glory He appeared to one of His friends in the olden days He named some of the keys, but not all. He said, "I am . . . the Living One; . . . and I have the keys of death and of Hades."

But there are other keys upon His girdle; they are all there —the keys of knowledge and wisdom, the keys of light and of love. My Friend can admit me into the mystic meaning of the daisy and lift this poor frail life of mine into fellowship with the rhythmic order of the infinite universe of God. This world is His. There is never a bank of flowers but that they exist through His power. There is never a glorious sunset that flames upon my vision but that His hand has painted it. There is no music worth the name but that He presided over its first thinking. There is no color but that is an expression of my Friend's beauty. I am seeing Him increasingly as the days go by in all the colors of life, and in all the grays moreover, and in the somberness. My Friend owns the world, and I am finding out that you cannot introduce me to anything that is in itself essentially beautiful but that at its heart my Friend is sitting as King. You cannot bring me to anything that is worth having in the world of things, moral or mental, of music or literature, but that I find my Friend will lead me a little deeper and swing the door a little wider, and fling the horizon a little further back. All the world belongs to Him, and more than that. If it be true that there are many keys at His girdle and He is Lord of the world, then He is Lord of the heavens, and there are many diadems upon His brow. When this soul of mine thinks beyond dust into the realm of deity, my Friend is still on the throne. When this life of mine, chained for the moment to the things of time and sense, flings itself out to the infinite and eternal, I find that in the midst of the glory is my Friend, and heaven is already familiar ground to me, for my Friend has gone to prepare an abiding place for me, and He whispers in my heart as I tramp the dusty road, "Where I am there you may be also." My Friend is Lord and Master of Time and Eternity, of this world and the next.

Once again—and now what word shall I use? I must use a commonplace for lack of something finer—my Friend is generous. He gives me all I need, and infinitely more, for He shares with me all He has. His very life He makes my life. His very resurrection glory is my inheritance.

If these things are too high and too far and too distant, let us get back again to the things of time and sense. He gives me the world that belongs to Him. This world is mine tonight, in its every spear of emerald green, in all the music of the thundering sea, in all the healthfulness of its blowing winds. They are all mine. You may put up a notice, "Trespassers are not allowed," but because my Friend holds all the earth I can look over your hedge and possess what you only own, and there is an infinite difference between the two things. He has given me Himself, and with Himself all things.

"Are you never lonely?" you ask me. Well, dear heart, never perhaps quite as you are, for today my path lies differently, and I have my home and my loved ones, but I have been alone as you are in the days gone by. I have been in a city where there was no one who seemed to know or care, and even today there are lonely hours. Even today there are moments when even my dearest and nearest—and how near and dear they are only my heart knows—are excluded, hours of mystery and questioning, hours when the heart grows faint; but I never have an hour now in which I cannot find my Friend if I will. In the midst of the city, right there in the place of business, He is close at hand, a lover "Who sticketh closer than a brother." How shall I say it? I cannot say it as it ought to be said. May God the Holy Spirit sing it into your heart tonight as the very Evangel of hope.

How may all lonely souls come into His circle of

friends? It is quite easy for you to enter the circle, because this Friend is your Friend long before you are His, and He wants your friendship. The advance is on His side, not on yours. Listen to the tender and strong words He spoke to the first group of His earthly friends, "Ye have not chosen me but I have chosen you." That is still true. Is your heart turning toward Him in its loneliness? Are you crying out for His comradeship? He has been seeking yours for a long, long time. There is the first message of hope I bring you in answer to your question. Let Him speak again if you would desire to know how to enter the circle of His friendship. This is what He says, "Ye are my friends, if ye do the things which I command you." You say that is difficult. Listen to the first thing He commands you to do. "Come unto me, and I will give you rest." Begin there, and He numbers you at once amongst His friends, and all the rest of the commandments He will give you one by one as you are able to bear.

You need not understand the mystery of His Person, you need not be able to formulate a theory of His Atonement, but you are to come to Him and give yourself to Him. You are to say, "Is this the Friend who seeks my friendship? I will be His." And then, bending over you, He will say to you, "No longer do I call you servants . . . I have called you friends."

> Behold, a Stranger at the door!
>   He gently knocks, has knocked before;
> Has waited long; is waiting still:
>   You use no other friend so ill.
>
> But will He prove a friend indeed?
>   He will: the very friend you need;
> The friend of sinners, yes, 'tis He,
>   With garments dyed at Calvary.

O lovely attitude! He stands
  With melting heart and open hands;
O matchless kindness! and He shows
  This matchless kindness to His foes.

Admit Him, ere His anger burn,
  Lest He depart and ne'er return:
Admit Him, or the hour's at hand
  When at His door denied you'll stand.

Admit Him, for the human breast
  Ne'er entertained so kind a guest:
No mortal tongue their joys can tell,
  With whom He condescends to dwell.

Sov'reign of souls! Thou Prince of Peace!
  O may thy gentle reign increase:
Throw wide the door, each willing mind;
  And be His empire all mankind!

CHAPTER X

AMAZING LOVE!

But God commendeth His own love toward us, in that, while we were yet sinners, Christ died for us.
ROMANS 5:8.

DURING THE PAST WEEK I RECEIVED ONE LETTER WHICH ESPEcially arrested my attention. It was unsigned, and I want to read it to you. It is very brief, very pointed, and seems to me to breathe the spirit of restless and disappointed rebellion. The writer says:

> The writer begs leave to call to the Rev. Campbell Morgan's remembrance a statement he made last Sunday evening, viz., "My Friend has proved His love to me so as to bring conviction to my heart." Then why does He not convince every person of His love? Why is He not just to all?"

The text I have read tonight is my answer to that question, and I was very careful last Sunday night to state that fact. In speaking of my Friend I said two things concerning His love. First, He has declared His love to my surprise, and then I made use of these actual words:

> He has demonstrated His love so as to bring conviction to my heart. Whether I have responded or not is not the question for the moment. I simply state the fact. "God commendeth His own love toward us, in that, while we were yet sinners, Christ died for us."

Thus it will be seen that when I said that my Friend had brought conviction of His love to my heart I made the statement upon the basis of the text which I take tonight. I do not think the thinking of that letter is lonely, even though the writing of it is singular. I can well imagine that many people would go away last Sunday evening saying in their hearts practically the same things. "The Preacher declared that God had demonstrated His love to the conviction of his heart; but He has not done so in my experience, and if not, why not?" To that attitude of mind I want to say that the proof given to me of the love of God has been given to all. I did not mean to say that in some flaming vision of the night or apocalypse of the day God had done for me what He had not done for others. I suppose there are people even in this age who do see visions. I have never seen them. I suppose there are even today those who seem to hear, and perhaps do hear, voices which others do not hear. I am not one of such, and I should be very sorry for any man or woman to imagine that I intended to say that I had been privileged by God in any way that they had not. My Friend's proof of His love is given not to me alone, but to all men. No proof in mystic words spoken in loneliness to my own heart and no proof by some sudden and exceptional vision of glory could begin to be so conclusive to my reason as the great proof which belongs to all quite as much as it belongs to me. I venture to say—I know I speak within the realm of the finite, and limited and human, and yet I say it of profoundest conviction—God Himself could not have thought of any other way to prove His love so conclusive as the way He has taken. Will you let me, in all love and tenderness, and yet with great earnestness, say to you, my friend who wrote to me, and to all such, that if God's love has not carried conviction to your heart, I think it is because you have not taken time to consider that great proof? You have heard of it, you have sung of it. You could recite the proof texts, my text and the text in John, and many other such. "God so loved the world that He gave His only begotten Son." That is the proof. "God commendeth His own love toward us, in that, while we were yet sinners, Christ died for us." That is the proof. I have no other. Hear me, that is not idly spoken. I have no other. I do not find the proof of God's personal love to me in nature. There are proofs in nature when once I have found His heart of grace. Then every flower seems to me to sing of His love, and all the rhythmic order of the universe becomes one great anthem of His tenderness. I never heard the song of the flowers or the anthem of the universe until this proof had brought me low and convinced me of His love. I have no proof but this, and yet I say to you again, speaking experimentally, my Friend has proved His love to the satisfaction of my heart in such full and perfect measure that I have no alternative, so help me God, other than that of yielding myself to Him, spirit, soul, and body, lover to lover in an embrace that makes us one forever.

I cannot help thinking, if you will let me repeat it, that if this proof has not carried conviction, it is because you have not taken time to think of it and consider it. You may believe it theoretically. You may never have quarreled with the simple statement, with the perpetual, almost monotonous, message of the evangel; but have you ever considered the proof of God's love? To ask such a question as this, and to make such a suggestion as this, is, of course, at least to carry to your minds the thought that I am going to try to lead you in the way of consideration. So I am, and yet I feel I never had a harder task or a more impossible. What can be said when the Scripture has spoken? There is nothing to be added to the text. There is great danger of detracting from its infinite music by any attempt to analyze it and break it up. Oh that we may hear it sung into our deepest heart tonight by that infinite spirit of music, the Spirit of God. "God commendeth"—recommendeth, demonstrates, proves—"His love toward us, in that, while we were yet sinners, Christ died for us." I cannot add to that. There is nothing more to be said. It is the speech of infinite and eternal love. When I read it I am inclined to bow my head and say, "The Lord is in His holy temple: let all the earth keep silence before Him." Yet I must deliver my message, tremblingly and falteringly, and honestly wishing I need not say any more.

Notice first the persons involved in the declaration—God and the sinner. The spaciousness of the text is its difficulty. The infinite distances appall us when we begin to attempt to traverse them. We sometimes speak as though the supreme thought of distance were expressed in the words, "at the poles asunder." The poles asunder! That is but a handbreadth, but a span! God and the sinner. That is the supreme distance.

Notice, in the next place, the fact declared. Four words declare it. Four words that any little child who has been to school for one year could spell out—four words in our language all so tiny that a child can lisp them. Yet heaven is richer for their utterance, and all the thunder of the music of the seraphim is as nothing to that contained in them. All the mystery of human pain through piled up centuries is only palest gray by the side of the deep, dense darkness of this announcement, "Christ died for us." Finally, notice the truth declared in the text: "God commendeth His own love toward us." I cannot, I do not, believe that if you will quietly try this evening to traverse that threefold line of consideration you can write to me again and say, "God has not demonstrated His love to me."

Notice first the persons involved. How shall I speak reverently and yet with boldness of God? It seems to me that the great Apostle of love, John, the mystic, the seer, the man of vision, has given us in the briefest sentences the sublimest truths concerning God. I am not going to attempt to deal with these sentences, and yet I want to quote them. John tells us the story of the essence of deity in this brief word, "God is love." That is the subject in question tonight. John tells us the nature of God as well as His essence in words equally short and simple, "God is life." And once again John tells us the character of God in another sentence as simple, "God is light." How dare I drape such declarations with the verbiage of explanation? It seems to me as though the Spirit through the chosen apostle of love took up the simplest words of human speech and lifted them above all rhetoric and eloquence and explanation and exposition, and focused in them all the light and splendor and glory concerning God which it is possible for man to stand in the presence of and live. God is life, essential life, and in the word is included all the facts of power which we try to express in other ways: all the facts of wisdom which so often appall us when we have tracked its footsteps through immensity, and that overwhelming fact of His sovereignty which we are so slow to learn and acknowledge. God is life. Not that He has it, or has been it, or even lives it, but He is life. This I am not considering now, for it does not seem to me that we shall catch the marvel of my text if we simply consider the fact of the life of God as it is manifest in all power and wisdom and supremacy. To be told that a Being of infinite power loves is not astonishing, even though His love be set upon a finite thing. To be told that a Being of infinite intelligence loves does not appall me, even though His love be set upon some foolish creature of His own hand. To be told that a sovereign, supreme Being loves is not amazing, even though His love be set upon those who are subject to His throne. Therefore I pass from the sentence that speaks of the essence, "God is love," and the sentence that speaks of the nature, "God is life," to the final sentence which speaks of character, "God is light." The moment I have uttered it or read it, the moment the thought it suggests passes before me, I begin to be astonished at the declaration that He loves me.

"God is light, and in Him is no darkness at all." How shall I speak of that light and what it really means? It is best of all to catch the words of Holy Scripture and let them suggest, at least to my heart, something of the infinite and awful purity of God. He is holy and righteous. He is true and faithful. Holy—right in character. Righteous—right in conduct. True—the essential fact concerning Himself. Faithful—His loyalty, in all His dealings with created things to the uttermost bound of His universe, to that essential fact of truth in His own being. The God of the universe, infinite in power, infinite in wisdom, is, above all else, infinite in holiness. If the statement of the truth does not appall us it is because our sensibility to holiness is blunted by our own sin. If these words can easily pass our lips and we never tremble, the lack of trembling is evidence of paralysis in all the higher sensibilities of the spiritual nature. If only we knew what holiness meant, if we could understand what righteousness essentially means, if only we understood the real meaning of "truth in the inward parts," of faithfulness in the least detail of the activity of power, we should be appalled by the thought of the essential holiness of God. God, infinite in holiness. Let the broken and incomplete sentence suffice.

AMAZING LOVE!

Then I pass to the end of my text and find this word "sinners." What are sinners? Those who in character are the exact opposite of God, though they are kin to Him by nature. Here is the marvel. By nature man is kin of God. Do not be afraid of the great word which the Apostle quoted on Mars Hill. By first creation man is "offspring of God," kin to God, related to God. As in His nature there is essential power, in my life there is power. As in His nature there is wisdom, in my life there are knowledge and wisdom. As in His nature there are supremacy and government, so in every human being there is the capacity for government, for man is the crown of creation, the king of the cosmos, made for co-operation with God in government and dominion over all the far-reaching life that stretches—a lost territory—beneath his feet.

Such is man in his nature. But what of his character? Though he is kin to God in nature, all his character is unlike God. Unholy instead of holy. Unrighteous instead of righteous. Untrue instead of true. Unfaithful instead of faithful. Contrary to God in choices and conduct. I am not going to discuss the theory of the "how," I am simply stating the fact of human life. Even though in these days some of us may be inclined to quarrel with the phraseology of sacred Scripture and the terminology of the older school of theology, the fact remains, men "go astray as soon as they be born, speaking lies."

There is no man here who will test his past character and conduct—I will not say by the white light of God's existence, but by his own ideal of truth and uprightness and purity—and dare stand erect and say, "I have never sinned." There is no man in this house who dare say that, whatever his religion, or lack of religion. Men everywhere are ready to admit the fact of sin. We have been told quite recently that in these days men do not want to hear about sin, that men are putting sin out of their vocabulary as a word, and are attempting to put it out of their thinking as a fact; but they cannot put it out of your experience. Drop it out of your vocabulary if you will be so foolish. Cease taking account of it in your arrangements if you will be so mad. It will be the madness of the ostrich that hides its head in the sand of the desert and dreams it is unseen because it cannot see.

Now mark what this means as to contrast. By the highest standards of human experience the sinner ought to be objectionable and loathsome to God. Purity—and we are down on the low level of human thinking—does and ought to hate impurity. The man of high ideals must hold in supreme contempt the man of base and ignoble ideals. To me it is first of all inconceivable that infinite purity can care for me because I am impure. Apart from the cross of Christ you will never persuade me that God loves me. I am not blaming God for not loving me. I would not suggest that He ought to love me. I would not lend my lips to the blasphemy of saying that He ought to love me because He made me. He made me kin to Himself with environment in His own being and the inheritance of His own might, stronger than any other environment and inheritance I have entered into. Still, I am impure. I have been selfish, and sinful, and am undone in the fiber of my moral being, and it is inconceivable to me that the pure can love the impure. I cannot, save as His love enters into my life and enables me. The measure of my purity—it is faint, God knows—but the measure of it is the measure in which impurity is hateful. Here are the supreme mystery and the supreme miracle, not only of the evangel as it is declared, but of the experience of all such as share its mystery and become themselves like God in that they, too, love those who are unlike Him and unlike themselves. Mark the persons involved: God, infinite in holiness and purity and uprightness, and sinners such as are kin to Him in nature and utterly unlike Him and opposed to Him in character.

Now come to the fact declared in this text, the central fact of all your Bible. The fact, the first dreams of which you find in Eden, and the last glory of which flames in the Apocalypse. "Christ died for us." "Christ died." How am I going to speak of that? Do not be angry when I say that some of you are almost weary of hearing this. You are almost inclined to say, "Is this all? We know all this." We do not begin to know it. There is nothing else to say when this is said. Therefore, God help us to be careful how we say it, and how we hear it. The matter of first importance is that we are very careful what we mean when we say "Christ." It is of equal importance that we are very careful what we mean when we say, "died." If I take this simplest phrase in holy Scripture "Christ died," and utter the word "Christ," I think simply of a peasant of Galilee, and when I utter the word "died" I think of such a death as I have seen when my own loved ones passed, but I have not heard the music, have not seen the wonder, have not begun to understand how God commends His love.

With great solemnity, and speaking under deep conviction, I warn you never to forget that when you speak of Jesus you also speak of God. God was in Christ, not as He is in me even by His grace, but in that fuller and infinite sense which the Apostle expresses in the grandeur of that word in the Colossian Epistle. "It was the good pleasure of the Father that in Him should all the fulness dwell corporeally." Oh, I cannot understand it. No philosophy man ever invented can contain it. If you rob the word "Christ" of that significance your Gospel will fall to pieces. Remember that this is God in Christ. The Man of Nazareth, very man, perfect man, man as I am man, was God's revelation to me of Himself. The Son of God was incarnate in the Man of Nazareth, and the Son of God is today still related to that selfsame Man of Nazareth in the place where men gather in the home of God; but you have something larger here than the mere Man of Nazareth, you have Christ, and the name is the mystic symbol of Godhead bent in humility to redemption's work. Christ, the Son of God Who is of the essence of God, Who was with God in the measureless deeps and infinitudes of bygone eternity, Who was God, and Who, in a mystery profounder than the mystery of the rolling ages, became flesh and dwelt amongst men. "Christ"—do not put any small human measurement upon this word, or you will rob the evangel of its music. You may well sit down and tell me that God has not proved His love to you if you think little of Christ. It is little thinking of Christ that has degraded our conception of the meaning of His death. "Christ died," and if you stand in front of the Roman gibbet and watch the ebbing of the life of the man until presently you say, "He is dead," and if you imagine that is all that is meant, your eyes are very blind. You have seen very little. He Himself said that the physical is not death. He did not ever speak of such as death, but always as falling asleep. In His thinking and teaching, and in the Apostolic thinking and teaching which immediately succeeded it, death was something profounder than physical dissolution. What is death? Death is that in which a man may be, while yet alive, in the physical realm. A man can be dead in trespasses and sins. Death is that condition in which a woman may be while in the height of the London season. "She that giveth herself to pleasure is dead while she liveth." Death is not dissolution of the body.

It is severance of the spirit from God, the sense of homelessness, the sense of friendlessness, the one all-inclusive agony of loss, of lack and failure. Christ—and do not forget the meaning of the word—died. Listen, "My God, my God, why hast Thou forsaken Me?" The sense of homelessness, loss, the infinite agony of loneliness. But you say to me, "You told us a moment ago that this was God." Yes, I repeat it. Then you say, "What can He mean when He says, 'My God, my God, why hast Thou forsaken Me?' How can God say that to God?" Here are the mystery and the marvel of the unveiling of infinite love as you will find it nowhere else. I pray you do not imagine that this Person on the Cross is other than God. After hearing that human speech in which the Infinite and Eternal sobs itself out in the little language of a fallen race, what do I find? I find that God has lost Himself to find man. I find that God has gathered into His own consciousness the whole unutterable issue of sin. Christ died. He did not cease to be. God in Christ, Who had blessed men with a touch, and had wooed men with winsomeness, now dies as He finds the place of loneliness, of homelessness, of infinite lack. Yea, verily the old prophetic word is fulfilled there in the sight of heaven and earth and hell in the experience of God, "The pains of hell gat hold on me." "Christ died." And yet you say that God has not proved His love to you.

Now mark the infinite reaches of this Gospel—God and the sinner. We see the infinite gulf, and we state, according to the very highest and best conception we have of things, that God ought to count the sinner loathsome. What is the truth? When there was no eye to pity, His eye pitied. When there was no arm to save, His arm brought salvation. What is the truth? Hear it, man, woman, doubting of God's love. The God of infinite purity bent in the mystery of incarnation, and in the cross, to the condition of the impure. He gathered into His own experience and consciousness all the immeasurable and unutterable issues of sin. "God commendeth His own love toward us, in that, while we were yet sinners, Christ died for us." "Oh, for such love let rocks and hills their lasting silence break!"

"God commendeth His love." Can you explain to me in any other way than by the answer that love was the inspiration, the mystery of that descent and that great death? I say to you tonight that to me there is no other explanation of that death. "Scarcely for righteous man will one die: for peradventure for the good man someone would even dare to die." Such is the prologue of my text, and mark the emphasis, "But God commendeth His own love toward us, in that, while we were yet sinners, Christ died for us." "His own love"—there is no other like it. Here is the quality found nowhere else—"His own love." You cannot commend anyone else's love in this way. I ask you again, Does that truth prove anything other than love? You tell me that that truth is proof of God's righteousness. I tell you, No. You tell me that truth is proof of God's wisdom. I say, No, not supremely. You tell me that truth is proof of God's power. Not finally. Yet God's righteousness is vindicated in it, wisdom is manifested, power is operative. You tell me that the Atonement was necessary because of righteousness. And I say, No, God's righteousness might have been vindicated by the annihilation of evil. All the infinite righteousness of God might have been perfectly satisfied if He had swept out the things that insulted His righteousness. But listen, "How can I let thee go?" That is the language, not of righteousness, but of love. "He commendeth His own love." The Apostle understood the deep truth. Though this is the great Apostle of righteousness he does not say, "He commendeth His righteousness," but "He commendeth His own love toward us." I stand in the presence of my text, and in the presence of that eternal wonder, and I say my Friend has demonstrated His love to the satisfaction of my heart, and I know now that He loves me.

Surprised? Oh, my God, how growingly surprised I am. Amazing love! Why did He love me? I really do not know; but He did, and He does. Why should He care for me? I have been so selfish, so impure in my thinking and desire. Why I cannot tell; but this I know, He loves me. You may persuade me on many things, and you may dissuade me from some convictions; but I challenge you to dissuade me here. My Friend loves me. I am in His heart as well as in His power. I am in His love as well as in His light. You ask me how I know it, and I take you, not to the infinite spaces where stars march in rhythmic order, not to the hedgerow where God smiles in flowers; but to the rough and brutal cross of Calvary, to the hour of the dying of the Christ. "God commendeth His own love toward us, in that, while we were yet sinners, Christ died for us." My brethren, such love is royal, and royal love makes claims upon loyalty. What shall I do in answer to that love? We have often sung together:

> Were the whole realm of nature mine,
>   That were a present far too small;
> Love so amazing, so divine,
>   Demands my soul, my life, my all!

Have we not sung that wrong in two ways? Have we not sung it first as though we would say, I cannot give Him so great a thing as the realm of nature, I can give only myself to Him? That is wrong. It is wrong in His thinking if it is not in yours. He counts you, bruised and broken, sinful, dying man, He counts you more than the whole realm of nature.

When one day He held the infinite balances in His hand, He said, "What doth it profit a man, to gain the whole world, and forfeit his life?" That is His estimate. God so loves you that He would not feel Himself enriched if he could save the whole realm of nature and lose you. How do I know that? Because He gave something infinitely more than the whole realm of nature, He gave Himself in His Son for you. If you want to know your value by the measurements of love, God measure you by Himself. When next you sing that verse, do not sing it as though you had nothing to give—if you have yourself to give. If you have yourself to give, give yourself. That is all He wants. Have we not sung that verse wrongly in the next place by singing, "Love so amazing, so divine, demands my soul, my life, my all," without the answering abandonment? My brother, my sister, answer that love tonight, not only by singing of its demands, but by giving all you are to it. Give yourself, with all your wounds and bruises, with all your weakness and frailty. Answer that love, and that love will remake you until at last you shall be meet for the dwelling of the saints in light. May God in His infinite grace speak this word to us as no human voice can speak it.

CHAPTER XI

IF CHRIST DID NOT RISE—WHAT THEN?

If Christ hath not been raised, then is our preaching vain, your faith also is vain. . . . If Christ hath not been raised, your faith is vain; ye are yet in your sins. . . . If we have only hoped in Christ in this life, we are of all men most pitiable.

I CORINTHIANS 15:14, 17, 19.

IN THESE WORDS WE HAVE THE APOSTLE'S ESTIMATE OF THE place and value of that great event which we commemorate today in common with the whole Catholic Church of Jesus Christ. It is a most startling statement, made without apology and without condition. Everything depends upon this one central fact: a risen Christ, or empty preaching and false faith, and a state of abject misery. This man did not think for a single moment that there could be any continuity of the Christian fact and force if the resurrection were disproved. Now, we must understand in considering so startling a declaration as this that we do not occupy exactly the same ground as Paul did when he wrote these words. The difference between his position and ours is a very great one in some respects. He wrote these words somewhere about a generation after the death of Jesus. The Gospel stories were not all then in circulation, but men had gone out from Jerusalem through Judea and Samaria, and with new force and power from Antioch to the regions stretching beyond, and as they had passed out they had everywhere told the same story of Jesus of Nazareth, who had lived a sinless life, had died a sorrowful death, and had risen again in power and in glory. A generation only had passed. Consequently Paul's statement in this letter to the Corinthian Christians, who were familiar with questions rife in Corinth concerning the possibility of resurrection under any circumstances, makes its appeal to a generation of experience, and therefrom gathers its greatest force as a challenge. We go back to these words and read them with a slightly different accent. Their essential meaning is not changed, but we are not gathered together at the close of one generation of the telling of the story of the life and death and resurrection of Jesus. The generations have multiplied themselves into centuries, and the centuries have rolled onward until nineteen have run their course, and through all of them the messengers have been pressing on, telling the same story with like results. Consequently, there is something less of the argumentative in the text for us than for the men of Corinth. We take these words and read them, and there is but one conclusion. The Apostle says if Christ did not rise, then "preaching is vain"; but preaching has not been vain, therefore Christ was raised. He says, if Christ hath not been raised, "faith is vain"; but faith has been fruitful for nineteen centuries, therefore Christ hath been raised. He says, if Christ hath not been raised, "we are of all men most pitiable"; but we decline the pity. We have marched through nineteen centuries with banners floating and songs lifted, and today we are a jubilant host raising songs of gladness that thrill through all the world. We are not pitiable, and with charity and tenderness, and yet with scorn, we decline the pity of the man who lives in dust and ashes. Therefore Christ hath been raised. If these conclusions are not right, then the Apostle's statement was

IF CHRIST DID NOT RISE—WHAT THEN? 141

wrong; he made a false deduction. According to the statement he made, the victory of preaching, the fruitfulness of faith, and the jubilation of the Church are final evidences of the fact of Christ's resurrection. We believe that they are. I submit to you that the surest evidence of actual and positive resurrection from the dead is not documentary evidence, is not argumentative evidence, and I will include in that the sermon I am about to preach. The final evidence is the Church, that holy company of men and women, and, thank God, little children, gathered from among all nations, irrespective of geographical boundaries or temperaments, or times or seasons, gathered as the result of the foolishness of preaching Christ crucified and risen. The supreme demonstration of the fact of the resurrection is in the fruitfulness of faith. Faith has fastened upon the Evangel, with what result? Impurity has perished, and purity has resulted. Selfishness has been smitten to death, and sacrifice has been the order of life. Bonds have been broken, and men have gone forth into freedom. Faith has taken hold upon this Evangel of the resurrection and believed it, and, lo, chains have fallen, the burden has rolled down the hill into the valley, and Christian has set his face toward the Celestial City with a new song and a new victory. The final demonstration of the fact of the resurrection of Jesus Christ is the joy of the Church: may I pause to say, alas, and alas, that we give so little of it to the world! We ought to be a singing people. We do occasionally hear people break out into song about their household duties, and in the streets, but all too seldom. One of the greatest curses of our age is that we are afraid that kind of thing is not respectable. Do not ever again hush the emotion that wells in your heart, whether you are in the train or on the street, or wherever you are. It is not that the song is not there, but we have tried to check it with respectability. In spite of all false checks, however, we are a singing people. You talk to me of musical London. There is more singing in the sanctuary than anywhere else. You tell me of the development of music in the history of the ages. There is no music yet quite equal to "The Messiah." When you have sung your Hallelujah Chorus, let there be silence. The Church has given the world its music. We are not pitiable. I claim that these things are the final demonstration of the truth of the resurrection of Jesus Christ.

Understanding, therefore, that we approach our subject from a slightly different standpoint, having all the added testimony of the passing centuries, I yet desire to take you back to Paul's affirmation, and, if I may, intimate the changed position we occupy by slightly changing the form of his declaration. To indicate the fact that we are looking back rather than that we stand in the presence of a newborn Gospel, I want to consider this theme thus—if Christ had not been raised, what then? Was Paul right when he said that faith would have been fruitless? Was Paul right when he intimated that upon the very children of song there must have come an inevitable sadness which would have made them the most pitiable men in the world? Was he right? I affirm at once that I believe he was absolutely right. Let us think of it for a few moments.

Suppose Jesus had not risen from the dead, what would it have meant so far as He Himself was concerned, so far as His work was concerned, so far as His avowed purpose to build His Church was concerned?

If Jesus Christ had not risen, what would it have meant so far as He Himself was concerned? It would have proved, first, that the greatest claims He ever made were valueless. It would have resulted inevitably in the demonstration of the fact that the work upon which He set His heart in absolute sincerity of endeavor He was utterly unable to accomplish. If Jesus of Nazareth, Whom they "slew, hanging Him on a tree," and Whom, with tender, loving solicitude, some disciples robed for burial and laid in the tomb, never came out of that tomb, what then? Then the greatest claims He made were valueless. I do want to state this carefully. I will not even suggest that the claims He made were false, that is to say, I will not hint that when He made them He did not mean them. I cannot consent to adopt that position even for the sake of a passing argument. But I say they were valueless, and all He meant to do according to His own teaching He failed of in His dying. He said to the crowds when they criticized Him for that first cleansing of the Temple, "Destroy this temple, and in three days I will raise it up." They did not at the moment understand Him. The interpretation of His meaning came by way of the resurrection. He said upon another occasion to the cynical seekers after a sign: "There shall no sign be given to it but the sign of Jonah the prophet. . . . For as Jonah was three days and three nights in the belly of the whale; so shall the Son of Man be three days and three nights in the heart of the earth." He said upon another occasion, speaking in the hearing of the critical multitudes, "I lay down my life that I may take it again. No man taketh it away from me, but I lay it down of myself. I have power to lay it down, and I have power to take it again. This commandment received I from my Father." None of these things was true in issue unless He rose again. According to the appearance of things, if you deny the resurrection, His life was taken from Him by cruel hands that mastered His weakness and hammered Him to the cross with brutal nails, and He never took it again if He never rose. If I had been, which is not at all likely, more patient than His own disciples, I might have waited for the three days to pass, and if the seal had still been upon the tomb and the Roman cross successful, I should have gone away with agony in my soul. I should have said, He meant to come back, but He is as frail as I am. He is mastered as I shall be mastered. He is beaten. If He did not rise, His own supreme and glorious claims are all valueless.

If He had not risen, what would it have meant concerning Himself and His actual work from the standpoint of the history which has been written for us of those days? When He was crucified all the little company of people that had been gathered about Him left Him. I am not criticizing them; the more I know of my own heart, the less I can do that; I am stating the fact. One disciple betrayed Him, another denied Him, then at the end of three years' public ministry we have the whole tragic story in this one sentence, "They all forsook Him and fled." That is the end of the whole thing—unless He came back. The reverberation of the hammer that drives the nails is the thunder that scatters His followers. They have all gone. The Christian ideal has perished. It was fair and glorious and beautiful. It captured a few hearts and held them, but it is over. He is dead. He is in the tomb. "They all forsook Him and fled," not through lack of love, but because they felt that He could not do the things they had hoped He was going to do. With the death of Jesus the whole movement is at an end. Men are hurrying back to fishing nets, to farming, to sit at the receipt of custom, to hide the shame and disgrace of having associated themselves with a Man, Who, however good, was still a failure. If Jesus had never been raised from the dead, there in Joseph of Arimathaea's garden lay the dust of the fairest dream that ever broke upon the throbbing, surging heart of humanity; but it was past; the whole thing was absolutely over. It was merely that the

IF CHRIST DID NOT RISE—WHAT THEN?

great dreamer had been murdered, and that is the only meaning of His cross.

We talk of the atonement. We do not perfectly know all its method and its meanings, but we know its victory. Where is the Atonement if this man has gone down to death to abide in death? Where is the proof that in the death grapple in the darkness betwixt old systems and the Word, the Word was triumphant? He hated sin. He claimed to be sinless. He flung Himself against sin. He made other men ashamed of sin; they blushed in His presence, and blanched with fear as the lightning of His denunciation smote them in their hypocrisy. But sin is still rampant. Sin has smitten Him to death. Sin has laid its grasp upon Him and has put Him in the tomb. He is mastered by sin. How can He break my bond, or set me free, or blot out my transgressions? If He rose not, preaching is empty. If He rose not, your faith is vain; you are yet in your sins, held by them, bound by them, mastered by them, damned by them.

If He rose not, His was an ordinary death, and the doctrine of justification is unutterable nonsense. Men often say about existence beyond death, "No one has ever come back to tell us." If He rose not, that is true. There is no certainty of the life beyond if He came not back.

There would have been no justification, and there would have been no song in the cemetery if He had not come back.

If He had not risen, what of the Church? The Church could not have existed. Two things have made the Church. First, the Church consists of a multitude of people who have seen the vision of perfect life. Secondly, the Church consists of a company of people who have received power to enable them to realize the pattern. Jesus was at once pattern and power. Pattern in the glory of His life, power by the fact of His resurrection. If He rose not from among the dead —and now hear me carefully—I affirm that the Church has lost her pattern. Deny the resurrection of Jesus, and I can no more admire the beauty of His life. But you say to me, "Why not? You have already admitted that He may have meant well." Think again. The things He uttered were things in which He, with great distinctness, laid claim to such relationship to God as no other man ever laid claim to. If men murdered Him and He remained under the bands and bonds of death, no more able to break them than other men, then He was none other than other men. We are compelled ultimately to the conclusion that unless He was the Son of God, He lacked modesty, He lacked meekness, He lacked in the deepest fiber of His personality the simple elements of truth. He was the Son of God or the most disastrous deceiver that ever trod the earth. If you put Him in the grave and leave Him there, murdered by other evil men, and never see Him rise again, then He was indeed only man as I am man, and if He was only man as I am man, I repeat, He was the most successful, the most awful, and the most tragic impostor that ever trod the earth. How is He demonstrated the Son of God? By the resurrection from among the dead!

Once again, if Christ did not rise, what did happen? The living Church proves that something happened. What did happen? How were men deceived? I take the Bible up and find the story, and read the things these men affirmed to be true. You say they are not true, that He never rose, that He never presented Himself in that upper room while the doors were closed, that He never stood upon the shore and built a fire and prepared breakfast for cold, tired fishermen, that Mary never saw Him, but that she saw the vision of her own imagination. Tell me, then, what did happen? I have been told that the whole thing was a fraud, that the disciples invented the story to save themselves. But from all earthly standpoints the invention of that story ruined them. If they had abandoned the story they could have saved themselves. All the persecution, all the stripes, all loss and agony came because they would say, "He is alive." I think that needs to be stated today, and to be carefully considered. If the Christians going back to the Temple had said, "We have found a new system, a new ethical teacher, and we propose to form a school around His name," Judaism would never have been angry. It would have taken them in, and there might have been a School of Jesus to this day within the Hebrew economy. Judaism flung them out because they said, "He whom ye slew is alive." I submit to you that they lost everything from the worldly standpoint, and I have yet to be convinced that for nineteen centuries men would continue to suffer pains, imprisonments, loss, agony, death for a lie. Men will occasionally suffer a little while for a lie, but if this thing were a fraud, either cowardice or courage would have declared it ere many years had passed. Cowardice, to escape the scourge, the dungeon and the cross, or courage, as conscience awoke, would have said, "The thing is a lie." The first witness was Peter himself, when, as is chronicled in the fifth chapter of Acts, he stood before the High Priest—who was a Sadducee, believing neither in resurrection, nor angel, nor spirit—and said, "The God of our Fathers raised up Jesus, whom ye slew, hanging Him on a tree. Him did God exalt with His right hand to be a Prince and a Saviour, for to give repentance to Israel, and remission of sins." And hear him now, "We are witnesses of these things." By which he meant not merely, "We are the men who talk about these things," but rather, "We are His proofs, His credentials, His arguments." He meant to say to the rationalism of his own age, as it was represented by the High Priest, "You have no right to deny the fact of the resurrection until you have accounted for the change that has been wrought in us by our belief in it." When you tell me the story of the resurrection was a fraud, it was a fraud which made men pure and strong, and this is to reveal the absurdity of the charge.

If it was not fraud, what then? To take only one other suggestion, I am told it was a visionary appearance. We are told that people see what they expect to see, and I believe there is a great deal of truth in that. I have been for a great many years looking for a ghost, and I have never seen one. I have not joined the Society for Psychical Research, although I am greatly interested therein. I have read all Mr. Stead's ghost stories. I have walked churchyards at night and seen all sorts of uncanny things, but I have never yet seen a ghost. I will tell you why: I never expected to see one. Some of you who have seen one may pity me. You did expect, and you saw it. That is it. So I am told today by a cheap philosophy that these people saw what they expected to see. They thought about Jesus and hoped to see Him. They thought they saw Him, and there He was. But the facts are against that. They did not expect to see Him. They were startled when they did see Him. The most astonishing thing that ever came to them was the news that others had seen Him, and Thomas was not alone when he said, "Except I see and feel I shall not believe." They did not expect Him. And it was to men not expecting that He came. And it was a man who did not expect who said, "My Lord and my God." The visionary appearance argument does not hold, because you cannot deceive five hundred people with a visionary appearance. If it had been only the women, Mary of Magdala, Mary the mother of James, Joanna, and Salome who saw Him, these latter-day philosophers might have had some ground. I hardly like to admit it, but you remember that the two men walking to Emmaus said, "Certain *women* of our company amazed us . . . saying,"—and that emphasis lasts until this moment. Yet be very careful how you use the emphasis. Augustine said a very beautiful thing of Mary of Magdala, that she was *Apostola Apostolorum*, because she was the first sent with the Gospel of the Resurrection. Do not forget this. Sometimes when you are struggling along by logical processes your wife will see the thing long before you. Do not be angry because women see more than you do. But it was not to women only that Christ appeared, but to five hundred brethren at once! Did you ever hear of five hundred people being deceived in that way, and they not for long? But five hundred people at once on a mountain side in broad daylight cannot be so deceived. That idea must be absolutely abandoned.

If you say it was a lie I can at least argue with you, but when you suggest that it was a visionary appearance you make an appeal to a credulity that I do not possess.

I end where Paul ended his argument, "Now hath Christ been raised from the dead." The testimony of the disciples, already referred to, is our first line of proof. These varied appearances, the unequivocal testimony of the witnesses in spite of their own previous unbelief, involving all manner of persecutions, upon the basis of which they suffered, and served, and won, that is the first line of proof, but not the final one. The testimony of Paul himself is also proof. Paul is such a living force today that in one of the most recent books issuing from the more rationalistic side of theological thinking it is suggested that Christianity is more the religion of Paul than of Jesus. I do not quote that as accepting it—I think it is unutterable folly—but to show the influence this man has exerted on the thinking of the centuries. We all know how he sought letters from the High Priest which should empower him to send to prison and death men who believed in the resurrection, and in the Corinthian letter he tells how "last of all, as to one born out of due time, He appeared to me also." One has heard in these recent days that what happened on the road to Damascus was that Paul had an epileptic seizure in a thunderstorm. Supposing that were true, then I should set to praying for epilepsy and thunderstorms at once. Oh, the unutterable folly of it. What changed this man? What made Saul the persecutor, the champion of the old, into Paul the flaming missionary of the new? He saw Jesus and heard Him, and found out that He whom he had thought of as dead was alive, and so forevermore the motto of his thinking and preaching was, "It is Christ Jesus that died, yea rather, that was raised from the dead."

The final line of defense is that to which I referred at the beginning—the Church of Christ today. Its very existence demonstrates the fact of the resurrection, or else you have this strange anomaly in human history, a great institution making always for purity born in a lie, for it was the proclamation of the resurrection of Jesus that gathered the scattered disciples together.

There is another demonstration of the fact of the resurrection which is personal. Individuals who trust Him share His life, and that life is manifest as it masters them and changes them, until today on thousands of faces wherever you go you may see the very lines of the grace and beauty of the Son of God. There are men and women here tonight by the hundred able to bear witness, and if there were no other, hear me as I speak reverently and make my boast in the Lord—I know He rose, for His life has come into this poor life of mine, and while mine has still much to do, His is already changing it, and forces that harmed are mastered, and new desires, new aspirations, new outlooks are mine. If

Jesus were only such as I am, a man who died and passed to the dust in Joseph of Arimathaea's garden, He could not do these things. I can admire the genius of Milton dead, but I cannot share his life and see the vision he saw. I can admire the very melancholy of Dante, but I cannot see with his eyes. Jesus has come into me, and I have seen the Father to be what Jesus said He was, and my brother to be what Jesus said He was, and the world to be what He said it was. I know that Christ rose, because His life is in me. I am not admiring a dead thinker. I am living and walking and singing in comradeship with the living Christ.

Christ is risen! Our preaching is not vain. Pardon follows it. Peace comes after it. Power results from it. Your faith is not vain. The Living Person is the demonstration of its truth. The proof of pardon is in your heart, though it defy logical statement; the pledge of immortality makes you challenge old death as he rides upon his pale horse. These are the final proofs. Preaching is not vain. Faith is not fruitless. We are not pitiable.

We go back once again in thought to the grave in the garden and look at it that we may believe, that we may preach, that we may sing. Oh, wonderful garden, wonderful grave.

> Seals assuring, guards securing,
> Watch His earthly prison.
> Seals are shattered, guards are scattered,
> Christ hath risen!
>
> Now at last, old things past,
> Hope and joy and peace begin;
> For Christ hath won
> And man shall win!
>
> Where our banner leads us
> We may safely go;

Where our Chief precedes us,
We may face the foe.

His right arm is o'er us,
He our guide will be.
Christ hath gone before us;
Christians, follow ye!

CHAPTER XII

THE SPIRIT'S TESTIMONY TO THE WORLD

Nevertheless I tell you the truth; it is expedient for you that I go away; for if I go not away, the Comforter will not come unto you; but if I go, I will send Him unto you. And He, when He is come, will convict the world in respect of sin, and of righteousness, and of judgment: of sin, because they believe not on Me; of righteousness, because I go to the Father, and ye behold Me no more; of judgment, because the prince of this world hath been judged.

JOHN 16:7-11.

WITH THE AWAKENING OF THE SPIRITUAL SIDE OF A MAN'S nature there ever comes to him a threefold consciousness: a consciousness of sin, a consciousness of righteousness, a conciousness of judgment. All this is, after all, but one: it is the consciousness of God, with the things resulting therefrom. Though it may not be formulated, tabulated, expressed, the awakening of the spiritual in a man is always, first, the consciousness of God; and the consciousness of God in the soul of a man is always the consciousness of righteousness, and the consciousness of righteousness in the abstract is forevermore the consciousness of sin as a fact, and the consciousness of sin carries with it the consciousness of judgment. In this passage we have something which touches us very closely and very intimately in this matter of spiritual consciousness.

Such an awakening may occur in very varied circumstances in the life of a human being; indeed, it may occur again and yet again without producing any very definite result. The awakening of spiritual consciousness does not necessarily mean the regeneration of the spirit of the beginning of a new life. By the awakening of the spiritual consciousness I mean the sense of the fact of the spiritual. Very often it comes to the most godless men in circumstances of peril and danger. A ship at sea is suddenly in peril of sinking, and it becomes a house of prayer. Men are suddenly overwhelmed in some great calamity, such as the earthquake in San Francisco, and they think of God. It is idle to speak of such seeking after God in times of peril as cowardice. It is not cowardice. It is rather that the essential within the man wakes and realizes itself. It may be a passing emotion, but is a very real one. I have sometimes attempted to illustrate what I mean out of my own experience, an experience very much on the material basis it would seem, and apparently for the moment quite apart from the line we are pursuing. The first time I became profoundly conscious in my own life that I am a spirit and not a body—I had believed it long and had attempted to live in the power of the fact, and had known much of the joy which comes from the conviction—was in an hour of peril. It was in New York, in the Murray Hill Hotel, within five minutes of a fearful explosion which occurred there a few years ago, when the whole building was shaken. In a room on the third floor of that building was my wife. I was attempting to reach that floor, and felt that my spirit was hindered by my body. I became positively conscious that this body was a clog, a hindrance. In that moment I understood what people sing about in higher realms, "This robe of flesh I'll drop," and I wished I could. I knew in the moment of peril, and of desire, that I was a spirit. These moments of awakening come to men in different circumstances and in different places. They have come to some of you in this house in the singing of a hymn, in the reading of the Word, in some message delivered, in some holy silence when the material has faded, and you have been conscious of the spirituality of your own personality. A man never comes to that consciousness and attends to it, listens to it, thinks of it, but that these things pass through his mind in quick succession—sin, righteousness, and judgment, and if this be dwelt upon and faced honestly, squarely, it becomes in each case a double consciousness—of sin as an actual fact present in the life, and as a paralysis which man cannot overcome; of righteousness as a true ideal, something which can be admired in spite of his uttermost degradation, and yet an impossibility, something he cannot realize; of judgment as a verdict found, not by a jury of his fellow men, not merely by an assembly, or the consensus of universal opinion, but in his own soul, a verdict of guilty, not only a verdict of guilty, but a sentence impending, that of the disaster and death which must overtake sin. This consciousness of the spiritual with its sense of sin, or righteousness and of judgment, is not peculiar to Christianity. When Jesus said that the Holy Spirit would "convict the world of sin, and of righteousness, and of judgment," He did not mean that the Spirit would give men to know the fact of sin and the fact of righteousness and the fact of judgment. They knew these things while He was still among them. They had known them long ere His advent in time. Today, where the presence and power of the Spirit through the Church have never yet come, all these things are known.

What, then, is the testimony which the Spirit bears concerning sin, righteousness, and judgment?

First, the Spirit sets this threefold consciousness in relation to Jesus Christ. The Spirit "will convict the world . . .

of sin, because they believe not on Me; of righteousness, because I go to the Father, and ye behold Me no more; of judgment, because the prince of this world hath been judged." While there are notes of severity and searching in this testimony of the Spirit concerning sin, righteousness, and judgment, it is the one great evangel of hope.

He came to convict the world in respect of sin. What is it that He has to say to us about sin? First of all, He reveals the fact that in this Gospel age sin has a new center and a new responsibility. "Of sin, because they believe not on Me." The Spirit, instead of dealing with men about their own specific sins, the varied and thousand forms all manifesting the one central malady, reveals the very heart and root of sin, not as it is where Jesus is not known, but as it is when a man has heard the evangel, has seen Christ, has had his opportunity of believing and being saved. "Of sin, because they believe not on Me." The Spirit creates a new center for sin. When the Spirit has exercised His ministry in the life of a man, sin is a new and different thing, yet the reasonableness of it will be seen if we follow for a moment this simple line of thought. What is sin essentially? Sin is rebellion against the government of God. You may speak of your particular sin, your impure nature, your passion, lust, your tendency to lie, to cheat, to embezzle. What are all these things but the results of a cause, but branches springing out of one essential root? What is the root from which all these things spring? Rebellion against the government of God. Sin in the life of a man is high treason against heaven. Sin in the life of a man is not an inheritance to be pitied, not an infirmity to be excused. It is the lifting of the hand in an attempt to smite God Almighty in the face. It is the turning of the back of man upon God.

Jesus Christ lived a life which was directly opposed to

that. He bound Himself by bonds of perpetual dedication to the throne of God. He did only the things that His Father willed. The story is an old one. We will not stay to refer to the great words which fell from His lips, proving this to be true. We know it and accept it. He lived in unceasing and undeviating loyalty to the throne of God: perfect amid imperfection, sinless amid sinners, pure amid impurity, loyal amid treason. Such was the life of the Son of God. There are a hundred ways in which you may speak of His death. Let me follow the line of my argument and say that in that death He accepted—I know how impossible it is to state it all, yet hear this one-sided statement very reverently—He accepted the responsibility and consequences of the sin of the race and made them His own. When He walked unknown among the crowd on the banks of the Jordan the last prophet of the Hebrew line pointed Him out and uttered words concerning Him which ought to be carefully pondered. "Behold the Lamb of God, which taketh away the sin of the world!" It was then a prophecy of hope which has now become a fact of history. He took the responsibility of sin, and because He did that He has provided an absolution which is justification, infinitely more than pardon, and he has provided a purity for man which cleanses his nature and energizes him for new life. I have sinned the sin of rebellion against God and the poison and virus of it have entered into my life, and when I "would do good, evil is present." I see righteousness and admire it, but in my nature is the poison and paralysis of sin. What am I to do? Jesus Christ stands confronting me, and says to me, "All the guilt of the past I have put away. All the weakness of the present I am waiting to energize." If I refuse Him, that is sin. There is no other sin left. He has put it all away. There is no sin in my past life that He has not dealt with in the mystery of His passion. There is no sin in my present life that He cannot deal with in the might of His Holy Spirit. He waits, and plenteous redemption is at my disposal. If I turn my back on that I remain the slave of the sins which bind me. I remain guilty of all the sins which are against me. The central sin, the one holding all these within its grasp, and binding them upon me, is my sin of rejecting Him. "Of sin, because they believe not on me." You tell me, my brother, that your sin consists in some particular failing. That is not your sin. Your sin is that you believe not on Him. If you would believe on Him, if you would believe on Him with abandonment of the life, all the guilt would be put away, all the power of the sin would be broken. If you refuse the remedy that is your sin. The illustration which is simplest is best. Here is a man lying sick of a fell disease. I bring him the one absolutely sure remedy for his disease. He puts it away and dies. You tell me he died of his disease? In some senses you are right; but he died because he declined the remedy. That is the story of sin in the light of the mission of Jesus and the ministry of the Spirit. Whatever sin you are in the grip of, that sin must loosen its hold in the moment when you believe on Him and He commits to you the efficacy of His cross and the dynamic of His resurrection.

You say, "My besetting sin is my temper, my love of drink, some form of impurity." Nothing of the kind. You have not named your besetting sin. Your besetting sin is your persistent unbelief in Jesus. Sin is unbelief. If you would believe on Him your evil temper would be changed, the very fire and force of your love of alcohol would die out, quenched by the power of the Spirit. If you would but believe on Him the feverish fire of your impurity would be dealt with. Some of you go mourning all the days, with a mourning which insults heaven and grieves the Spirit, over some besetting sin which you cannot cure. If you would but believe on Him! The Spirit comes to give sin its relation to Jesus Christ, to reveal to men the perfect Saviour in order that they may understand that if any suffer the penalty of sin it is because they have refused God's one great all-sufficient remedy for sin.

Following that is the testimony of God's Spirit to righteousness. He "will convict the world in respect . . . of righteousness, because I go to the Father." The Spirit's testimony concerning righteousness reveals Jesus in two ways: first as a perfect pattern, and secondly as an all-sufficient power—a perfect pattern.

When Jesus said, "I go to the Father," so far as He personally is concerned He meant, "I came forth from the Father. I have walked the earth and the ways of men in the light of the Father. I am going back to the Father. There is nothing to keep me out. There is no barrier shutting me out of God's heaven. I go to the Father. I challenge heaven's light because of the purity of my life. I challenge the very holiness of God because I have never sinned. I am at home with the Father." That is Holiness challenging holiness and defying God's light to exclude Him. "I go to the Father, for I love the Father and my home is with the Father. The place of all my affinities is with the Father." Thus there emerges a new ideal of righteousness. We have said righteousness is for a man to pay his debts, and never to do his neighbor any harm, imagining that it consists in all that morality which is conditioned by the policeman. Jesus Christ says that righteousness consists in such relationships with heaven as make relationships with earth high and holy and noble. Righteousness consists not merely in the keeping of the laws written upon tables of stone, but in life which finds its center in the heart of God, and finds its home in the home of God. The Spirit reveals to us the true meaning of righteousness, and delivers us from false conceptions. The Spirit says to you righteousness is rightness, and rightness is right, and right is the proper relationship to the will of God, so that a man finds himself at home only when he finds himself with God. There are a great many men who are boasting of their righteousness who are not at all at home if you talk about God. There is a difference between the boasted morality of the sinner and the righteousness of Jesus Christ. If you are going to measure things by the standard of the street and the police court I respect your respectability; but here in the sanctuary where His Name is proclaimed your respectability is as far below God's righteousness as hell is beneath heaven. "I go to the Father." That is human speech. It is the language of a man who has walked here amid earthly things, amid the flowers and birds, and children, and in the dusty highways, yet forever more homed in the bosom of the Father. This is righteousness. "Of righteousness, because I go to the Father."

That is not all. If that were all I would be afraid, more afraid than ever before. Let me speak for my own heart. If I had nothing other than this revelation of righteousness I would be hopeless, desperately hopeless. I pity with all my heart the man who tells me that Jesus is his ideal and nothing more. Either he is so blind as never to have seen Jesus' glory, or else if he has seen, and is honest, the comprehension of the distance is in itself the consciousness of perdition. When Jesus said, "I go to the Father," He was not speaking personally merely. He meant more than that. He meant, "I go to the Father for you." In stately language, in the second chapter of the Acts, Peter traces the way and issue of His going. "Jesus of Nazareth, a man approved of God unto you by mighty works and wonders and signs which God did by Him in the midst of you, even as ye yourselves know; Him, being delivered up by the determinate counsel and foreknowledge of God, ye by the hand of lawless men did crucify and slay: whom God raised up, having loosed the pangs of death: because it was not possible that He should be holden of it. . . . Being therefore by the right hand of God exalted, and having received of the Father the promise of the Holy Spirit, He hath poured forth this, which ye see and hear." When He sent to the Father, and there in high heaven challenged holiness by the purity of His life, and found Himself at home with love ineffable, He came there not merely as the perfect Man. He came there wounded, with scars in His hands, and feet, and side. I see this Man of Nazareth coming back to heaven's high court, and I hear the song of heaven as it tells of His victory, and I am afraid, for I am left here amid my sin. Yet as He comes I hear Him say, "I am He that liveth." I understand that. Purity always lives. Holiness cannot die. "And was dead." Why did He die? I give you the answer in the first person singular. You must make it your own. "He loved me and gave Himself up for me." When the Man of purity came back to heaven, when the Man of right challenged heaven's light and was as unsullied as it, in His hands and feet and side were the arguments which told of the passion by which He had made it possible for the impure to come home, for the lost to be found, for the ruined to be redeemed. Now the Spirit has come to "convict the world in respect . . . of righteousness, because I go to the Father." Conviction by the Spirit is not only the revelation of a new pattern of righteousness, it is the declaration of a new power whereby men can themselves become righteous, and can themselves become holy. I think we must see that or we miss the very heart of the evangel. What is man's salvation? If by God's grace I stand in the light by and by—and by God's grace I shall—how shall I stand there? Not merely because He pardons sin. That is so, or I never could stand there. How, then, shall I stand there? First, because He pardons sin; and, secondly, because He makes me perfect. No one will misunderstand me. I speak not as though "I have already obtained, or am already made perfect." The work is not yet done. My patient, tender Lord has much to do, but He will do it. He "will perfect that which concerneth me." Jesus Christ is not proposing to lead into the courts of heaven an army of crippled men and women. He is not proposing to bring back to God's dwelling place vast companies of incompetent spiritual beings. What, then, is He going to do? Let inspiration tell us. He will "set you before the presence of His glory without blemish in exceeding joy." This is what the Spirit says to a weary world about righteousness. Have the true pattern and see it in Jesus. Have the power, and have it in Him.

Once again, note what the Spirit says to the world concerning judgment. "Of judgment, because the prince of this world hath been judged." This is a new emphasis upon judgment. It is a new warning from a somewhat strange angle of thought, and yet a very true one. It is, first of all, a new emphasis. In His victory over sin borne, and in His ascension and enthronement, God's final judgment is pronounced against sin. It surely has occurred to you that whereas the gospel of the resurrection is a gospel of hope, it is the severest gospel of condemnation which men have ever listened to. When on that Easter morning long ago God Almighty raised Jesus from the dead, selecting Him from among others, choosing Him and making Him the approach to Himself, what was He doing? He was saying in the sight of all the race, "This is the Man, the anointed Man. This is the Man I accept." What more, then, was He saying? "All men unlike Him I reject." The resurrection of Jesus was the evidence in human history of the type, the pattern, which God accepts.

THE SPIRIT'S TESTIMONY TO THE WORLD 163

The resurrection of Jesus was the proclamation to men everywhere that it is only as men are like Him that they can hope to rise as He rose, and ascend as He ascended, and come into the light and glory as He came into the light and glory, so that the fact of the cross and resurrection of Jesus is God's verdict against sin. "The prince of this world hath been judged." The verdict was found, and the sentence passed in the morning of resurrection. By the acceptance of this One, all unlike Him are rejected and judgment is pronounced against the prince of this world. Mark the emphasis. We cannot afford to miss anything that Jesus says. Who is it that is judged? The *prince* of this world. The master of worldliness. Worldliness is a great deal more and other than some of us think it is. Some people think that worldliness consists in playing cards and going to theaters and balls. There may be a great deal of worldliness that never plays cards and never goes to theaters or balls. Worldliness is that which never stretches out into the spiritual. Christ judges the world, pronounces it a failure, and condemns it to its own death in dust. By that material cross on which cruel and bloody men have nailed God's ideal "the prince of this world hath been judged."

Where are you living, my brother? Are you living here in London as though London were the last thing? Are you living on this one little planet amid the spaces as though it were all? Whether you play cards, or go to the theater or not, is nothing for the moment. Where do you live? How far does your horizon stretch out? How much do you know of the eternal? Your heart is capable of being full of God. What is it full of? If it is full of anything less than God, do not forget that "the prince of this world hath been judged."

Thank God, it means more than that. It means that the prince of this world hath been judged, and therefore his captives are free. "He came to break oppression and set the captives free." You have been mastered by the foe. He masters the foe, and if you will, you can go out; your prison door is open, the prince is judged. He bruised the heel of the Lion of the tribe of Judah; but the Lion of the tribe of Judah put His foot upon the neck of the roaring lion. The prince of this world plunged his venomous dart into the side of the Prince of glory; but the Prince of glory quenched its venom in blood, and you are free if you will be so. The Spirit is not here to convince you of judgment *to come*, unless that is your choice. He is here to convince you that judgment is accomplished. The monster is dead. His power is broken. The foe that held you has been despoiled in the mystery of the cross, and you and I may be free. If you choose to abide in slavery, if you choose to make this world the beginning and the end and the all of your life, then you must share the hell of the prince of this world. But it is your own choice. It is not God's choice for you. If you make it your own you must abide by it.

The Spirit's testimony is the most solemn and searching declaration that men can ever receive concerning sin, righteousness, and judgment. Yet my heart bids me declare to you that if it be solemn and searching, it is the one evangel of hope that is worth having. It does not seem to me that to preach Jesus as an ideal is an evangel at all. It does not seem to me that if He told me He was willing to forgive my sin without any reference to myself or my state it would be enough. When I learn by the ministry and witness and testimony of the Spirit that if I will believe on Him the sins that bound me shall bind me no more, the fierce fires of passion that burned shall be quenched. When I hear that if I will believe on Him Who went to the Father, Who bends out of His high heaven, and says, "I will that ye also shall be with Me where I am, though I know the worst of you—that you will deny me on the way—let not your heart be troubled, you believe in God, trust Me and I will bring you home," then I have an evangel! When I hear that He Who calls me to follow Him is not asking me to escape and run away from a foe that may dodge my footsteps and may overtake me, but is asking me to follow Him, has met the foe, and has broken his power, and has delivered me, then I hear the evangel.

What shall we do with the evangel? If you reject Him tonight that is your sin. Will you believe on Him tonight? That is your righteousness as pattern and power. Will you reject the Christ of Whom the Spirit speaks? Then you choose the judgment which follows upon the prince of this world. Will you crown the Christ of Whom the Spirit speaks? Then you share His victory over the prince of this world, and instead of being vanquished you shall be victor. Do not give this away in generalities. Shut yourself up to yourself in these last minutes. Forget me, and forget your neighbor, whoever that may be, friend, husband, wife, brother, sister, child. Be alone one moment with God. Now confronting you stands the Christ. What will you do with Him? May God help you to decide.

CHAPTER XIII

THE FRUIT OF THE SPIRIT

The fruit of the Spirit is love, joy, peace, long-suffering, kindness, goodness, faithfulness, meekness, temperance; against such there is no law.

GALATIANS 5:22-23.

"THE FRUIT OF THE SPIRIT IS LOVE." WHILE PERHAPS THE sublimest statement the Bible contains concerning God is the brief monosyllabic declaration of the Apostle of love, "God is love," I am inclined to think this is the sublimest statement it makes concerning the issue and finality of Christianity.

It is quite impossible to exhaust so broad and spacious a statement in one meditation. If we take the widest outlook, that of the purpose of God in the race, Christianity will have won its victory finally and perfectly when love becomes the sole law of life and conduct. It is certainly true in the narrower realm of the Church, in which is deposited and through which is communicated the dynamic which moves toward the larger realization, that in proportion as Christ's Church lives in love it is able to fulfill its mission in the world. Again, Christianity wins its final victory in the individual life when that life becomes love-mastered, love-driven. That is the first meaning of the text, although I have set it last in order.

The Apostle here has been describing the difference between the works of the flesh and the fruit of the Spirit. He gathers up the whole truth into this one brief sentence, which he afterwards explains by the other words which lie within the compass of my text. Everything is written when this is written, "The fruit of the Spirit is love."

Let us examine this statement in three ways, passing very rapidly over the first two and giving the greater part of our time to the last.

The declaration is, first of all, a revelation of the method of Christianity in its use of the word "fruit." "The *fruit* of the Spirit is love." It is, in the second place, a revelation of the dynamic of Christianity in the use of the word "Spirit." "The fruit of the *Spirit* is love." And, finally, it is a revelation of the issue of Christianity in its use of the word "love." "The fruit of the Spirit is *love*."

Our thoughts gather round the three outstanding words, "fruit . . . Spirit . . . love," the first indicating the method, the second revealing the power, and the last declaring the issue.

"The fruit of the Spirit is love." The word "fruit" presupposes life. There can be no fruit apart from life. The word "fruit" indicates cultivation. Fruit comes to perfection only in answer to the touch of cultivation. Fruit, finally, suggests sustenance. Fruit is a food. In these simplest thoughts concerning the word we have a revelation of the whole method of Christianity.

Fruit suggests life. The Apostle writes, "the *works* of the flesh," but "the *fruit* of the Spirit." As my friend, Samuel Chadwick, of Leeds, once forcefully put it, "The word *works* suggests the factory: the word *fruit* suggests the garden."

Works, the works of men, are always operations in the realm of death, and they forevermore contain within themselves the elements of disintegration. Fruit is always an operation in the realm of life, containing within itself the power of propagation.

The finest works which man has ever wrought are all operations in the realm of death. If your quickly moving mind questions me about the flowers and tells me that they are man's work, I reply that it is where man's work ceases and God's begins that life proceeds. Man's work is always an operation in the realm of death. Take the building in which we are gathered. It is useful, necessary, proper, but it could not be erected save as man handled dead materials. The tree in the forest with its rising sap and its budding life was no use to the builder. It must die before man could begin his work. Man's works being operations in the realm of death, they contain within themselves the elements of break-up. While this building was being erected, long ere the builder put on the final stone with rejoicing, old mother nature with mossy fingers had begun to pull it down, and, notwithstanding the fact that we have reconstructed it, she is busy destroying it at this moment. As quickly as man works, his work crumbles and passes. That is the figure the Apostle used when he was speaking of the flesh. The works of the flesh are operations in the realm of death. The finest thing a man can do within his own self-centered life is a thing of decay and break-up, which perishes and passes and cannot abide.

Fruit is an operation in the realm of life, that mystic fact, which we all know by observation and none of us knows by final analysis and explanation. Life is of God as much in the flowering of a daisy as in the blossoming of stars. It owes its origin to God as surely in the sparrow as in the seraph. Fruit is God's work. You may paint fruit, but it fades upon your canvas though you mix your colors with the skill of a Turner. You may make your fruit of wax, but it perishes, notwithstanding the fact that you put it under a glass case.

Fruit has in it the properties of perpetual life: "the tree bearing fruit, wherein is the seed thereof, after its kind." There is the potentiality in all fruit of unceasing propagation. It is a thing of life. Christianity is a thing of life. The love which is its final fruitage cannot be manufactured; it must grow, and it must grow out of the principle of life.

Fruit implies cultivation. There can be no perfection of fruit without cultivation. Let the tree in your garden run wild, never use the pruning knife, and all the fine quality of the fruit will pass away from it. The fruit of Christianity, which is love, comes to perfection only by the processes of cultivation, not your cultivation, but Jesus'. "I am the true vine, and my Father is the husbandman . . . ye are the branches." Let me turn aside for one brief, passing message to some heart in trouble. You are passing through the fire, you are overwhelmed with sorrow. You crept up to the assembly of the saints feeling inclined to say, "Has God forgotten me? Why this pruning, this beating, this buffeting?" Hear this: The perfection of Christian character comes only by cultivation. "My Father is the husbandman." He holds in his hand the pruning knife. "All chastening seemeth for the present to be not joyous, but grievous: yet afterward . . ." God help you to look to the afterward, and to know this, "whom the Lord loveth He chasteneth," and to see that by these processes of cultivation He is perfecting the fruit.

Finally, fruit suggests not merely life and cultivation, it suggests sustenance—sustenance for God. "God is love." God's heart hungers after love. God can be satisfied only with love. Listen to the wailing minor threnody of the old Hebrew prophets. They are from beginning to end the sighing of God after the love of His people. I shall never forget what a revelation of God came into my own life when a few years ago I gave myself to the study of their writings. I had thought of them as men of thunder and found them to be men of tears. I had thought of them as men of wrath, uttering denunciation of sin and proclaiming the terrible judgment of God's holiness. They are all that; but I found that at the back of all the thunder was the infinite disappointment of God because men did not love Him. "How shall I give thee up, Ephraim?" That is the cry of a Being hungry for love. If you go a little further back in your Bible to the old story in Genesis, you find God saying to Adam, "Where art thou?" That is not the arresting voice of a policeman. It is the wailing voice of the Father Who has lost His child. God is hungry for love. Take a figure nearer home. We believe He is here in this house. He has come to His garden. He is among the branches of His own vine. What is He seeking? Love. The proportion in which he finds love in your heart, dominating, flourishing, mastering, is the proportion in which God is satisfied with you. The fruit of the Spirit which is for the sustenance of God's own heart in its hunger is love.

Pass to the second of these thoughts, and I dismiss this even more rapidly. Our text is a revelation of the dynamic of Christianity in the use of the word "Spirit." Let me only take the thought that Christianity is a life. How is life generated in man? By his being born of the Spirit. If that life needs cultivation toward perfection, how is it cultivated? By the ministry of that Spirit Who is grieved when we violate the law of love. If Christianity is indeed the fruit which is sustenance for the very hunger of God's heart, how does it come to its perfect fruitage? Only as my spirit becomes by close identity the very Spirit of Jesus Christ. "If any man hath not the Spirit of Christ, he is none of His." But if he have the Spirit of Christ it is the Spirit of love, and God finds the answer to His hunger in me as He finds Christ formed in me by the ministry of the Holy Spirit. The fruit comes through the life which the Spirit gives. The fruit is cultivated toward perfection by the Spirit in all His tender, gracious work in the heart. Love is sustenance for God's hunger, and it is His Holy Spirit in perfect co-operation that makes my spirit Christ's Spirit, and the fruit for which God seeks.

Now we come to that which is the plain meaning of the text. "The fruit of the Spirit is love." I can well understand that some of you are saying, "Why do you take this one word 'love'?" Because when this one word is uttered there is no more to say. It is perfectly correct to take all the words which follow. The Apostle wrote them under inspiration and with deep significance. You will see at once there is difficulty in the text. It reads, "The fruit of the Spirit *is* love, joy, peace, long-suffering, kindness, goodness, faithfulness, meekness, temperance." You feel there is difficulty in saying, "The fruit of the Spirit *is*," and then reciting nine words. Men have recognized the grammatical difficulty of the "is," and quote the passage, "The fruits of the Spirit are . . ." That is grammatical. That reads smoothly. Hence the popular supposition that there are nine fruits of the Spirit.

But we have no right to interfere with the text in that way. Our business is to find out what the text really means. The Apostle wrote, "The fruit of the Spirit *is* love . . ." It is one, not nine! It may be objected that the affirmation does not remove the difficulty in the text. The one thing in your Bible which is not inspired is the punctuation. If I were writing this text out for myself I would feel I was perfectly warranted in changing the punctuation, and I would read it like this: "The fruit of the Spirit is love," and then I should indicate a pause by some means other than a comma, say a semicolon and a dash, and then read on: "joy, peace, long-suffering, kindness, goodness, faithfulness, meekness, temperance." The Apostle reaches his climax, and he writes the full and final fact concerning Christian experience in the words, "The fruit of the spirit is love." Then there breaks upon his consciousness the meaning of love, and in order that we may not treat the word as a small word, that we may not pass it over and imagine there is nothing very much in it, that it is merely a sentimental word, he gives us the qualities and quantities and flavors of the fruit by breaking it up into its component parts. To change the figure, the Apostle writes the word "love," and there surges through his soul all the harmonies of the Christian life. It is a great orchestra—love— and he listens and picks out one by one the different qualities of the music, joy, peace, long-suffering, kindness, goodness, faithfulness, meekness, temperance.

If you have love you have all these things. If you lack love you lack them all. If that can be proved, then I think it is proved that love is the all-inclusive word, and the words which follow break it up and explain its meaning.

"Joy." This is a commonplace word. It does not signify an ecstasy which occurs once, and passing leaves the soul on a deader level than it occupied before it came. It does not indicate one of those red days in one's life aflame with high passion. These are not to be undervalued; but this word does not indicate any such experience. "Joy" is a simple word which means cheerfulness, gladness, common delight, that peculiar and wonderful quality which, present in the life, transmutes everything into light and peace and happiness; that consciousness in the life which sings through all the livelong day; that happy cheerfulness, alas! too sadly absent from our life today, which sings in the midst of a November fog just as much as on a glorious June day. What is equal to keeping a man cheerful in all circumstances? Nothing other than love. I make no apology for taking my illustration from that wonderful realm—the newborn love of youth and maiden, of Christ and the Church, of the bridegroom and the bride. It is God's own illustration. I read in the old prophets, "I will betroth thee unto Me forever." Let such love take possession of the heart of youth and maiden, and they are perpetually cheerful. You button your coat around you and say, "It is a drab day." They say, "No, it is saffron." If you say the sky is gray they say it is purple. They are cheerful from morning to night with the cheerfulness which comes with love's first young dream. If you would be cheerful through all vicissitudes of life you must have love in your heart. Love is a singer that never tires. Love is a nightingale which sings while the sun flames, and keeps singing when the rains descend. *Joy is love's consciousness.*

"*Peace.*" This word indicates not stagnation, but the peace which follows battle—the harmony of opposing forces. What is equal to making peace after battle? Nothing other than love. Two nations are at war. The stronger defeats the other by force, and I take up my newspaper and read that peace has been declared. Is it peace? For all national and political purposes, yes; but in the deepest fact of things it is not peace. If—and it is a great if—the stronger nation can so deal with the conquered nation as to make that conquered nation feel that the conqueror loves it, then you will have peace. Two people are at strife in the Church. Forgive the illustration, but these things do exist. They come to me as their pastor and say, "We have settled this business." "How have you settled it?" I ask. "We have agreed that it cannot be settled, so we have decided to bury it and never talk of it again." Then, in God's name, dig it up. That is not peace. The buried hatchet can always be unearthed. Learn to love, and you will have peace. *Peace is love's confidence.*

"*Long-suffering.*" May I put that in another form and say long-temperedness. I very seldom find people who easily understand that word. Let me suggest another, "short-temperedness." I find most people understand that. Long-temperedness is the exact opposite of short-temperedness. Long-temperedness is the great and marvelous quality which endures. You heard the great love poem which I read to you from the Corinthian letter, "Love suffereth long." That is the same word. Love is long-tempered. That is not all Paul said. "Love suffereth long *and is kind.*" That is the marvel of it. You have suffered long, the sense of your own dignity has made you silent; but there comes a day when you say, "I have suffered this long enough, and now . . ." We all know what you mean. That is not love. "Love suffereth long *and is kind.*" Love is the overplus of patience. Can you think of anything else that would make you long-suffering? I suppose you will agree with me that the most long-suffering people in the world are mothers. Why? I can give you the answer in a word. Because they love. There are all sorts of foolish proverbs abroad. Men tell me that love is blind. Nothing of the kind. Love sees most keenly and acutely and correctly. You tell me I am wrong, and say, "Look at that woman. Her son is going wrong. We have seen it for a long time. She is blind. She does not see it." Let me tell you she saw it long before you did. Then you say, "Why does she not heed us when we try to tell her?" Because "love beareth all things, believeth all things, hopeth all things, endureth all things." That is the story of a mother's love. That is long-temperedness. *Long-temperedness is love's habit.*

"Kindness." The Greek word here is one which refers not to sentiment, but to service. Kindness is usefulness in a good sense, and always in small things. The word "kindness" refers to that attitude of life which makes men see the little thing which, being done, will minister to some other soul. I submit to you, is there anything equal to maintaining you in the kindness of doing little things except love? I am afraid it must be granted that there may be motives for great philanthropies other than that of love. Amos was a wonderful prophet, and he, when he was dealing with the men of his day, said, "They proclaim freewill offerings and publish them." Love is not necessarily behind the published gift. It is told of Sir Moses Montefiore that after he had passed away there was found a little book in which were entered gifts which far surpassed those which had been publicly acknowledged during his lifetime. On the front page of this book these words were written, "The gifts which men acknowledge do not count in the ledgers of heaven." That was Hebrew, but it was coming very near to the heart of Christianity. Here is a young man who, if he were talking to me, would tell me he loves his mother. He would even tell me that he was willing to die for her. Nonsense! Stay at home tomorrow night and read to her for half an hour. Kindness is the willingness to do simple things to help other people. When Jesus approaches a subject He says the last thing. According to Him, the cup of cold water, which costs nothing but the trouble of seeing that it is wanted and the giving, counts in heaven. What will make a man keen-eyed enough to see the thousand and one little needs of life and meet them? Nothing but love. *Kindness is love's activity.*

"Goodness." Goodness is—just goodness. I wish we used that word more than we do. We have been talking much about holiness—not too much—but we have been talking a great deal too little about righteousness. What is holiness? Rectitude of character. What is righteousness? Rectitude of conduct. What is goodness? Both. Goodness is the greatest of all the words. That is one reason why I love the hymn:

> There is a green hill far away,
> Outside a city wall,

Where the dear Lord was crucified,
Who died to save us all.

He died that we might be forgiven,
He died to make us *good*,
That we might go at last to heaven,
Saved by His precious blood.

There was no other *good* enough
To pay the price of sin;
He only could unlock the gate
Of heaven and let us in.

What is the inspiration of goodness? Goodness is a word which we have relegated to the nursery. We still tell the children to be good. What, then, is the inspiration of goodness in a child? Love. You may keep your boy good in the externalities by being a moral policeman. If you want to bind him to goodness through the coming years you must make of him such a boy that when he comes up to the city and sin confronts him he will say, "No, I cannot do it. It would whiten father's hair and break mother's heart!" Love is the only sufficient inspiration of goodness. "If ye *love* me, ye will keep my commandments." That is the whole philosophy of goodness, and you will never be good while you are aiming to be good because you may lose your respectability by badness. When love is in your heart, and you can say, "I cannot grieve my Father," that is the true inspiration of goodness. *Goodness is love's quality.*

"Faithfulness," which may with perfect accuracy be translated "fidelity," is the good old-fashioned virtue of being true to your compact and your duty. What is equal to keeping a man true in the sense of being faithful to his compact? Nothing but love. You talk to me about infidelity —of infidelity in the marriage relationship, or in business.

What is its reason? There is no love. Love makes such infidelity impossible. Where love is sentinel I shall always be at the post of duty. Where love is the inspiration, I shall never fail in faithfulness to my compact with friend, or lover, or acquaintance. I shall never fail in my business integrity if love stands sentinel over all my actions. *Faithfulness is love's quantity.*

"Meekness." What is meekness? Active humility. Unconscious humility. Believe me, it is good sometimes to use that word "unconscious" before humility to see what humility really is. Humility is always unconscious, and that is meekness. There is a so-called humility which parades itself. It is not humility. There are people who are always willing to take the lowest room at the feast, provided they come late enough for everyone to see them do it! There are people who say to me sometimes when they are talking about their work for God, "Well, yes, we are doing what we can in our humble way." And I always know they are the most conceited people for five miles round. The man who is humble does not know he is humble. Meekness is the ability to stay doing the commonplace drudgery of the carpenter's shop for eighteen years. Meekness is the ability to leave the carpenter's shop and face the crowds and deliver God's message when He so wills. Meekness is the unconsciousness of self that bears to Calvary the rugged cross in the sight of all the world. The Master said, "I am meek and lowly in heart." What was the inspiration of His toiling in the carpenter's shop, the driving power in His preaching, the reason of the cross? There is only one answer. Love. It was love that made Him true in the commonplace of the carpenter's shop, that made Him true to the prophetic message, that made Him true to God's purpose even in the mystery of His Passion. *Meekness is love's tone.*

"Temperance." What is temperance? Not merely the thing with which we so often associate the word today. Teetotalism may be intemperate. Temperance is a greater word—no one need be anxious, I am a total abstainer—it is self-control. Tell me, what is the power of self-control? What alone is sufficient to induce anyone to attempt self-control? I think you will find by long testing of my question that it is nothing but love. A man comes to me and says, "You should not indulge in any excesses, you will injure yourself, you will spoil your chances in life." All very right and proper, but it is not a final argument. I am inclined to say to the man, "Mind your own business and leave me alone." But if a man should come to me and say, "Sir, walk carefully. You have four boys who are coming after you, and what they see you do they will do." That is my motive for self-control. Self-control is the victory of love, and the victory of love is the issue of the work of the Spirit. Do not be misled into imagining that you can control yourself in any way other than by the Spirit's interpretation of love to you and the Spirit's realization of love in your heart. That is the secret of self-control. *Temperance is love's victory.*

That analysis is rapid. I have attempted it only that I may bring you face to face with the real meaning of the statement, "The fruit of the spirit is love." If you have love you have all these things. Joy is its consciousness. Peace is its confidence. Long-suffering is its habit. Kindness is its activity. Goodness is its quality. Faithfulness is its quantity. Meekness is its tone. Self-control is its victory.

How shall I love? I take you back to my first word. "The fruit of the Spirit is love." I cannot love so as to have this joy, this peace, this long-suffering, this kindness, this goodness, this faithfulness, this meekness, this self-control by any way other than by handing my whole life over to that Spirit Who comes to communicate the very life of Jesus that there may spring up within me the first moving of love. Someone says, "I am far away from all that." Let me ask such a one: Do you know this first movement within? Have you felt the first thrill of love? Have you felt a tenderness born within you? Then remember God's order, "First the blade, then the ear, then the full corn in the ear." This fruit of the Spirit can be perfected only through cultivation. Thank God if the first movement is in your heart. If at the back of all your thinking and planning and doing lies selfishness, then yield yourself tonight to Him Who alone is able to give you the victory over self by the inflow of God's own love.

CHAPTER XIV

THE SPIRIT OF LIFE

The Spirit of life.
ROMANS 8:2.

THE SPIRIT IS DESCRIBED IN THE NEW TESTAMENT AS "the Spirit of truth," "the Spirit of promise," "the Spirit of grace," "the Spirit of glory." "The Spirit of life" is a suggestive and comprehensive phrase, indicating the relation of the Spirit of God to all life. Two words are here placed together, both of which refer to life. The word "Spirit" suggests life at its very highest. Here, as always, where the reference is to God, the word indicates the originating cause. The word "life" marks rather a manifestation or a form of the essential than the origination and power thereof. This word translated "life" is a very interesting one. The Greek language is richer than ours in this particular, that it has more words than one to describe life. Where we use our word "life" to include many conceptions, there are at least two words in Greek literature, words that we have become familiar with by their adaptation into our language in scientific usage—the words *bios* and *zoe*, from which we have derived our words biology and zoology. These two Greek words indicate two thoughts about life, but in Greek classical literature they are other than the thoughts that they indicate in the New Testament. The order of suggestiveness is reversed in the New Testament, and this is an arresting peculiarity which demands attention. The Greek use of the word *zoe* indicated the purely natural—I may almost say the animal—side of life. The other word, *bios*, had in it something of an ethical value and a spiritual conception. In all Greek literature you find this contrast is maintained.

But when I take up the New Testament, uniformly I find the order is reversed, and when life is referred to by Jesus, by New Testament writers, the higher word in Greek thinking and Greek writing is relegated to lower uses and the lower word is elevated to higher uses.

Such a fact arrests attention, and a man is immediately driven to ask why this peculiar change—not a studied change, not a change of language adopted after some council had met and decided to adopt it. Then we might have questioned it. We are always open to question anything councils do. It was a change that came into the thinking of all Christian men so quietly, and yet so powerfully, that when you gather up the arguments of the Christian writings and put them into one, you find the strange uniformity. Jesus Himself, so far as the records reveal His teaching, adopted this change, and all the writers conformed to it. A new thought of life lies at the back of this change of word, a new conception of life is its originating cause. These New Testament writers saw life as the Greeks saw it, and yet quite differently. They saw the same things, the same men, the same women, the same animals, the same flowers, the same landscapes, the same seas, the same everything; and yet, without collusion, without decision of Pope, or Council, or Presbytery, or even Congregational Union—I suppose that was the only ecclesiastical court in existence then—without any of these things, I find these men made a change in terminology.

I believe the explanation will be found in the fact that the Christian man recognizes the original sanctity and holiness of every form of life. He has discovered that behind the "natural" of theology—even Paul's theology—is the "natural" of Divine intention, and the "natural" of Divine intention is holy, and is directly due, always and everywhere, in every realm of life, to the activity of the Spirit of God. Without resolution, without decision of Council, the early Christian consciousness made its protest against the idea that life in any form is essentially evil. The early Christian consciousness is perfectly plain in declaring that life has become evil, that man has fallen into willful and rebellious wrongdoing; and it is in this very epistle that you have the most glaring and terrible revelation in literature of what the heart of man is by the choice of his sin. Thus Christianity, powerfully and pervasively, has taken hold of a word in current Greek literature, which always had upon it the taint of sin, and changed its meaning because Christian thought has been remade by the advent and presence of Jesus Christ.

But now, concerning the conception that this presents to our view as Christians, the relation of the Spirit of God to all life is too often forgotten by Christian people. Let me make this broad and inclusive proposition. All life is due to the direct action of the Spirit of God. The Bible never loses sight of that fact. As we take up this ancient literature of the Hebrew people and study it, we find a recognition of the relation of God and the Spirit of God to all life. That is the meaning of the first chapters in Genesis. "In the beginning God created." "Darkness was upon the face of the waters," but "the Spirit of God moved upon the face of the waters." The original creation has behind it a spiritual explanation. Travel back as far as you will through æons you cannot measure, and Genesis still sings the anthem of the beginning, "in the beginning God created"; and when there was to be a remaking of a disorganized and chaotic world, again "the Spirit of God moved upon the face of the waters." If you study this ancient literature you will find perpetually that the Hebrew heard the wheels of God in the thunder of the storm, and saw the flash of His chariot when the lightning illuminated the heavens. He saw at the back of all life the presence of the Spirit of God. The whole truth has been beautifully expressed by one of our more modern writers:

> One Spirit—His
> Who wore the plaited thorn with bleeding brows—
> Rules universal Nature! Not a flower
> But shows some touch, in freckle, streak, or stain
> Of His unrivalled pencil. He inspires
> Their balmy odors, and imparts their hues,
> And bathes their eyes with nectar; and includes
> In grains as countless as the seaside sands,
> The forms with which He sprinkles all the earth.

You say that is poetry? That is scientific fact to the Christian soul, and science is always poetic if you know it. Think of that conception; what is it? That all the fragrance of the flower is the result of the breathing of the Spirit of God, and every touch of delicate beauty upon its petal is the direct, immediate, actual, absolute workmanship of the Spirit.

That outlook is wide, and radiant, and spacious. Let us confine our attention to the thought suggested in this spacious outlook as it affects man. We suffer today from too constant contemplation of man as he is, and a consequent failure to understand man as God intended he should be. We have been gazing so long and so intently at ruin that we have forgotten the fair lines of the Divine ideal and the plan toward which God is moving and working in all such as are submitted to His Spirit.

In my Bible I have two glimpses of this in human life. The first is spoiled ere I can see it in perfection. The second grows with increasing glory the longer I gaze upon it. I have the "first Adam" and the "last Adam." When I look at the "first" I see the picture of what the Spirit of God means in human life.

You will remember verse 7 in Genesis 2, which runs thus: "Jehovah . . . breathed into his nostrils the breath of lives," that suggestive Hebrew plural which is used poetically to indicate the fact of spaciousness and breadth which cannot be expressed in the singular number—"the breath of lives; and man became a living soul." Man is made in the image of God and given dominion over the creation of God. There are no details. The broad poetic facts are stated in that chapter. I turn to chapter 2, and I do not find a contradiction, but an explanatory account of a certain fact and phase of human life which had not been dealt with fully in the first chapter. Here there is revealed to us the nature of man. Man is dust and Deity; of the dust, God in-breathed; linked to the material, offspring of the Spirit, of the earth, of the heavens. It is all poetry, but it is true poetry. Man becomes the conscious and capable ego, when by this mystery, baffling all explanation, the God of heaven by breath Divine makes man.

What is this man's consciousness? First, he is subject to the government of God. That is the first consciousness of personality, as Genesis reveals it. Secondly, he is conscious of the creation that he finds about him. He is able to name things, able to till the soil, able to touch the resources of nature and make them blossom more perfectly. He is a being capable of co-operation with God, and all this in the power of the Spirit.

But I turn from the story. It is disappointing, it is heartbreaking. Just as the glory of it is growing upon the imagination, the vision is clouded and spoiled, and we leave it, and, passing through the centuries, come into the presence of the "last Adam." The story of the human life of Jesus from beginning to its unending condition—for there is no end to it—is the story of this truth, that the Spirit of God is the Spirit of life. All the human life of Jesus, naturally—not supernaturally—was life in the Spirit. His very existence was by the Spirit. He was a Man of the Spirit by processes different from those by which man at first was man of the Spirit. But God may change his methods, and yet do the same thing in the underlying principles of His government in exactly the same way. Once again, the breath of God, and the dust of earth, and the "last Adam," come into human life. His was development in the power of the Spirit—physically, mentally, spiritually, not spiritually alone, but mentally and physically, developing, growing by this very spirit life which He lived.

In His ministry it becomes more patent. He was anointed for ministry by the Spirit of God. He went down into the wilderness to temptation, driven by the Spirit of God. He came out of the wilderness and went back again to ministry in the power of the Spirit of God. He wrought miracles, as the record declares, by this selfsame power of the Spirit. He came to the sublime mystery of His death, and we hear the word again, "through the eternal Spirit He offered Himself without blemish unto God." He came to the morning of resurrection, and by the power of that Spirit He took life again, and came back into human consciousness and being. He tarried for forty days among His disciples, and, as Luke, the accurate Greek, the cultured scholar, tells us, He instructed His disciples by the Holy Ghost long before the Spirit was poured upon them. I open the Gospel of John, and read: "In Him was life"—essential life—"and the life was the light of men." What is the life of Jesus? Spiritual life, not spiritual life as we too often use the phrase, as though it were something distinct from human life; but spiritual life in the simplest, and broadest, and profoundest sense of the truth that all life is life by the Spirit of God.

It is this conception which reveals how deadly and dastardly a thing sin is. If I had a life apart from the life of God and the Spirit of God, even then sin would be ungrateful. But when I find that the very life I live is by the Spirit of God, then how dastardly a thing it is to take this in-breathed life of God and use it for purposes that thwart Him, and hinder His Kingdom, and spread the poison all abroad amongst humanity, insulting His love, and hindering His purpose.

The life of Jesus is life in the Spirit from beginning to end, and when I read that "in Him was life, and the life was the light of men," I understand the evangelist to mean that if I want to know what life really is, I must look at Him—physically, mentally, and spiritually—and see this truth, that all life is by the Spirit of God. Man's being, in all its complex wonders, is the creation of the Spirit of God, and the proper use of all the powers of the being is possible only in submission to the Spirit of life.

So that when we speak of regeneration, or of the filling of the Spirit, or of the anointing of the Spirit, or of spiritual life in the deepest and profoundest sense of the term, we are not asking men to enter a range or realm of life for which they were not made. We are calling them back to normality, to naturalness, to the fulfillment of the deepest and profoundest meaning of their own first creation. A man does not by his new birth become something other than himself. He becomes himself, as he never has been until by that new birth he finds himself. Not angels did Jesus Christ come to make; and if His terms are drastic and hard, if ere He can baptize a man with the Spirit of life the man must consent to death, it is in order that he may find by the same new life, not some foreign life, but his own life. If you differ from the exposition, hear the actual words: "He that loseth his life . . . shall find *it*," the very life he is willing to lose. The very life which I lose by submission to Him, the life which I deny in order that I may find Him as my Lord and King, is the life I find. The baptism of God's Holy Spirit, and the filling and the anointing of that Spirit mean, first, the correction of the thing that is wrong, the putting away of the sin, the breaking of the power of sin, the subjection of the rebellious territory to the power of the Lord. But they mean infinitely more. They mean the cultivation of the rebellious territory, they mean the restoration of the thing over which the weeds have spread themselves, and where the briars and the thorns are growing. Not merely that the desert life of man is handed over in order that it may be possessed by Him, but that the desert life, being possessed by Him, shall be made to blossom as the rose. Not that the dry and arid distances of the wilderness are simply to be given to Him, but that He will make run through them the rivers of God, which bring life wherever they come.

I do not want by any generalization to dissipate the impression on my own heart that I fain would transfer to yours. I mean that the Spirit of life brings a man into the realization of the highest and best of all the facts of his life. When this physical part of me is really handed over wholly to the indwelling King, because it is originally also of God, it finds itself, and lives at its highest and best.

The Spirit of God is the Spirit of life also in the mental sphere. It is only in the illumination of the Spirit that you obtain the finest literature, or the most perfect poetry, or the most matchless art, or the sublimest music, or the most correct science. Even the men who turn their backs upon revealed religion, in the measure in which they have been successful in music, art, poetry, or science, have been so in the life the Spirit created. Never forget that in the far country all that the prodigal spent was his father's property. You may be wasting your life, my brother, but the life you are wasting is the life God made, and the life you are wasting is the life which the Spirit of God has created and conditioned.

The second birth is that by which a man enters into the meaning of his first birth. Jesus Christ brings me by the Holy Spirit of His outpouring into an understanding of my own life, into realization of my own life, because He puts my life back into harmony with God. Regeneration is the first fact in the process by which the Spirit of life operates through grace for the renewal and restoration of man to the Divine intention.

There may be some of us who are very near, and yet have never had the baptism of this Spirit of life. Paul came down to Ephesus, and he found men naming the name of Jesus, and I do not know what he saw, but it is evident that he saw something that made him ask a very strange question. He said to them: "Did ye receive the Holy Ghost when ye believed?" "Why," said they, "we have not so much as heard that there is any Spirit given." Then his question, "Into what, then, were ye baptized?" And do not forget their answer: "Into John's baptism." Do not misuse that text to preach a second blessing. There is no such authority in it. These men had never been baptized with Jesus' baptism. They were men who probably had heard Apollos preaching the baptism of repentance only. Paul said, "There is more than repentance. There must be faith, and if there is faith in Jesus then there is the baptism of the Spirit, and in that moment they were baptized by the Spirit and entered into life."

Some of you may be as near as were these men of

Ephesus. Some of you may imagine that you are Christians because you have gone as far as John's baptism can take you. You need to be born again, to yield yourself wholly to the Christ Himself, and believe on His name, and receive regeneration as a free gift of God's infinite grace. Wherever that is done, the Spirit of life, the Spirit to Whom you owe your first life, Whose dominion you have not recognized or acknowledged, Whose illumination you have lost, Whose energy you have so sadly failed to appropriate, will come back and remake you, not as an angel, but as a new man. God's meaning in you will be fulfilled as the Spirit of life takes possession of you.

But if we have received that Spirit, if we have yielded to Christ, and have been baptized by the Spirit into union with Him, the verse still has a call for us and a suggestiveness. Let us yield ourselves absolutely to the Spirit of life, that all His gracious purposes may be accomplished in us.

Do not let us be satisfied with so much of realization as will ensure us, as we think, entrance presently into the home of God. Rather let this Spirit of life, Who is in us, have perfect dominion, and then every part of the being—physical, mental, and spiritual, suffused with light, baptized with power —will begin to find out how broad, and generous, and spacious life really is.

CHAPTER XV

THE SIFTING OF PETER

Simon Peter answered and said, Thou art the Christ, the Son of the living God.
MATTHEW 16:16.

He began to curse, and to swear, I know not this Man of Whom ye speak.
MARK 14:71.

THE CONTRAST IS A STARTLING ONE. IT IS AT FIRST SIGHT ALmost inconceivable that these are the words of the same man, and yet we know that they are. Then surely we have placed them in the wrong order, and ought first to have read "I know not the man," as language used in the days before he met the Christ; and his declaration, "Thou art the Christ, the Son of the living God," must have been made subsequently. We know, however, that this is not the case. If, indeed, they have been read in their right order a long period must have intervened between affirmation and denial. As a matter of fact, not many months had passed between the hour in which Peter rose to the height of that most wonderful confession and the hour in which he denied any knowledge of Jesus. So startling an association of texts compels us to inquire the meaning of the change which has come over Peter since that glorious and radiant hour when, amid the rocky fastnesses of Cæsarea Philippi, in answer to the challenge of his Lord, he had said the one thing the heart of Christ had been waiting to hear, "Thou art the Christ, the Son of the living God."

I do not propose to consider particularly that confession of Peter, nor do I intend to dwell at any length upon the final words. I am desirous rather of asking you to consider with me the awful possibility of passing in brief time from the most blessed confession to the most dreadful denial. I think perhaps I might take another text from which to preach tonight, and if I did so it would be by way of application at the beginning as also at the close. The text would be, "Let him that thinketh he standeth take heed lest he fall." The story of Peter's denial is the story of backsliding, and it is a story which reveals the truth which we perpetually need to remember, that no man openly backslides at once. The open blasphemy is always preceded by heart backsliding. If we would understand how it came to pass that from that height of affirmation to that depth of denial a man could pass in those few brief months, we must go back to the occasion of the affirmation. We must see what happened immediately afterwards, and then attempt to trace the downward progress of this man, until from mountain height we find him in the depth of the valley.

You will remember that immediately after Peter's confession our Lord told him of His purpose concerning His Church and His Kingdom.

For the first time He introduced the band of disciples, in so many words, definitely and plainly to the fact of which He had been conscious all the while, that He could win His crown only by way of the cross. Immediately, while the light of the glory of the confession and the annunciation concerning the Church was still about them, I find the first movement in Peter's backsliding. He said to Jesus, "Be it far from Thee, Lord: this shall never be unto Thee." As we hear him we are inclined to sympathize with him. We feel that we would have said exactly the same thing under the circumstances, and in all probability we would have. That, however, does not prove Peter to have been right. We may make every excuse that we will—and it is better that we should—for his limited light, for his fickleness and feebleness of character, but the fact remains that in that moment he passed out of immediate and close fellowship with his Lord.

When this man could not see Christ's method he withdrew from absolute and unquestioning loyalty to his Lord. So long as Jesus had spoken to him of building a Church, Peter remained loyal; but the moment Jesus ceased to speak about keys and began to talk about a cross he was puzzled, astonished, disappointed, confused. He could not see how suffering could be the way to the throne. He could not see how his Master's going to Jerusalem and being ill-treated, and finally—for he would use no other word—murdered, could issue in the building of that glorious Church to which his Lord had just made reference. He could not see how keys of any kind could be of use to him if the Master were to pass into the shadow and lose His life. Neither could I have seen it, nor could have you. So far, let us confess our perfect sympathy and fellowship with this man. It was a strange thing Jesus said to him. He had so hoped for the coming of a Deliverer. The Deliverer had come, and at last, Peter, in a moment of supreme, divine illumination, had looked into the face of the long-hoped-for Messiah and confessed Him. In his confession there was the outpouring of his soul's hope of triumph, and victory, of the breaking of chains and loosing of the captives, of the restoration of order and the setting up of the Kingdom of God. I am growingly reluctant to criticize Peter, but for our own soul's profit let us see wherein lay his mistake. It lay in the fact that he was not prepared to accept his Master's estimate of necessity, was not prepared to follow his Lord simply, even when he could not understand his Lord's method. That is the common mistake of the saints. We have all made it, and therefore, sooner or later, we have found ourselves at a distance from Jesus.

The great lesson of Peter's denial is that wherever there is arrested development of Christian life there must follow deterioration of Christian character. Life must make progress to higher levels or sink lower until it pass away. I must follow Jesus Christ wholly and absolutely without question, or there will be an ever widening breach between Him and myself, until I, even I, presently shall deny Him with blasphemy over some flickering imitation fire. "Let him that thinketh he standeth take heed lest he fall."

Your affirmation of loyalty is God-inspired. Your confession of Christ is true to the deepest within you. You are perfectly honest and sincere. God help you to follow Him all the way, whether you understand Him or not. God help you at least to keep by His side when clouds almost obscure the vision of His face, for if once you let yourself question His wisdom and His word there will be distance which must increase. Let us trace this in the history of Peter. The whole subsequent story is written for us in chapter 14 of Mark's Gospel. I am not going to read the whole chapter, but I desire to take you from stage to stage, that you may see how this man passed away from Jesus ever a little further, until we come to the open denial in our second text. Remember that the first step was taken when Peter shunned the cross because he did not understand it, and questioned his Lord's wisdom when He declared the method necessary to His crowning. You will find the next step in verse 29 of this chapter. "Peter said unto Him, Although all shall be offended, yet will not I." Then going on to verse 37, I read, "He," that is Jesus, "cometh, and findeth them sleeping, and saith unto Peter, Simon, sleepest thou? Couldest thou not watch one hour? Watch and pray, that ye enter not into temptation: the spirit indeed is willing, but the flesh is weak." Notice, the Lord did not call him Peter then. He went back to the old name. The next step is to be found in verse 47. "A certain one of them that stood by drew his sword, and smote the servant of the high priest, and struck off his ear." Mark is Peter's friend, and does not mention his name, but we know that the "certain one" was Peter. There we have the next step, and increased distance. I pass on to verse 54 and read, "Peter had followed afar off," and I think he seems yet a little further away from his Lord. At last he was sitting with the officers and warming himself in the light of the fire. Then, in verses 68-71, a serving maid charges him with being a Galilean, and tells him that his speech betrays him, and thrice, and finally with curses, he denies his Lord. Let us now notice the stages.

First, refusal to follow his Lord into the mystery of pain and refusal to believe that his Lord knew best. Next, boastfulness. "Although all shall be offended, yet will not I." What follows? Failure in the devotional life, inability to watch, and the cessation of prayer. Then zeal without knowledge, hastiness, the drawing of a sword, not under the command of his Master. What next? Following afar, because his Lord had rebuked him for his zeal without knowledge. Then in the chill of the night we see him warming himself over a fire which the enemies of Christ had built. And then a laughing serving maid and a lying Apostle. Christ is denied, and the man of the mountain is in the depths, the man who thought he stood has fallen. The first refusal to follow Jesus has culminated in dastardly and blasphemous denial.

These things need looking at a little more closely, that we may see how perfectly natural is the story. After the refusal of the cross Jesus Christ sternly rebuked Peter. "Get thee behind me, Satan: thou art a stumbling-block unto me; for thou mindest not the things of God, but the things of men." From that moment there was in the heart of Peter a consciousness that his Master was not able to trust him, a strange sense of distance between friends which is the most agonizing consciousness that can ever come either to one or the other. This man, knowing his Lord's attitude to himself, will endeavor to lessen the sense of distance by loud profession. John tells us the story far more fully than it is stated in Mark. Peter said, "Lord, whither goest Thou?" Jesus looked at him and said, "Whither I go, thou canst not follow Me now; but thou shalt follow afterwards." Then Peter asked, "Lord, why cannot I follow Thee even now? I will lay down my life for Thee." Jesus answered, "Wilt thou lay down thy life for Me? Verily, verily, I say unto thee, the cock shall not crow, till thou hast denied me thrice." Then Peter said, "Although all shall be offended, yet will not I." I pray you notice the principle which questioned his Master's knowledge working itself out. Peter said, in effect, "You do not know me, although You think You do. You are suspicious of me. You think I will deny You, but I will never deny You." Moreover, his boastfulness is of that most objectionable kind which puts itself into contrast with other people. "Although all shall be offended, yet will not I." In that moment Peter went further from Christ. Jesus set His face toward the cross even though there was not a single soul able to sympathize with Him. He gathered Peter, James, and John, and took them to the somber shadow of the Garden of Gethsemane, and, withdrawing Himself from them, told them to watch. He returned to find them asleep, and going up to the man whose profession had been so loud He said, "Simon, sleepest thou? Couldest thou not watch one hour? Watch and pray, that ye enter not into temptation." Peter boastful had become Peter unwatchful. Peter confident in himself had become the man who did not feel his need for watchfulness or for prayer, and thus in the presence of the very agony which the Lord had predicted he fell asleep. Suddenly, upon the darkness of the night there flashed the torches of the foes of Christ who had come to arrest Him. Peter was there. He had been boastful and unwatchful, and now he must make up in zeal for what he lacked in devotion. He drew his sword and smote Malchus, cutting off his ear. The Lord immediately rebuked him, "Put up again thy sword into its place: for all they that take the sword shall perish with the sword." Then we read that "Peter followed Him afar off." Oh, the humanness of it. Peter said in his heart, "I can do nothing right. Whatever I say is objected to. Whatever I do is wrong. Very well then, I will drop behind." He "followed afar off." Do you see the growing estrangement? He still followed, but it was "afar off." It was a cold night, and there was a fire in the court, round which the soldiers and enemies of Christ were gathered, in all probability laughingly discussing the arrest they had made, and perhaps wondering what it all meant, for in the garden they had seen the glory flame from His eyes and had fallen to the ground. They were now perhaps laughing at their own stupidity and superstition. Peter was cold, and he warmed himself at their fire. When a man gets there it is so easy for a laughing servant girl to make him swear that he never knew his Friend at all.

Let us turn from the picture, keeping it in our minds

only as a parable and a teaching. Let me say to you that the steps of Peter's downward career as here revealed are always the steps manifest in backsliding from the Lord. It begins at some moment when it is impossible to follow Him by sight and we decline to follow Him by faith. It begins in some crisis when He calls to something higher than we have known, and because the way to the higher level is the way of the cross and shame we draw back. Backsliding begins in some moment when we think we understand the genius of Christianity better than Jesus Christ does. You say, "Does man ever so imagine?" Ask your own heart if you have not come there often. I believe and confidently affirm that the fact that you have left the Church of God and have turned your back thereto does not constitute the first thing in your backsliding. You were disobedient to the heavenly vision. Some of you have entered only today upon that first phase. The cross has confronted you, and you have shunned it. You did not believe that could be the pathway to the higher life of crowning and victory, and you have put your own thinking concerning Christian experience over against the clear command of your Lord and the word of your Lord, and immediately there begins to be distance between you.

The next thing inevitably will be boastfulness. I want to put this as practically as I know how. I am always afraid of the man who tells me he is never going to deny Christ. I have been in experience meetings, in testimony meetings, in fellowship meetings, and I have heard men say, "Whoever else turns his back upon Jesus Christ I am never going to do that." If a man should so speak in a Church meeting over which I presided he is the man I would watch over and pray for, because he is in danger. The moment a man says "I will never leave Thee nor forsake Thee, O Christ, though everyone else shall," that man already has passed a little way out of communion with his Lord. The trembling soul in the Church who says, "I walk fearfully, I am afraid lest I should grieve Him, I am afraid lest there should grow distance between me and my Lord," I need not watch over. That trembling soul will be found close to the Lord all the way.

What follows boastfulness? Always the same thing, lack of prayer and lack of watching. Young man, when you commenced your Christian life you were very regular in your habits of prayer, you were afraid of yourself and watched constantly for the coming of the enemy. You burned bridges behind you which, alas, you are beginning to reconstruct today. You dared not walk down certain streets after you broke with evil and set your face toward following Jesus Christ, but you are beginning to frequent those old paths again. You are not quite so watchful as you were, and you excuse your lack of watchfulness by saying that there is no necessity for that carefulness and narrowness which characterize some people. There is great need for narrowness when you are walking amid precipices. The man who is sure he is safe, and who ceases to watch and drops prayer out of his life, who imagines he can live an independent life as a Christian soul, is falling already.

What follows? Again, always the same thing as in the case of Peter—zeal without knowledge. The Church of God today is cursed by zeal without knowledge. This is the age of fussy feverishness, and there are multitudes of people who are attempting to overtake their lack of spiritual life by service. It is not very long since a young lady came to me and said, "I feel my Christian life is at a very low ebb. I feel that there is distance between me and my Lord, and I do not know how to improve matters. Do you not think it would be a good thing for me to take a class in the Sunday school? I replied, "A thousand times, no. In the name of God leave the children alone until you are right with God yourself." The same thing expresses itself in the invitations which sometimes reach me. People write, "Will you come and conduct a few days' special services? We want to see a deepening of our spiritual life, and we think if you came and held some evangelistic services it would help us." I invariably reply, "Get right with God first and then, if I have time, I will come." You cannot make up by doing for what you lack in being. It is well for us to remember that the last act of Divine surgery which the hand of Jesus ever performed was made necessary by the blundering zeal of a distant disciple.

What follows zeal without knowledge? A slackening of the zeal, following afar off. Let us speak in the language of the day—one attendance at church on Sunday instead of two! On Sunday morning looking out to see whether it is wet, a thing you never do on Monday morning. I do not say these things to raise a smile. If they amuse you, God have mercy on you. Following afar. Following, yes, I will not deny you are following, but afar.

If you are far from Jesus you get cold, and then you want to warm yourself, and you begin doing it at the world's fires. There are all sorts of fires—they are called fires, but they are not, they are only painted. You begin to talk of narrowness. Your father did not allow you to play cards or go to the theater, but you are so chilly you want something to warm you. There are scores of men who ought to be tramping to Calvary with Christ who are playing with the devil's fire trying to get warm. That is what I mean, nothing more and nothing less. What right had Peter at that fire? It would have been better for him to have been starving outside in the cold night than getting warmth there. The world knows you. You cannot drop the speech of Jesus all at once. You are of the same country and kin as He is, and your speech will betray you. You will have someone say to you when he meets you at one of the world's fires, where you are trying to get a little warmth, excitement, enthusiasm, "I thought you were a Christian."

Where ought we to draw the line as Christian people? Where the world draws it for us. The worldly man has a very keen and accurate estimate of what the Christian man ought to be. You will have some servant maid, someone in the world, say to you, "Really, I thought you were a Christian." God have mercy upon you—that is the moment of your last peril. You may not curse. You may not take any oath on it. You may adopt the method of the age in which you live, and smile, and say, "Yes, I used to be." You may just as well swear at once. I do not think any worse of Peter for swearing that day. It is the fact that he denied his Lord which is the tragedy. The blasphemy was the expression of his nature. If he had remained true to Christ the same impetuous, impulsive nature would have expressed itself in a song instead of an oath. It is the relationship that is wrong, the distance is wrong. It is the tragedy of denial that is the agony of the story.

To you who have drifted away from nearness I might use the Apostle's words, "Ye were running well; who did hinder you?" This is the final thing, that you break with the Church and break with the ordinances of religion, and break with the external manifestation of Christianity. You are now known among your friends as a man who once held religious views. God have mercy on you! The swearing word was the accident of a temperament; the denial was the sin of a soul. The fact that you do not swear is simply due to your temperament, and yet you may even do that. It is not long since a dear and beloved friend of mine, a Christian minister, sheltered in his own home for the last weeks of his life a man who had been a preacher of the Gospel, an evangelist, winning souls, but who, when my friend found him, was preaching his sermon and praying in a public house for a pint of beer. You say, "I will never do that." Beware, that is what Peter said. You say, "I could not sink to such a level as that." "Let him that thinketh he standeth take heed lest he fall." You have made a glorious confession. It was sincere, true, high, noble, God-inspired, Christ-approved, and yet close to you is the depth of denial.

Another thing I would say to you is that if you have wandered the slightest distance from Christ your only hope of safety is in immediate return. You may return now, if you will. Listen to me—and God forgive me if there has been anything of undue and un-Christly sternness even in my tone—have you denied Him? Have you actually gone so far as to say you never knew Him? He will take you home now if you will come. Next Sunday evening I hope to speak about Peter's home-coming, but you need not wait for next Sunday, you can get home now. You have gone a long way from Him, but He has not left you. You say that is a contradiction. There are all sorts of contradictions in Christianity, and its paradoxes are its most blessed things. You are as far off from Him as denying Peter, but He is close to you; and tonight, without sign or sound for man's knowledge, fling yourself back upon His heart and He will blot out all your sin and love you freely. You are not as far as that perhaps. Where are you? Place yourself. Warming at the world's fire? Quit it. I am talking to those of you who have confessed Him and known Him, but have lost your power for witness because you are at a distance from Him. Are you warming at the world's fire? Leave it. Jesus can make fires for you if you are cold. He made one for Peter by and by. I know you are tired. I know the drab drudgery of the life that some of you live, but do not make the mistake of trying to warm yourself at painted fires. Go back to Him. Walk with Him. Talk to Him. Serve Him. Let Him talk to you. Then, suddenly, in the midst of the chilliness, you will say, "How my heart burns within me when He talks to me by the way." Or are you following afar off? Is the old first love, the love of betrothal and espousal gone? Press back to Him. It is you who have changed, not He. It is your love that has cooled, not His. Press back to Him, and you will find Him ready to receive you even now. Or are you among the number of those who are neglecting prayer in order to do more work for God? Do less work for God and pray more. Are you neglecting the hour of devotion because you have so many things on hand in connection with the Christian Church? Get some of the things out of your hands and hold your hands empty to heaven for a longer space, I charge you. I often think it would be a blessed thing for the Church of God if for a little while she attempted to do less and worshiped more. The doing, in the end, would be not less, but more and mightier. I pray you hasten back to the mountain top, the place of quietness and seclusion, of keen watchfulness and prayerfulness, which marks your sense of dependence. Perhaps you have not come so far as this, and are a little angry with me tonight. You are saying, "Why does the preacher so talk to us? We shall never do this thing. I am never going to deny Christ." Is that the language of your heart? Then it proves you are a distance from Him. The nearer a man is to Christ, the more conscious he is of his own frailty, and the more is he possessed of strength, though he hardly knows it. The nearer a man lives to Jesus Christ, the more acutely conscious is he of distance between him and his Lord by reason of his Lord's superior strength and his own frailty, and the more he presses closely to Him.

Are you shunning some cross which His will appoints,

setting up your own estimate of His will and method as against His? Do not shun the cross. He sees the cross as a means of grace. It is an old word and we have made a proverb of it. We used to engrave it upon bookmarkers—"No cross, no crown!" It is the whole philosophy of Christian life. Remember the cross there is not His cross, but your cross. Did He not say, "If any man would come after Me, let him deny himself, and take up his cross daily, and follow Me." It is when a man shuns the cross that he passes out of intimate fellowship and begins the downward course.

My final word is that already twice said. Wherever you may be, you need go no farther. Turn back to Him and to His love, back to His heart ere you rest tonight, and you will find Him the same loving, almighty Saviour.

CHAPTER XVI

THE TURNING AGAIN OF PETER

From that time began Jesus to show unto His disciples that He must go unto Jerusalem, and suffer many things of the elders and chief priests and scribes, and be killed, and the third day be raised up. And Peter took Him, and began to rebuke Him, saying, Be it far from Thee, Lord: this shall never be unto Thee.
MATTHEW 16:21, 22.

Verily, verily, I say unto thee, When thou wast young, thou girdedst thyself and walkedst whither thou wouldst; but when thou shalt be old, thou shalt stretch forth thy hands, and another shall gird thee, and carry thee whither thou wouldst not. Now this He spake, signifying by what manner of death he should glorify God. And when He had spoken this, He saith unto him, Follow Me.
JOHN 21:18, 19.

LET US READ THESE PASSAGES AGAIN, OMITTING ALL SAVE THE actual words of Peter as recorded in the first, and those of Jesus as recorded in the second. "Be it far from Thee, Lord; this shall never be unto Thee." "Verily, verily, I say unto thee, when thou wast young, thou girdedst thyself, and walkedst whither thou wouldst: but when thou shalt be old, thou shalt stretch forth thy hands, and another shall gird thee, and carry thee whither thou wouldst not. . . . Follow Me."

THE TURNING AGAIN OF PETER

Last Sunday evening I spoke to you on the subject of the sifting of Peter. This evening we turn our attention to our Lord's method in restoring him. Ere we trace the stages in his turning again, I would notice the significance of the two passages we have read. The one reveals the first movement of Peter out of harmony with his Lord, when for the first time Jesus definitely told His disciples that He must needs go to Jerusalem and suffer and be killed, and the third day be raised up. Peter stood in the presence of the announcement astonished and afraid, and instead of following his Lord, though unable to understand Him, he said, "Be it far from Thee, Lord: this shall never be unto Thee." The Master immediately rebuked him in the sternest terms, "Get thee behind me, Satan: thou art a stumbling-block unto me: for thou mindest not the things of God, but the things of men." When I come to the scene at the seashore, and to the final movement in it, I hear Jesus saying to him, "When thou wast young thou girdedst thyself, and walkedst whither thou wouldst; but when thou shalt be old, thou shalt stretch forth thy hands, and another shall gird thee, and carry thee whither thou wouldst not. . . . Follow Me." Thus Jesus brought Peter back to the cross, to his own cross. Peter failed in following when his Lord's cross was presented to him. He was restored to following when his own cross overshadowed his life. Yet there are many stages between that movement out of fellowship and that perfect restoration. This evening, to magnify His grace and to attempt to set forth the patience and persistence of the Lord in seeking after and restoring His wandering ones, I shall ask you to follow me as I attempt to trace the stages of the restoration, for the man turning his back upon the cross is not immediately transformed into a man who consents to the cross and comes presently to glory in the fact that he is counted worthy to suffer shame for his Master's Name. There was much—I speak it very reverently, although the much of human speech is an awkward word to use of the Divine activity—there was very much for the Master to do for this man. While we shall see Peter all through our study tonight, I pray you attempt to fix your eyes, not on him, but on the Lord, marking the method of His mercy and His patience, how He commenced to make a highway home for this Peter, and how He went after Peter persistently until He set his feet once more upon the broad highway of His commandment, and commissioned him to all the toil of the coming years.

Last Sunday evening we were able to trace the downward steps of Peter in the first chapter of Mark 14. In order to follow consecutively the method of the Master's restoration we cannot confine ourselves to one chapter, but shall attempt to follow it by turning to different passages in the Gospel writings. The first to which I shall draw your attention is to be found in Luke 22:31, 32. Here the Master is speaking to Peter, and says to him (and here I very deliberately use the marginal rendering), "Simon, Simon, Satan hath obtained you by asking, that he might sift you as wheat: but I made supplication for thee, that thy faith fail not: and do thou, when once thou hast turned again, stablish thy brethren." That is the first step in Peter's restoration. The "you" is plural and the reference is to all the disciples: "but I made supplication for *thee*, that *thy* faith fail not." That is singular and personal and immediate. This does not mean that Jesus did not pray for the rest, but it is a special word for Peter. While He tells Peter that he, in common with all the rest, has been obtained by Satan for sifting, He singles Peter out because he is especially in peril.

The first step our Lord took toward the restoration of this man then was that of storing up in his mind words which would be of service to him in the days to come. In one flash of light He revealed a most startling situation. A human soul stands between two forces, the forces of evil and of good. "Satan hath obtained thee by asking . . . but I made supplication for thee." Satan has been asking about this man. Jesus has been asking about him. Over against the asking of Satan, Jesus has put His own asking. All that will pay for further consideration, and we postpone it. What I now want you to notice is that Jesus told Peter He had prayed for him that his faith should not fail. Was that prayer answered? Certainly. You say, "But his faith did fail." Never. He denied his Lord. Yes, and believed in Him all the time. What did fail? His courage, his hope, his obedience, not his faith in the Person. The faith of the disciples of Jesus never failed. The two men walking to Emmaus had lost hope and courage and confidence, but not faith in Him. They had lost faith, in the sense of having certain convictions about Him weakened, but they had not lost their faith in Him personally. They thought He had been mistaken. They thought He had failed. They said, "We *hoped* that it was He which should redeem Israel." Their use of the verb "to hope" was in the past tense. They had lost their hope, but they said He "was a prophet mighty in deed and word," and that suggests that they still believed in Him. The faith which saves is not faith in anything heard about Jesus, but faith in Jesus. Peter's faith never failed. His courage failed, his obedience failed, his hope died out; but he never lost his faith in Jesus. I think the hour came when he thought his faith had failed. A great many people come there. But Jesus had prayed for Peter before his denial, before the outward and evident manifestation of the inner heart backsliding. He had taken an advance march against the enemy, had garrisoned the soul of His child against all the sifting of hell. Thank God, that is my Saviour. I hope He is your Saviour, dear heart. So He begins His method of restoration.

In this same 22nd chapter of Luke we find the next step in verse 61. "And the Lord turned and looked upon Peter." Just a look. I cannot interpret it. There was no theology in it. There were tears in it. Have you ever asked yourself quietly when you were alone how Jesus looked at Peter? I think I know how I would have looked at him. I am very much afraid, from what I know of my own heart, that if my bosom friend had denied me in answer to the give and take of a servant girl and the mockery of brutal soldiers just when I most needed him, when my life was being sworn away, my look might have been one of anger. Jesus did not look that way. I know He did not. If there be anything of His grace in my heart I might not have looked in anger, but I think the highest thing that could ever have been said of my looking would be that I looked reproachfully at Peter. Do you think Jesus did that? Do you think that day in the judgment hall He looked back where Peter stood by the fire cursing and swearing, and there was something in his look which said, "Peter, is that you? Can you add to my sorrow? Can you help to break my heart?" I do not think He looked like that. I think He was too self-emptied. I do not think there entered into the thinking of Jesus the sorrow caused to Him by His friend's denial. I think His was a look aflame with the pity of God. I think it was a look ineffable in its tenderness, which said to Peter, not, "What sorrow art thou causing Me," but "What sorrow art thou causing thyself?" I think it was a great look of compassion, full of tenderness divine. Overwhelmed with personal sorrow, He forgot His sorrow in pity for the grief which this foolish man was bringing to his own heart. That interpretation may not be correct. Therefore I simply remind you of what happened and ask you to find out when you are alone what the look meant. Of this at least I am sure, that look broke Peter's heart. I do not think a look of anger would have done that. I almost question whether a look of reproach would have done it. But, oh, the pity of those eyes! The unveiling of God's compassion in those eyes! Peter hurried out into the night. He is coming home. A man is always coming home when he quits the world's fire for the dark night in penitence. There are many tears and sighs and dark hours to go through, but he is coming home. My dear man, are you broken-hearted because you have denied your Lord? Have you quit the world's fires? Are you very dark and desolate and lonely in this house tonight? You are on the way home.

What is the next thing? We turn to chapter 16 of Mark's Gospel and find it in the 7th verse. An angel is speaking to the women, and in the midst of his speaking we hear these words: "Go, tell His disciples . . . He goeth before you into Galilee: there shall ye see Him, as He said unto you." I am so glad you have Bibles and have noticed the omission. "Go, tell His disciples *and Peter*." I do not know how much that means to you. Have you ever thought how much it meant to Peter? The message was all wrapped up in two words, one of which was his own name, and the other the little conjunction which linked him to the other disciples—"and Peter." Imagine for a moment, if you can, what Peter had been passing through. Think of the judgment hall where they swore His Lord's life away, and condemned Him to the brutal death on the cross. Think reverently how they had buffeted Jesus and bruised Him: and think all the while, if you would understand it, from Peter's standpoint. Think how they nailed Jesus to the cross, how they watched Him die, and remember that Peter was saying in his heart, "He is dead, and the last thing He ever heard me say was that I did not know Him." May God deliver every man and woman in this house from the unutterable sorrow of losing a loved one, which loved one last heard you say an unkind thing. If you said an unkind word as you left home tonight, get up and go home and put it right. It may become the agony of your life. Think of it in Peter's case. Cannot you hear him saying, "I denied Him with curses, and swore I did not know Him, and He heard me, and He looked, and I have never had a chance to say another word. He is gone. He is dead. Those eyes cannot look at me now. Those lips cannot speak to me. The hand that leaned on me as we walked will never rest on my shoulder again. He is dead." I have sometimes tried to go with Peter through those days and nights after the Lord looked at him, and I cannot help feeling that they were days and nights of unutterable sorrow.

It is the resurrection morning. The women are early there. They have seen a vision of angels, and are coming with swift steps to the disciples. Peter is somewhere among them, on the outskirts. He felt he did not belong to them. They had all run away, but he alone had denied his Lord. The women are delivering their message and Peter is listening with the rest. Suppose the women had said, "We have seen an angel who told us to tell His disciples that He has gone into Galilee, and we shall see Him there." Peter would have said, "That is not for me. He wants to meet the disciples, but I have denied Him. I have cut myself off from the disciples. I have put myself outside." The Lord knew it. The Master of angels, while yet in the spirit world, charges His angel to tell the women to deliver His message to the disciples *and Peter*. The women come to the disciples and say, "The angel said we were to tell His disciples *and Peter*." Immediately there is new hope in the heart of that man, or I do not know human nature. I am not sure that the sorrow did not grow. There is nothing breaks a man's heart like the sign of forgiveness. If I have wronged you and you are hard with me, I shall be sorry; but if you are kind to me you will break my heart. Peter is saying, "He has something to say to me. I wonder what." So the Lord has taken another step towards bringing him home. He has sent him a message.

The next step in the restoration is found in Luke 24:33, 34, "And they rose up that very hour, and returned to Jerusalem, and found the eleven gathered together, and them that were with them, saying, The Lord is risen, and hath appeared to Simon." The Lord had revealed Himself to the two men walking to Emmaus, and they hastened back to Jerusalem with the news that they had seen Him, and found the eleven gathered together, and it was the eleven who said, "The Lord is risen, and hath appeared to Simon." I do not know how you are going to place that chronologically. I am not sure whether He appeared to Simon before He walked to Emmaus with the two men, or somewhere in the interim between His breaking of bread with them and their getting back again to Jerusalem. I think probably it was before the walk to Emmaus. When the two men from Emmaus got back to Jerusalem to tell what they had seen they found all the disciples filled with wonder and saying, "The Lord is risen, and hath appeared to Simon." Where He appeared to Simon I do not know. What He said to Simon, I dare not tell you dogmatically. There is no record of it. The fact that He appeared to Simon is chronicled, and it was so important that Paul knew about it, and when he mentioned the appearances which demonstrate resurrection, he included this, "He appeared to Cephas." This is the Lord's next step in bringing Peter home, a private, lonely interview. I am so glad I do not know where it happened. I am so thankful there is no record of what passed between them. There are things which pass between a penitent soul and Christ which no third man ought to hear. When Jesus is restoring a soul He is sure to get that soul alone somewhere, and when all others—apostles, prophets, and teachers—are outside, He will talk with that soul face to face. So He talked with Peter. I wonder if you will be patient while I try to imagine one thing He said to Peter. I am almost reluctant to do it. I would not do it if I had not had some such experience myself. I think, among other things, there would be something like this: "Peter, I told you I must go to the cross." Only you must not imagine that Christ said it as you say to people, "I told you so." It was not said in a triumphant tone, to rebuke him. "You did not want me to go to the cross; but, Peter, I have been to the cross, and by My blood your sins are forgiven." I think He said something like that. I think Peter learned in that private interview the meaning of the cross. I think he felt the virtue of the cleansing blood. I think in that hour Peter found out the folly of his own mistake and the wisdom of his Master's method.

Thus finally we come back to John 21, in which we have the last movement in the restoration of this man. May I remind you of the steps already taken? First, Jesus prayed for Peter. Second, He looked at Peter. Third, He sent Peter a message. Fourth, He had a private interview with Peter; and now, in the story of the events which took place on the shore of the lake, you will find the fifth, sixth, and seventh steps. What is the fifth? He challenges Peter's love. The sixth, He gives Peter back his work and commissions him. The seventh, He puts the cross in front of Peter and says, "Follow Me."

First, He challenges Peter's love. There is such wonderful fitness in all our Lord does, and in all His ways. I know it is an old story. We have often read it, but it will not harm us to look at it once more. There are contrasts and similarities in this story which I think are very wonderful. Peter had denied the Lord in the city. Jesus takes him away from the city, with its rush and roar and all its seductions, to the sea. Peter had denied Him just past midnight. Jesus meets Peter there by the sea in the early morning hour, just when men are beginning to see clearly, and from the boat they looked and saw a stranger on the shore. Peter had denied Him by a fire which Jesus' enemies had built. Jesus builds a fire now for Peter, and calls him to confess Him over that fire. Peter had thrice denied Him. Thrice our Lord calls him to confess. Is there any picture in all the Bible more full of beauty? How does Christ begin? Is this a formal court to which He brings Peter? No. It is an informal breakfast. No ecclesiastical commissioners these before whom Peter is arraigned, but fishermen with the tang of the sea and the weariness of the night upon them, and the hunger of robust physical health. The risen Christ has built a fire, and cooked fish and prepared bread, and He said to them, "Come and break your fast." He waited on them. You did not miss that, did you? He made them sit down and He waited on them. When they had broken their fast, and the light of the morning was all about them, the fire glowing there, and no sense of chilliness, Jesus looked at His servant and said, "Simon, son of John, lovest thou Me?" It is somewhat wearisome and academic, yet one must point out the difference between these words translated love. When Jesus asked that question He used a high word, which indicates love upon an intellectual plane. "Lovest thou Me with the love of illuminated intelligence?" That is not what He said, but that is what is in the word. Peter did not use that word but took a lower word, a warmer word, an emotional word. "Yea, Lord, Thou knowest that I fondly love Thee." Immediately Jesus said to him, "Feed My lambs." Then once again He said, "Simon, son of John, lovest thou Me?" And still the word is the high word with all the light of

God upon it. Peter again got down to his lower word, a very beautiful word nevertheless. "Yea, Lord, Thou knowest that I fondly love Thee." Peter dared not climb to Christ's high word. Then listen, the third time the Lord came down in great grace to Peter's lower word, and said, "Simon, son of John, fondly lovest thou Me?" That is why Simon was grieved. Not because Jesus asked him three times if he loved Him, but because the third time He descended to the lower word. He did not like His Lord to come down, but he had learned such a lesson that he dared not climb to the high word. "Lord, Thou knowest all things; Thou knowest that I fondly love Thee." Did Peter ever climb to the high word? Yes. Read his Epistles. He never uses the lower word, always the high word of Jesus. That morning by the lake he just kept on the level of the love he knew he possessed. Mark the contrast in this man. A little while ago he had said to Jesus, "Thou dost not understand me. Though all should forsake Thee, I will not." Now he says, "Lord, Thou knowest all about me. Thou knowest all things, Thou knowest that I love Thee." A little while ago, over the fire the enemies of Jesus had built, Peter had denied Him thrice. Now, in the sunlight of the morning, in the warmth of the fire Christ had built, Peter thrice confessed Him, and every time Jesus restored him to his work, and so brought him back into full and perfect fellowship and communion.

I am bound to stop for a moment to say, in God's name get away from the fires Christ's enemies are building for warmth. He knows how to build fires. There is in your nature no demand that He cannot supply. You want enthusiasm, passion, fire? Let Him build it and kindle it and inspire it. Man, if you go to the world's fires, you will burn your passion out until it is nothing but ashes and dust upon the world's highway. Go to Christ's fires and He will take your passion and make it flame and burn. That seems to me to be the value of this fire which Jesus built. He is saying to men for all time, "If the morning is chill and you want warmth I can build your fire." So He has called for His child's confession, and has given him back his work by the fire which He Himself has built.

There is one other step. He looked at Peter once more and said, "Follow Me." "When thou wast young, thou girdedst thyself, and walkedst whither thou wouldest: but when thou shalt be old, thou shalt stretch forth thy hands, and another shall gird thee, and carry thee whither thou wouldest not." I think we may interpret that, "When you were young you were your own master, and had your own way, and went whither you would. You made your own choices and decisions. Presently, when you are old, when you most need comfort and help, there is a desolating experience waiting for you, Peter. You will stretch out your hands and another will gird you and carry you whither you would not." John listened, and he understood these mystic sentences better than any other man, so he put in a parenthesis, "Now this He spake, signifying by what manner of death he should glorify God." Accepting that word of John as true, when Jesus said these words to Peter He meant to say to him, "When you were young you had your own way. You have been impulsive, girding yourself in great independence; but there is an hour coming when someone else will gird you, and bind you and crucify you." It is as clear a picture of the cross as came to Peter at Cæsarea Philippi. But that is not all Christ says. Do not go away and think that is all. "Follow Me." What does that mean? "Peter, you were afraid of my cross. I have endured the cross. I have despised the shame. I have risen from among the dead. I am your Lord and Master. Peter, you are coming to the cross. Follow Me. Come My way. My cross leads to My crowning. Your cross will lead to your crowning. My dark day of shame issued in My glad Easter morning of glory. All the perils of your pathway and its pain but lead you out to the Kingdom and to life. Follow Me." And Peter followed Him. He was not changed into an angel, for the very next thing he tried to do was to interfere about John. "What shall this man do?" He is still the same impetuous, impulsive Peter, but he has heard the supreme word. I take his Epistles up presently and read them and find in all of them the glory of his knowledge of his Lord. I find in all of them his consciousness of the infinite meaning of the cross. I find in all of them his consent to the cross and his abandonment to its claims, and I find in all of them his triumphant, glorious victory.

The Saviour who brought Peter back is waiting for you. How shall I say it? Now the crowd hinders me as it always does. I cannot say it, but thank God that while I am witness of these things so also is the Holy Ghost. Listen now to the voice of the Spirit Who is speaking in your heart. Far away are you? Broken-hearted, disappointed with yourself? You have denied Him and He has looked at you. He sends you a message, He is at your side. He wants to talk to you all alone. Let Him. There has been no cooling of His love, no failure in His faithfulness. Where are you, man? Wandering yet? Are you broken-hearted and disappointed? You have gone very far from Him. You have been very mean toward Him. You have dragged His name in the dust, but still His arm is about you. His hand is on your head, and it is a pierced hand. He presses you to His heart, against His wounded side. Trust Him. God help you to trust Him. At last, by the way of the cross, He will bring you also to the crowning. Is there distance between you and your Lord? Cancel the distance. Get back to Him. His love is stronger than death, mightier than the grave. No waters can quench it, and He loves you. I have no other word to say. God help you to see it for yourself, and to obey it by returning to Him now.

CHAPTER XVII

LOVE'S PROOF AND PRIZE

He that hath My commandments, and keepeth them, he it is that loveth Me: and he that loveth Me shall be loved of My Father, and I will love him, and will manifest myself unto him.

JOHN 14:21.

I CANNOT READ THE SUBLIME THINGS OF JOHN WITHOUT FEELing that I am listening to the man who leaned his head upon the bosom of Jesus. They are not set and dignified discourses, as was the Manifesto of the King which Matthew records; but they are discourses broken in upon by the interruptions of familiar friends, interruptions which reveal the blunders of the men who interrupted, and yet which lead to new unveilings of the heart of the interrupted Teacher. Take this discourse in the midst of which the words of my text occur, and you find that Jesus was interrupted four times, and yet there is no interruption to the stream of revelation which flowed from His lips. Peter interrupts Him, then James, then Philip, and presently Jude. Through all Jesus' replies runs a perfect system, and in the midst occur the words of my text. How simple these words are and yet how searching. They are so simple that perhaps when I read them they produced no blush of shame, no blanch of fear. They are all commonplace words, yet, somehow, there was something in them which lingered with us, creating a sense of discomfort, and almost compelling a stricter self-examination. Jesus says two things. First, "He that hath My commandments and keepeth them, he it is that loveth Me." Secondly, "And he that loveth Me shall be loved of My Father, and I will love him, and will manifest myself unto him." First of all, Jesus sets love and obedience in relationship. "He that hath My commandments, and keepeth them, he it is that loveth Me." It is a statement that has at least a twofold meaning. First, that my love is proven by my obedience, and, secondly, that love to Christ produces obedience. That is but to state the one declaration in its twofold application.

Love, how we speak of it, how we sing of it, how we imagine we understand it! We hardly care to formulate its terms or declare its requirements. We talk of it as a symphony, a song, a sentiment. Jesus Christ analyzes it. It seems an almost ruthless touch that He puts upon love as He declares its terms. We are accustomed to think of love as vaporizing itself away, or expressing itself in a fragrance which cannot be analyzed. We are called Philistines today if we begin to analyze love. Jesus the One Revealer puts His hand upon love and says, "Love is demonstrated by obedience." Obedience is the outcome of love and consequently its fairest blossom and fruitage. Jesus says to us, "You can express love perfectly only in the terms of law." Jesus says to us, "Love that is lawless is not love." "He that hath My commandments and keepeth them, he it is that loveth Me."

Jesus, having expressed the truth concerning love in the terms of law, rose to another level: "He that loveth Me shall be loved of My Father, and I will love him, and will manifest Myself unto him." If love be most perfectly manifested by obedience to definite and positive commandments it has as its answer visions, voices, revelations, unfoldings, manifestations. Love's one supreme desire is to comprehend being loved. Thus love will obey the law, keep the commandments, and the loved One will answer the search by revealing Himself. "I will manifest myself unto him."

Let us look at the first thing more particularly. "He that hath My commandments and keepeth them, he it is that loveth Me." Some attempt to prove love to Christ by professing it, others by unceasing toil in His service, still others in a higher and better way, by the cultivation of a meek and lowly spirit, by the humility that does not obtrude itself, by manifestation among their fellows of that spirit which has learned sweetness and tenderness and gentleness at the very feet of our Lord Himself. No one in this congregation will for a single moment imagine that I am saying these things are wrong in themselves. I say that they will all be present in the life of the true lover of Jesus, but that none of them demonstrates love. All spring out of other causes and other reasons than love. Untiring zeal in the business of the Kingdom and the work of Jesus Christ does not prove love, nor does even the cultivated humility and meekness of spirit. Christ mentions none of these things. He says simply and prosaically—forgive that word, I do not quite like it, but am at a loss for a better—"There is only one way to prove that you love Me—keep My commandments." "He that hath my commandments and keepeth them, he it is that loveth me."

What are these commandments? First of all, the great kingly words which Jesus uttered while He was here that make for men the way of entrance upon the life of loyalty to Himself: "If any man would come after Me, let him deny himself, and take up his cross, and follow Me." That indicates the way of beginning in this whole pathway of loyalty. That one great word of Jesus covers the Christian pathway from its initiation to its consummation in the glory. What is the beginning? Denying self and taking up the cross. What is the progress? Following Him, until He lead us at last into the infinite light. There is, however, a larger application. His commandments are the words which He speaks in loneliness to the heart of everyone who really loves Him and leans upon His bosom, the simple words which He speaks in the silence of the morning or amid the rush of the noontide, or when the shadows of evening are falling; in the place of swift and subtle temptation, or in the quiet calm of that everyday life which becomes dreary because of its monotony. His commandments are given to all trusting souls immediately and directly.

Do you love Him? You do not prove it when, gathered in the sanctuary, you sing of Him. You do not prove it when in the busy hours of toil you are doing work for Him. You do not prove it when amid the men by whom you are surrounded you are attempting to reproduce the humility of His Spirit. You prove your love when in answer to His word you straightway do what He tells you. This is the demonstration of love for which He seeks. I may sing songs of praise to Him in the great congregation, or even in my loneliness I may lift to Him some psalm—and He seeks such singing and loves it—but it does not prove love. I may give my body to be burned. I may pour out all the fiber of my manhood in service and never prove my love. When because He says, "Do this," I do it; when because He says, "Go there," I go; when because He says, "Sit still and wait," I wait with happy spirit, then I prove my love. The final demonstration of love which He craves is not work or anything about which men will talk and sing, but the thousand and one little obediences which men never see and know, in which the heart pours out its gratitude. "He that hath My commandments." How fond Jesus was of sweeping out the interference of all middle men. "He that hath My commandments in his own soul, in his own heart, he that hears My words spoken in a whisper and immediately obeys and keeps the commandment, that is the man who loves Me."

You cannot tell whether I love Him, make no mistake. You cannot measure my love by my service or my lack of it. The final demonstration of love is not for the vision of any save the loved one. Love is always between two. I may sing and serve, toil and suffer, and yet never love; and while the world applauds the supposed evidences of my devotion, my Master may be hungry for the love I am withholding, pining for the affection I will not give Him.

He broods over me and says, "My child, that is the way." I walk in it. It is quite an average way. You see me walking along that way and you do not notice it. It means nothing to you. It is a common, ordinary way; but to Him it is the song of love because He sent me there. He says to a child of His love in some noonday of blessing and of joy, "Come apart into the darkness. Come with me. I am going by this *via dolorosa*; come with me." You see the passing out into that way of sorrow, and you do not understand it. To you there is no song upon the lips, no radiance, no heroism; but there is love because there is walking with Jesus. You cannot discover the love, but He finds it. "He that hath My commandments, and keepeth them, he it is that loveth Me." We cannot prove to each other our love for Christ, but we know that He is right when He says that love is proved only by obedience. We often sing, sing loudly to cover the tracks of our disobedience. Thousands of men are busy doing something for Jesus, anything except the thing He told them to do. While we admire their zeal, He mourns their lack of love. "He that hath My commandments, and keepeth them, he it is that loveth Me."

Again, love to Christ produces obedience. This is not a

contradiction. It is simply the statement of the same thing from the other side. If obedience proves love, it follows by logical necessity that love is the inspiration of obedience. Love to Christ is produced, first, by knowledge of His love. Do not forget that word which John wrote in his epistle, "We love, because He first loved us." If my obedience is the demonstration of my love, my love is always born of His love and is the response to His love. Nothing short of love will produce perpetual and glad obedience such as satisfies the heart of the Lord. Think of the things I have now referred to us illustration. Profession of love never produces obedience. A man's pride in his own profession will keep him following for a little while. A man will say, "I have said this thing and I will do it." As the darkness falls, the strain and stress become more terrible, and presently he will forget his profession and disobey.

Zeal for work for Christ will not keep him obedient. It will halt, and presently passion will cool, unless the passion be the passion of a burning love for his Lord. Humility, what of that? Humility may become cowardice. Nothing other than love will keep me obedient. It is love which makes obedience a delight, even when obedience means pain and suffering. There is no motive other than love powerful enough to maintain unswerving obedience.

Mark how these two things interact. Obedience is the demonstration of love. Love, therefore, is the inspiration of obedience. At the beginning it is a simple thing. One vision of His face and my heart answers love, and I begin to follow Him. He lays upon me some new word of His law. If I disobey, my love will cool and disobedience will become the order of my life. If I obey I shall find through the gateway of that obedience a new demonstration of His love, which will make my love profounder, and gradually, with the increase of my love, there will be an increase in my devotion, until at last nothing but love will possess my soul and nothing but obedience will express that love.

To these deeper things our Lord passes in the second statement of our text. "He that loveth Me shall be loved of My Father and I will love him, and will manifest Myself unto him." At first sight there may appear to be contradiction to something I have been saying. I have been insisting upon it that He loved us first, and that is why we love Him. Here the love of the Father is stated to be the result of our love to the Son. "He that loveth Me and proves his love by obedience, him My Father will love." There is no contradiction. It is forever true, and there is no escape from it, that God's love is the first thing, but it is when I answer that love with love and obedience that His love is able to flow on toward me unchecked in its manifestation and operation. It is possible, terribly possible for me, not to make God cease to love me, but to put myself outside the place where His love is consciousness and power. That is the meaning of Jude's great word, "Keep yourselves in the love of God." Being in that love, keep yourselves there. Keep yourselves bearing such relationship to Him that love may flow on unchecked. Illustrate it if you will by earthly love. I do not think you could possibly make your mother cease to love you, if she is a real mother, but you may do such things as to put yourself outside the operation of a mother's love. I know the Scriptures say a mother may forget her child, but they say so only because it is such a remote possibility, and to throw into clearer relief the fact that God never can. You may check the outflow of a mother's love, you may lose the expression of it. You may make it necessary for the mother, to the breaking of her own heart, to seal up her love because of your disobedience. So also with God. "My Father will love him," says Jesus, "and

I will love him," and by that He means to say, "Our love will flow on unchecked in all its expressions and all its operations." Mark the comfort of this word. We are beginning to touch the realm of poetry. We are coming to the place of vision and hope, of joy and strength.

Have I spoken of two things? Really, they are but the unfolding of one logical sequence. At the risk of wearying you, I will repeat again the words of Jesus, "He that loveth Me shall be loved of My Father, and I will love him, and manifest Myself unto him." Think of the comfort of it. This is the crowning glory which rests upon the path of obedience, the path of the man to whom God has spoken, and who has heard His word and has obeyed it. Jesus says, "My Father will love him, and I will love him." That fact makes the barren path blossom as the rose. That fact makes the dreary day shine with all the glory of God's uplifted face. Think of what this means: this dual consciousness of God's love and Christ's love set upon me in the path of duty.

The path of obedience for you may be a dreary path in many ways. It would be a great deal easier for you to be out upon the high places of the field doing heroic things, but you are needed here, working on the dead level of monotonous repetition as the days become weeks, the weeks months, and the months years. Start once again, my brother, on the same pathway, and start doing on that pathway the thing He appoints because of love to Him, and then what? "My Father will love you, and I will love you." Think of the inspiration of that in any hour of temptation and difficulty. Think of the moral force of it in a man's life if it once take possession of him. Think how the love of some dear one upon earth strengthens a man. There are young men in this house tonight who would have gone to the devil long ago if it had not been that their mother and father loved them. How often a man is saved and delivered in an hour of peril because he knows someone loves him, even though not then with him. We have known of those who have hung up before them the picture of a human friend to save them in the hour of great temptation, and it has saved them. Apply that in a higher realm. As you tramp the ordinary pathway of everyday duty, it may be with bleeding feet and burdened heart, know that because you are aching by His appointment His love rests upon you. I am increasingly convinced that this is the true force of holiness. It is when I come to say, "I cannot do this, it would grieve the heart of my Lover," that I shall live as I ought to live. It is as this great fact dawns upon the soul like sunshine, and possesses it like a force, that the pathway of commonplace obedience becomes one of perpetual joy.

If God loves me and Christ loves me and increasingly that love surrounds me, what then? Then the laws which govern my life will multiply. You say, "But you are going back to the severe tones." You always get back to the severe tones when you get near to the gentleness of the heart of God. The more perfectly He loves me and the more amenable I am to His love, the more I shall find restrictions multiplying around me. You say, "I thought I was coming to new liberty." So you are, but it is liberty to produce the highest and the best.

I remember that when I was pastor of a country church one of my friends married and went to live out on Cannock Chase. He procured a piece of land, rough and utterly lacking anything in the form of cultivated beauty. When his house was built I went out with him to look at it. His land was fenced in, the fencing consisting of rough poles and wire. That was all. I did not see him for some years after. When I went back I saw that the fence round his land was a great deal stronger than when I first saw it. It was a closer fence. The garden was cultivated now, and the more perfectly you cultivate the garden, the stronger you make the fence. At first it was a fence to keep out marauding animals, but afterwards it must be a fence which will keep out the little foxes that spoil the vines, because the vines have tender grapes. The more God loves me, the closer will His fence be round about me. The more perfectly I answer love, the severer will be the restrictions He sets upon me. That is His principle. It is gentle and tender, always closing up the fence a little because He would come into His garden and find it unspoiled, not only by marauding beasts, but by the little foxes and small things which spoil the garden of God. It is love which makes the fence a little closer. It is love which makes the law a little more severe. It is love which shuts us up more completely from everything, and to Himself.

Now take the other word, a gracious and beautiful word: "I will manifest Myself unto him." This answers the severe part of the last thought. If it be true that the severity has become greater, and the requirements of God more stringent in the case of the man He perfectly loves, do not forget this other thing: "I will manifest Myself unto him." Every new requirement of love is a new opportunity for my rediscovery of my Lord. Every time He confronts me and asks me to yield up something He has never asked me to yield before, there is my chance of a new vision of His face and a new unveiling of His glory; but the face is never seen and the glory never flames until I answer His commandment. He is waiting to give some of you great revelations. He is waiting to unveil before your astonished gaze a face more radiantly lovely than you have ever dreamed, but He cannot do it until you obey that last commandment He laid upon you and so demonstrate your love, for love can be revealed only to love. "I will manifest myself to him." Every new commandment is a proof of new revelation. The world does not understand it. Jesus could not manifest Himself to the world, because the world does not know Him and does not love Him. You say this is something at which proud, cold, rationalistic philosophy smiles, and yet in the higher reaches of spiritual life this is a scientific law. This is a wonderful philosophy of love radiant with beauty, that when Jesus makes a demand and the soul answers it, that soul sees Him as never before.

This manifestation of Jesus, let me ask you to remember finally, is not a manifestation on the mount of transfiguration. It is a manifestation which comes along the lowly pathway in the valley. There are people here who do not want me to talk about this. They know all about it. When they tell you that in the midst of their business yesterday they saw the Lord, you smile at them, and the angels smile at you. Get up tomorrow morning to do His bidding. What shall I do tomorrow morning? The thing you were going to do, do it only at His bidding. Go to your office, your business, your workshop because He bids you go. Do not talk any more of the drudgery of it. Cancel the word "commonplace." Keep His commandment. To do that will be to safeguard you in your calling from everything that is low and base, and it will be to transfigure the meanest calling of all into a thing of glory and beauty. In the office, in the home, on the street, in the hospital, amid its pain and fear, do each thing because it is His bidding, and you will see Him in His glory, toiling through your business vocation toward the building of His city, calling to you through the days of suffering for your help, whispering to you in the lonely hour of your watching, "Inasmuch as ye did it unto one of these My brethren, even these least, ye did it unto Me."

Earth's crammed with heaven,
And every common bush afire with God;
But only he who sees, takes off his shoes—
The rest sit round it and pluck blackberries."

You can see Christ in the street as well as in the sanctuary, on Monday as well as on Sunday. Wherever a soul obeys Him and demonstrates love He answers love with manifestation, and every manifestation leaves its impress upon your brow, its light in your eyes, its elasticity in your step.

So by the commonplace of obedience I climb to the mountain of vision, demonstrating my love by keeping His commandments, seeing Him where I did not dream He could appear.

CHAPTER XVIII

THE LACK OF THE SPIRIT

Did ye receive the Holy Ghost when ye believed?

ACTS 19:2.

"DID YE RECEIVE THE HOLY GHOST WHEN YE BELIEVED?" NOT, "Have ye received the Holy Ghost *since* ye believed?" There is no warrant for the introduction of that word "since" into the Authorized Version. The tense is the same in both the verbs. "The Holy Ghost received ye when ye believed?" The only difference is that the one is a question and the other an affirmation. Received ye? Ye believed. This is a distinction rendered necessary by a difference. The introduction of the word "since" makes the Apostle's question mean, "Subsequently to believing, have ye received the Holy Ghost?" The inquiry which he raised really was, "Coincidentally with believing, did ye receive the Holy Ghost?" The Apostle's question was not whether these people had received a second blessing. It was rather an inquiry into the nature of the first blessing. An examination of the context will, I think, throw light upon the meaning of this question and enable us to make that personal and present application of it which is important to us.

Apollos was a Jew, that is, a proselyte, for he was an Alexandrian by race. He was "a learned man," and he was "mighty in the Scriptures." This man had been instructed in the way of the Lord, which does not mean that he was perfectly familiar with all the facts concerning the mission of Jesus. He had been, as the margin more accurately has it, instructed by word of mouth in the way of the Lord, and being fervent in spirit he spake and taught carefully the things concerning Jesus, not all of them, for he did not know all the things concerning Jesus, "knowing only the baptism of John." In all likelihood, upon some occasion Apollos had listened to the voice of the forerunner, had heard him as he foretold the coming of Another. He knew the One of Whom John spoke through what John had said, and he knew no more. He knew that One was to come after John, whose fan was to be in His hand, Who was to thoroughly purge His floor: One so Kingly that John said of Him that He was not worthy to stoop down and unloose the latchet of His shoe, One Who would baptize men with the Holy Ghost and with fire.

Knowing these things and being fervent in spirit, Apollos taught carefully what he knew. Listening to him were Priscilla and Aquila, who knew a great deal more than the preacher. They recognized his power and sincerity, but they knew his lack. I never know whether to admire Aquila and Priscilla or Apollos more for what follows. They heard him, and "took him unto them, and expounded unto him the way of God more accurately." I admire them because they did not write letters to the newspapers about him, but took him unto themselves. I admire him because he was willing to listen to two persons who were members of his congregation. After this instruction he appears to have passed on to Achaia. There his message was changed. He knew far more than when he had begun to preach in Ephesus. "He helped them much that had believed through grace, for he powerfully confuted the Jews, and that publicly, showing by the Scriptures that Jesus was the Christ."

He had persuaded men during the early days of his preaching to take a certain position—the one he himself had taken. He had told them about John and his message, about the One Who was to come after, the One Who was to come with His fan in His hand to purge His floor, to gather the wheat into a garner and to burn the chaff with unquenchable fire. Some of them had believed and had been baptized with John's baptism, but nothing more. No preacher ever lifts his hearers above the level of his own spiritual attainment.

When Paul came into contact with these men he saw that something was lacking. They had a great deal, but not everything. They had come a certain distance, but had halted. Paul discovered that they lacked the power of the Holy Spirit. There were certain inimitable evidences of the Spirit's presence in human lives which were lacking in these people, and he said to them suddenly, and I think with a note of surprise in his voice, "Did ye receive the Holy Ghost when ye believed?" They said, "We did not so much as hear whether the Holy Ghost was given," which does not mean that they did not know of the existence of the Holy Ghost, because John had preached the doctrine of the Holy Spirit and the fact that One was coming Who would baptize them with the Spirit. It does mean, as our rendering gives us to understand, that they had not heard whether the Holy Spirit was given. John's teaching had declared that it should be given, but they had not heard whether the promise had been fulfilled. Then Paul asked another question, "Into what then were ye baptized?" And they said, "Into John's baptism." "Then," said Paul, in effect, "if you were baptized into John's baptism, you have not been obedient to John's message. John told you that you must repent, but he also told you that you were to believe on the One who was to come." Then most evidently Paul told them He had come, told them the story of His coming, of His work, and led them further on. They were then baptized in the name of Jesus. It was an act of faith, and following that, Paul laid his hands on them, symbolically, not sacramentally, and in that moment, as they were baptized because they believed in the name of Jesus, while Paul's fatherly hands lay still upon them, the Holy Spirit fell upon them.

Now look and listen. They spake with tongues, they prophesied, and from that day forward no apostle could ask them, "Did ye receive the Holy Ghost when ye believed?" The signs have come. The evidences are present. The something lacking is lacking no more. The inner life bubbles up into joy, ecstatic speech, tongues. The inner life pours itself out in testimony, prophecy. They had received the Holy Ghost because they had believed on Jesus in all the fullness of the apostolic message concerning Him. They had not until that moment received the Holy Ghost, because they had believed on Jesus only within the narrow limits of John's message concerning Him.

Now, I think with the light of that context upon the text, we see how this may be a very pertinent and absolutely important question today.

I am speaking to an audience the vast majority of which believes in Jesus. There may be some few here who have lost their faith in Him, and have lost their faith in revealed religion. With all sincere and honest respect for them, they are outside the scope of my present message. Were I to go from pew to pew and speak individually to man, woman, and little child, asking the same question, "Do you believe in Jesus?" the answer would be naturally, honestly, truthfully, "Yes." Therefore I bring you the Apostle's question, "Did ye receive the Holy Ghost when ye believed?" Is your belief of that nature which has resulted in the actual reception in your own life of the Holy Spirit of God?

If in the economy of God some of these apostles of the Early Church were called upon to face congregations such as we have to face, I think they would pause in astonishment in the first ten minutes, and would say, "Did ye receive the Holy Ghost when ye believed?" There are hundreds and thousands of people who in some measure believe in Jesus Christ who have never received the Spirit, who have never been baptized with the Spirit, who have never been born again, for the terms are synonymous. Ethic without enthusiasm, principle without passion, desire without dynamic, negation of the wrong things without position in the soil of the new life—this is a perilous state in which to live. It is a perilous state because to continue in that state is to become in the one tremendous word of the writer of the letter to the Hebrews, "hardened."

The ethic merely accepted as true becomes traditional bondage. The principle obeyed with no passion of fire burning through it becomes heartlessness. Desire for the higher life and the broadening of the outlook long unfulfilled become cynicism. The negation becomes chaos. This is what is happening everywhere. You believe on Jesus, yes, and you believe on Jesus very reverently; you have never taken His name in vain. So far from that, you have always attended what we call the means of grace, you have sung the hymns of the sanctuary, you have attentively listened to the message delivered by the servants of God. You have come so far as to believe the ideals of Jesus, you accept them; but there is no passion, no fire, no force, no light upon the mountains, no song in the heart.

> Faultily faultless, icily regular,
> Splendidly null.

Dead while you live. Our churches are crowded with such people, who have never received the Holy Ghost, who, if you begin to speak to them, will say, "We are not sure about this doctrine of the Holy Ghost. We do not even know whether the Holy Ghost is!"

May I press the examination of this passage of Scripture a little further for our own profit. What was the fault of the attitude of these people? They had halted. John had pointed them on to Jesus. They had not fully obeyed. I do not know that it would be fair for me to criticize them or to attempt to say they were blameworthy in this matter. It may have been that they had never heard the final facts about Jesus. Perchance Apollos had never heard them. It may have been that in the darkness which resulted from the crucifixion all hope in Jesus had been eclipsed. They may have heard of the death of Jesus, and may have heard rumors of His resurrection. They may have said, "We are not certain that this is the One. John said there was One to come, but this may not be the One." Be all that as it may, this is certain, they had halted after repentance. They had never taken the second step which John had commanded—to believe on Him Who was to come. When Paul came he preached Jesus to them in all the fulness of the apostolic message. They went beyond the messenger John to One of whom he spoke, and thus passed into the realm of life. They no longer waited for the operation of the fan and the operation of the fire, and the baptism of the Holy Ghost, they gave themselves over thereto, and immediately they did so, they felt the burning of the fire, the sweeping wind of the fan, the touch of a new life. The horizon was flung back, the windows were opened, the thrill of life for which they had waited came to them when they abandoned themselves to Jesus Christ.

What is the one thing lacking in all such as believe in

His ethic, in His ideal, who come so far as recognition of the beauty and glory of His purpose? In order to come into touch with His life, what is the one thing needful? Just the step further. Hand the life over to Him by an act of faith. In the case of these people it was an act which expressed itself in baptism. I do not think for a moment that the method of expression matters. I do think that the act of faith which drives a man to a method of expression is the important thing. I do not believe that these men received the Holy Ghost because they received water baptism. Nobody believes that the immersion in water was the medium of the baptism of the Spirit. By that baptism into the name of Jesus they gave expression to their faith in Christ. Answering that faith expressed in that act, the Spirit came upon them.

That is what you need. You have been for years on the confines of Emmanuel's land. You are familiar with all the songs, but you cannot sing them and feel the rapture of them. You are familiar with all the phrasing of Christianity, but it has never become the phrasing which beats your heart into infinite music. You need that faith which abandons itself absolutely and wholly, not to an ideal you would like to realize, but to a Person who will realize in you every ideal after which your heart is seeking. In order to receive the Holy Ghost we have to add to our conviction, confidence; to our repentance, faith; to our hope, appropriation, and all these things in relation to Jesus Christ. The living Christ has come. The Spirit has been poured out. Westminster Chapel, London, tonight is as full in every part of the Holy Spirit of God as was the upper room on the day of Pentecost. The mistake you have been making for years is that you have been waiting for Him to come in nights of prayer and lonely vigil, in speculative inquiry; waiting while you have been attending conventions and reading books about the Holy

Ghost. The Spirit has come. He is here. Every man, woman, and little child in this house is surrounded by the beneficent Spirit of God, waiting to come in, waiting to teach you the deeper music of life, its vision and glory. "How is it that I do not feel the thrill and do not see the light?" you ask. Because you have never believed in Jesus Christ. Convinced of the perfection of His ideal, put confidence in Him, and rank yourself by His side and under His banner. Repenting of sin, changing your mind about it, trust Him to give you victory in every department of life. Hoping for a better day, appropriate the day that has come. Wishing that you could be delivered, be delivered now by trusting Jesus Christ. Just where you sit, hoping, wishing, wondering, cast yourself upon Jesus Christ and say, "Here I am, now, just as I am." The Spirit of God will bring the living Christ into your own inner experience. That will end your infidelity, your skepticism, your wonder. You will pass into the realm of life, and all the signs following will be granted to you.

What were the signs following? "They spake with tongues and prophesied." I am not going to inflict upon you any elaborate discussion as to that "spake with tongues." It was a repetition of the Pentecostal experience, and yet not a repetition, but to them the very Pentecostal experience. Just what Peter, James and John and the rest received at Pentecost these men received then. Just as Peter, James and John, waiting for the Spirit when Christ's work was done, received it, and immediately spake with tongues and prophesied, so these men who had been waiting, when they received the Holy Spirit, did the same thing—they spake with tongues. My own conviction—and here is a speculation with which you need not waste time—is that the miracle of Pentecost was not a miracle of talking in different languages, but of hearing in different languages. I believe these were the same tongues of which you read in Corinthians, notwithstanding other opinions. I believe the gift of tongues was the gift of ecstatic utterance, in praise, in prayer, in gladness. Somebody said, "Hallelujah," a little while ago, and you did not like it. I am afraid it was a sign that you have not received the Holy Ghost. I do not mean to say that if you have received the Holy Ghost you will say, "Hallelujah," but you will be in sympathy with the man who is bound to say it. The deadly dullness of half our services is proof of the fact that we lack the Spirit of God. If that fire is within me I burn, and, somehow or other, either in the volume of congregational song or some other way, it must flame forth. "They spake with tongues." They could not help it. Don't you, dear intellectual soul of this twentieth century, be cynical with the man who breaks out into tongues. You know the story; it is told of half a dozen different painters. I do not know of which one it is really true. I will fix it on Turner. He was showing one of his pictures to a friend, who said, "Oh, but that is not real. I have never seen colors like these." Turner replied, "No, but don't you wish you could?" Do you, in your cold intellectualism, say you never feel inclined to shout? Don't you wish you could? There is pathos in my question. The dead, hard, cold profession of the present day is tragic, pathetic. We need again to hear the outburst of song, of praise. When these men received the Holy Ghost they spake with tongues. There were only twelve of them most likely, all speaking the same language. The rigidity of repentance had merged into the renewal of remission. All the hardness of waiting and longing had passed into the gladness of receiving. That is the difference between believing in Jesus intellectually and believing in Him so that the answer is the answer of the Spirit creating ecstasy that speaks with tongues and conviction that utters itself in prophecy.

That was not the only sign. Read the chapter further, and you will find that these people created an atmosphere of apostolic testimony; they became a propagative center from which the Word of God sounded forth through all Asia. You will find also that they became the objects of imitation. You will find, finally, that their presence in Ephesus meant the undermining of idolatry, and presently we see the flaming fires at which men are burning the things of their witchcraft. Even until this hour the same thing is true. Let there fall upon us tonight the great constraint to go a little further, a little beyond the repentance which is change of mind about sin, a little beyond the long, lonely waiting for something that comes not, a little beyond into personal definite submission to Christ, what then? First tongues and then prophecy, and then an atmosphere in which the preacher can preach in the coming months so that men shall be saved, and then a propagative center from which the Word of God shall sound through all the neighborhood, then spurious imitation and the force that lights fires which destroy the witchery and wizardry which are cursing our age.

In the name of God do not let us talk of the Day of Pentecost as though it were a day that came and went nineteen hundred years ago. This is the day of Pentecost. The Spirit of God is here. If I am not singing, living, prophesying, it is because I am like the twelve men at Ephesus—I have come so far and have halted. Man, dare to go further. Add to your present position the final thing of belief in Jesus Christ.

If we have received the Spirit, there is yet responsibility. I can express it in one word, Yield. Take that step of faith in Jesus Christ tonight, and the Spirit will come upon you, and immediately you will feel the burning of the fire, the rising of the song, the driving of the power. In the name of God do not quench that fire. "Quench not the Spirit." Do not stifle that song. "Grieve not the Spirit." In the name of God do not resist that power. Resist not the Spirit. Hear the ancient words again, hear them upon the fringe of a new winter's work, while doors of opportunity are opening before you. "Quench not the Spirit." "Grieve not the Spirit." "Resist not the Spirit."

What answer do you give to the Apostle's question, "Did ye receive the Holy Ghost when ye believed?" If you say honestly, in this hour of clear vision, "No," then receive Him now. You say, "How can I receive Him?" Not by opening your heart to the Spirit, but by opening your heart to Jesus Christ. Not by believing that Christ is the perfect example, but by enlisting under His banner and putting your whole life at His disposal. By trusting Him for yesterday, to-day, tomorrow, and the infinite forever, with your whole life, physical, mental, and spiritual. If your answer to the Apostle's question be "Yes," then in God's name remember your peril, for we are all in peril. If we have received the Holy Ghost and the tongues have begun to speak and prophecy has begun, what is our peril?

That was the foundation of the Ephesian Church. It was a wonderful church, so great a church that Paul wrote the last flaming glory of his letters to it. But that is not all about the church. There is another letter to the Church of Ephesus, which the great Lord, believing in whom, they had received the Spirit, sent to them through John from Patmos. In that letter He says such tragic things as these, "I have this against thee, that thou didst leave thy first love." As God is my witness, I can hardly take up my Bible and read these words without my heart being ready to break. It is the sigh of Christ over the lost love of people who had received the Spirit, and who once had tongues and prophesied. Is Christ sighing over your lost first love? Some of you business men years ago, before you were so well off, felt the fervor and passion of the Spirit's power. Have you lost it? Are you just a wee bit impatient with me tonight because I have taken this line? You would not have been ten years ago. You have lost your first love.

What did Christ say to the church that had lost its first love? "Repent and do the first works." I love that. It is His new opportunity for backsliding souls. "Go back. Begin where you began before. Repent; change your mind once more. Get back to the place where you stood when you left me. Do over again the thing you did at Ephesus when the sky became glorious and the song burst forth." Will you do it tonight? Many of you, lost lovers of Jesus, are you coming to Him tonight?

Hear me again patiently. Do not think this harsh, unkind. I deliver it as the message that is on my heart. I am not half as anxious about you as I am about the multitudes who are outside. I want you in order to reach them. I would far rather see this place in ashes than see it the tomb of a dead, lifeless mob that admires Jesus and feels nothing of His life pulsating in them. We stand upon the threshold of tremendous opportunities. Are we ready for them? The question we are to ask our own souls is, "Did we receive the Holy Ghost when we believed?" If not, here and now, let us yield ourselves to Christ, and we shall receive. If we have received and have lost the thrill, and the saffron of morning has become the gray of eventide, let us go back. Though the way be rough, even though it means the cross, even if shame attend our going, let us go back to the first works, and out of the valley of humiliation shall rise Emmanuel's land of light and love and service for every one of us.

CHAPTER XIX

HIS WORKMANSHIP

We are His workmanship, created in Christ Jesus for good works, which God afore prepared that we should walk in them.

EPHESIANS 2:10.

THIS VERSE CONTAINS A REMARKABLE STATEMENT AS TO THE Christian life. All other conceptions of life at its very best are idealistic, but the Christian conception is also dynamic. "We are His workmanship," not merely men and women seeing an ideal which we are attempting to realize. That is not the deepest fact of Christian life, though that also is true. The word "workmanship" in this connection immediately attracts our attention. If we very literally translate here, we shall not, I am perfectly well aware, get the truest sense of the Apostle, and yet I think we should gain some light upon that sense, for the word here rendered "workmanship" might read "poems." I do not mean to suggest that the Greek word *poema* means exactly what our word "poems" means, but there is a quality in the word which we must not lose sight of when we read the word "workmanship." It is the quality of perfection, and the thought which the word suggests is not only that of a piece of work, but of a piece of work which is perfect. The thought, therefore, is that of poetry in its deepest, broadest and truest sense. It is the thought of rhythm, of orderliness and of beauty. We are God's workmanship. All that would be said if we simply laid the emphasis upon the fact that we are *God's* workmanship. Everything He does is full of beauty. Everything He does is characterized by order. Disorder is not of God. Ugliness in any sense of the word is not of God.

The method of Christianity is thus revealed. "We are His workmanship, created in Christ Jesus." This phrase includes the whole mission of Christ in its application to trusting souls. It is in Christ that God is making us what He would have us to be. The sphere in which God operates to the creation of our lives and the perfecting of His thought in and through us is Christ. By the way of His incarnation man came into conscious nearness to God. By the way of His life there was unveiled before the eyes of men what was in the heart of God when He said, "Let us make man." In the death of Christ there was revealed that mystery of atonement whereby man's sin is dealt with, canceled, made not to be, that man may find his new opportunity. By the way of the resurrection of Jesus Christ power was placed at the disposal of man so that he not only finds himself in Christ Jesus a pardoned soul, but a being equipped with all resources for the accomplishment of the Divine purpose. By the way of the reign of Christ over the individual life through the Spirit there is the administration of the will of God and perpetual communication of both pattern and power.

Yet, again, the purpose of this new creation and of this new method is manifested in the text, "We are His workmanship, created in Christ Jesus for good works." "For good works" is not a narrow phrase referring merely to specific acts of so-called Christian service; it refers to the whole life. We are prepared for good works. The Apostle is contrasting the present with the past condition of these Ephesian Christians. He says to them, "Among whom"—that is the sons of disobedience—"we also all once lived in the lusts of our flesh, doing the desires of the flesh and of the mind." That description of the past covers the whole fact of life, the daily task and toil, specific acts of worship under the old idolatrous conditions, amusements, recreations, everything. All life proceeded in answer to fleshly passion and desire. Everything is changed when we are in Christ Jesus, so that all our life is to proceed, not in answer to fleshly passion and desire, but in answer to the highest motive and the highest reason, in brief, in answer to the perpetual inspiration of the Christ life which has now become our life. "We are His workmanship, created in Christ Jesus for good works."

I want to consider the practical application of this truth to our everyday life. We shall therefore proceed to consider the orderliness of the life of the Christian in the will and economy of God, and we shall attempt to apply the teaching of the text, asking what our responsibility as Christian people is in the presence of its great and gracious declaration.

There are two subordinate statements made in this text in explanation of the one all-inclusive declaration with which it commences, "We are His workmanship." They are, first, that we are created for good works; and, secondly, that good works are created for us. That is not the exact phrasing of my text, but I think that is its exact intention.

We are created in Christ Jesus for good works. That is one statement. Omit for a moment the sphere—in Christ Jesus—and take the clear, simple statement which remains. "We are His workmanship, created . . . for good works, which God afore prepared that we should walk in them." We are created for good works: good works are afore prepared for us. Thus in this verse there is a wonderfully gracious and tender unveiling of the fact that all the life of the trusting soul lies within the plan of God. Such a one is perfectly equipped for all God's will appoints, and all appointments within the will of God are prepared in view of the equipment which He has bestowed. If I can once accept this teaching and rest upon it I shall take my way into every new circumstance knowing these two things absolutely: first, God has prepared me in Christ Jesus for whatever the day has in store for me, and, secondly, all that to which I come, step by step as the veil recedes or the mists melt, though unknown to me, is not unknown to Him. Good works are afore prepared, afore ordained for us that we should walk in them.

For purposes of examination let us reverse the order of these statements, beginning with the last and returning to the first. Take the statement that good works are afore prepared for us that we should walk in them. What is meant by "good works"? Let me answer that question generally. I believe that the phrase refers to every crisis and commonplace of life, that the whole fact of life is included in the term "good works." In writing to Titus, the Apostle, speaking of the epiphany or the outshining of the grace of God, says, "For the grace of God hath appeared, bringing salvation to all men, instructing us, to the intent that, denying ungodliness and worldly lusts, we should live soberly and righteously and godly in this present world; looking for the blessed hope and appearing of the glory of the great God and our Saviour Jesus Christ; Who gave Himself for us, that He might redeem us from all iniquity, and purify unto Himself a people for His own possession, zealous of good works." I read the whole passage in order that we might set the final reference to "good works" in its proper relation to all that has gone before. It is one of the most glorious passages in the Bible concerning the manifestation of God's grace. It is one of the most wonderful passages unfolding before our minds the intent of the coming of Christ. "He gave Himself for us, that

He might redeem us from all iniquity, and purify unto Himself a people for His own possession, zealous of good works." That is the ultimate issue. Whatever the phrase "good works" may mean, it is here set in relation to the majesty and mercy of the manifestation of grace and glory by the work of Jesus Christ.

Then, again, when the Apostle is drawing his letter to conclusion, he writes, "And let our people also learn to maintain good works for necessary uses, that they be not unfruitful." You will notice that the marginal reading of the Revised Version suggests as an alternative rendering, "And let our people also profess honest occupations, that they be not unfruitful." One application of that term "good works" is honest occupations, daily callings, the profession a man follows, the business which occupies his time and attention, the everyday matters of the week days of life. "Honest occupations" is a perfectly fair translation of "good works" in Titus. When I get back to the Ephesian letter, I find that the word "works" is the same but that the word "good" is different. In Titus the word "good" refers to utility, or, as it is put there, "to maintain good works for necessary uses." I find the word "good" in Ephesians means that which is intrinsically good. What, then, is the meaning of the word "works"? It is a word which is applied to all kinds of effort. Work is an effort made. I care not whether it be for pleasure or profit, for the hope of gain, or for pure love of an object served, whether it be selfish or not. Work is an effort made. This word, which is applied to the highest and the lowest, the broadest and the narrowest, the most sublime and the most simple alike, is the word of my test. It includes all the activities of life, all the effort a man makes, not on Sunday only, but on every day of the week; not here in the sanctuary, in the pulpit, or in the Sabbath School, or in the Mission Hall, only, but in the countinghouse, the school, the office, or any professional employment. It is the effort of your life, whether, I repeat, for pleasure or profit. Whether you count it high or low, mean or noble, matters nothing. I go back to the Ephesian Epistle, upon which I never can look without seeing something of the glory of the ages yet unborn, the Epistle in which the Apostle has reached the topstone and is describing the glory of the Church; I find that he sets my life with all its works, its efforts put forth every day in every place, for pleasure or profit—he sets the works of my life in relationship to the infinite and eternal glory, in relationship to the great work of God in my character, in relationship to the fact that God is the Master Workman, making me through all these processes what He would have me be. This is a message of comfort if we will have it so. He has foreordained the works of the man He is making. He has been ahead of me preparing the place to which I am coming, manipulating all the resources of the universe in order that the work I do may be a part of His whole great and gracious work. God has foreordained good works. He has prearranged the forces of nature and the facts of life so that when I rise in the morning and begin to make my effort, it may be an effort in harmony with His character, a good work, whether I preach or play, whether I labor for pleasure or profit.

In the discovery of this fact lies the conviction which makes a man ready to submit wholly to the will of God. Joseph said to his brethren in the midst of their sorrow for the wrong they had previously done him, "It was not you that sent me hither, but God." In that moment—perchance previously he had seen it—in that moment he confessed the fact that the pit, the brutality, the exile, the imprisonment, and the long waiting were all foreordained of God. They were all part of the "good works" which God had prepared for him. Or, if I may most reverently quote the supreme instance of this thing, and bring you to that moment when Jesus of Nazareth stood confronting the power of the world in the person of Pilate, I hear Him saying, "To this end have I been born, and to this end am I come into the world, that I should bear witness unto the truth." The latter words I am not careful to deal with now, but I ask you to notice Christ's great conception that there was purpose in His life, arrangement made beforehand. There is another word which He said to Pilate, "Thou wouldest have no power against Me, except it were given thee from above." There He stood amid all the darkness and brutality, and travail and pain, and agony of an hour of overwhelming defeat, conscious that God had foreordained the works of all the days. He came to tragedy and to suffering and pain, regnant, mighty, sublime, because He knew that all were part of the "good works, which God afore prepared that He should walk in them."

Do not let these illustrations rob us of the one thing I supremely desire to say to my own heart and to yours. If we would say that as it ought to be said, I think we must come down from the larger outlook and take the more partial one. It is by seeing the partial thing sometimes that we gain understanding of the whole. Tomorrow is an absolutely unknown quantity for you and for me. I do not know what waits for me tomorrow of joy or of sorrow, of difficulty or of overcoming, of testing or of triumph. Is not that enough to affright me? Not at all. I know that God foreordains the pathway. I go back to the swan song of Moses, in Deuteronomy. He is singing to his people, the people he loves, and reminds them of many things in the Government of God. Among all the things he says to them there is nothing more gracious than this—he tells them that God led them through the "great and terrible wilderness." If that were all he had said it would have produced nothing other than a shudder of memory, but that is not all. He also said that God "went before you in the way, to seek you out a place to pitch your tents in." That lights the wilderness. That makes the desert blossom as the rose. That creates the anthem in the hour when a man cannot see one yard in front of him. The thought of God moving in front of His hosts, choosing them places in which to pitch their tents is sublime. We often sing,

> We nightly pitch our moving tent
> A day's march nearer home.

The teaching of my text is that that tent is never pitched at haphazard. I talk about tomorrow. I do not know about what remains of today. I am not sure about the next half hour. Yet I am absolutely sure that God is ahead of me preparing the works in which He would have me walk, planning the little things of my life, arranging the infinite mosaic, putting simple words into such harmony that if I will but obey and follow Him His poem shall be heard in all this life of mine. God is moving ahead and He foreordains all the crises and commonplaces of life. He is always in front of us preparing the works in which He would have us walk.

Now return to the first statement. If it be true that God has prepared works for us it is also true that He has prepared us for the works. "Created in Christ Jesus for good works." We are prepared for the works as the works are being prepared for us. Therefore, we are perfectly equipped for whatever the day may bring. "Then let the unknown morrow bring with it what it may, it can bring with it nothing but He will bear us through."

We do not know what tomorrow is bringing, but we know that God is preparing tomorrow, and not only that, but that He has laid up for us in Christ Jesus resources equal to whatever He brings us to. Who was it said something about tempering the wind to the shorn lamb? It is not true. God never tempers the wind to the shorn lamb. God has provided the lamb with fleece. The shearing of the lamb is a human invention. It may be right, or wrong—I am not discussing that. If you shear the lamb and put it out on the mountains you must take the responsibility. The wind will not be any warmer for the lamb. It is a wrong idea that God tempers the wind to the shorn lamb. What, then, is true? He tempers the lamb to the wind. He gives the lamb its fleece, and if I interfere with that rule I am responsible. He will not temper the wind to me. He will temper me to the wind. Is there not a phrase about finely tempered steel? You do not temper the things you want the steel to cut so that the steel shall be able to cut it. You temper the steel so that it may cut. So with me. I am tempered to the wind. Is there much of battle ahead of me? Then in Christ Jesus I have all the strength to enable me to overcome. Is there ahead of me some sorrow? Let me speak carefully, is there ahead of you, dear heart, some sorrow? God is getting you ready for that sorrow in a thousand ways you know not of, and He will never let you feel the burden of any sorrow until He has prepared you for it in Christ Jesus. That is His method. He said to Jeremiah when Jeremiah shrank back from the pathway of service, "If thou hast run with the footmen, and they have wearied thee, then how canst thou contend with horses? And though in a land of peace thou art secure, yet how wilt thou do in the pride of Jordan." There was no reference to death in either case, but to difficult service. God says to him, "You are shrinking here in a comparatively easy pathway, but presently you have to contend with horses." Yes, but with all reverence I say in the presence of God's own word, "Yes, Jehovah, great Master of us all, but Thou dost never ask a man to contend with horses until Thou hast practiced him with footmen." Think of God's method in the case of children. He does not let little children feel the amount of grief you are able to bear. Some years ago there was a railway collision in Wales. When they were rescuing the people out of the midst of the debris they found a mother, dead; but clasped in her arms was a little two-year-old child. When they extricated the child from its mother, it looked up with a smiling face and then they found it had clasped in its little hands a packet of chocolate. They unclasped the little hands and the child cried, cried over the loss of the chocolate, but not over the loss of its mother. Thirty years afterwards it would have forgotten its chocolate and cried for its mother. What does the story teach? That God does not allow a little child to feel all the force of sorrow until it has been prepared. The sorrow was there. The wind was not tempered. The agony was there. The mother was taken, but the little one was not ready for that sorrow yet. God was teaching it to bear the pain of its loss by letting it grieve over the loss of chocolate. That is God's method. He is always preparing and equipping me for the things which come by the processes through which He leads me. In Christ Jesus I am equipped for everything. I know He will not permit that to come to me for which I am not prepared. We are His workmanship. He is equipping us in Christ for all His will appoints. He is appointing in His will things for which we are created in Christ.

What effect ought this view of life to produce upon us? It seems to me that the first fact is that it brings to us the conviction of grave responsibility. Perhaps you hardly expected I would say that first. I might have spoken of the safety and peace, but I choose to name those last. I say that this conception creates grave responsibility.

The responsibility is a twofold one. First, that I should find the place His will appoints, and, secondly, that I should use the resources His grace provides.

First, that I should find the place His will appoints. What is the tragedy of my life, of yours, if there has been tragedy in either? The tragedy has been that while He has foreordained good works for me I have not discovered them and have gone my own way, and my works have been as were the works of the idolaters of old—answers to fleshly desire. That is the tragedy of life. The first thing, therefore, is that I should find, as each day breaks upon me, God's place for me in that day, as every new crisis confronts me; and as I look out toward the coming years I should find God's place for me. You say, "That is exactly what I want to do. How shall I do it?" The first thing that you and I have to do if we would find God's place for us is to destroy our own programs and give up forevermore the perilous business of imitating anyone else. I said something like this once in the United States at a convention, and a lady came to me afterwards and said, "Do you not keep a diary? Do you not enter any engagements?" "Oh, yes," I replied. "Then how do you follow your own advice to destroy your own program?" I am old-fashioned enough to write, and to mean, "God willing," over every engagement made. I am very tired of hearing men account for certain of their actions by saying, "The Lord led me to do it," when I am perfectly sure He never did lead them to do anything of the kind. That is not what I am asking for. In the deepest of you, and of me, in that inner shrine of the personality where the will reigns supreme, the program is to be always, "God willing"; the arrangement is to be of such a nature that it can be abandoned if He change the purpose. The symbols of Abraham's life were the tent and the altar. The altar was the symbol of God's grace, and of worship. The tent was the symbol of pilgrimage, something which could easily be struck and removed. It marked a man ready to be disturbed if God saw fit to disturb Him. That is the attitude of faith. When a man settles down at any point and says, "Here am I for ever," he is in great danger of missing the Divine guidance. When a man says about his work, his business, anything in his life, that it is the final thing, he is in peril. You and I have to say, "This is His will for me. What is next I know not. I watch only for His will."

There must be not only this abandonment of the final program in the thinking and will of the life; there must also be the abandonment of the attempt to imitate someone else and walk as someone else is walking. We must understand if we are to live this life that God deals with us as though there was no one else, and we must seek from Him direct and immediate guidance as though there were no others. It is the life devoted to God, waiting for His voice to obey its call, which find the good works which He has foreordained. I am to ask Him what His will is and I am to wait until He manifests it, and I am to use for the discovery of His will not merely my faith but my reason. When Jesus Christ said in His manifesto, "Behold the fowls of the heaven, that they sow not, neither do they reap, nor gather into barns; and your heavenly Father feedeth them. Are not ye of much more value than they?" He did not mean that the disciples were not to gather into barns. What He meant was, "If God feeds these fowls to whom He has given no forethought and prearrangement, how much more will He feed you to whom He has given forethought and reason!" When Jesus said that the lilies of the field were clothed in majestic beauty even though they could not weave and spin, He did not mean that men were not to weave or spin. If the lilies of the field are clothed in splendor by God, how much more will He clothe you to whom He has given the ability to weave and spin! We are not to sit down in the morning and open our mouths and say, "Give us this day our daily bread," and expect manna. We are to use our reason on the basis of faith. In proportion as we do this we shall find His way for us. We shall find His works afore prepared.

Then we are to use the provision, the resources which He has set at our disposal. Everything I need is in Christ. I need not ask the question, "What would Jesus do?" as though He were not here and I wanted to speculate as to what He would do if He were here. What will Jesus do now? For He is here and all I have to do is to follow Him.

Remember these two things are absolutely interdependent, obedience and progress. If I have missed my way what is the best thing to do? The only thing to do is to get back to the point where I lost my way and start again. It is a long tramp for some of us. How many years is it since you got out of the will of God? You must get back to that point and obey, and from that point you may start again and find the way of His appointing.

If that be the fact as to responsibility think of all it means. It means perfect safety for the man God-led and God-governed. There are no risks. Never again use the word "happen" in the infidel sense. Things do not happen in that way. There is no failure. "Oh," you say, "you must not tell us that. We have known men of faith fail." Never. To sit on a throne or to sweep a crossing may alike be fine in the thinking of God. It depends upon where He puts you. If God wants you in the carpenter's shop and you leave it to go into the House of Commons you will be a dead failure there. Or if God wants you in the front of the battle, and you are hiding in a business house, you will fail. You have to get where God wants you to be if you are to succeed. As it has been beautifully said, if God sent two angels to this world, one to rule an empire and the other to sweep a crossing, they would never think of arguing on the way as to which was the more important work. Each is equally important, because He appoints it. May we learn this lesson! The ultimate test is not notoriety, but fidelity. On that basis all rewards will be made in the light of the coming Kingdom. What follows? Safety, peace. Peace in misunderstanding, in defeat, and in triumph. In the majestic words of the New Testament, peace from God, peace with God, the peace of God.

Let us be very careful lest we mar the Divine poems. We are His poems. He wants to sing a song to the world through our life. He cannot lose His thought. If He cannot sing it through us He will sing it through someone else.

There is only one question which we need to ask in the presence of every new day:

> Only to know that the path I tread
> Is the path marked out for me;
> That the way, tho' thorny, rough and steep,
> Will lead me nearer to Thee.
>
> Only to know when the day is passed,
> And the evening shadows come,
> That its trials and cares have proved indeed
> A "day's march nearer home."

CHAPTER XX

THE CHILDREN'S PLAYGROUND IN THE CITY OF GOD

And the streets of the city shall be full of boys and girls playing in the streets thereof.

ZECHARIAH 8:5.

ONE ALMOST EXPECTS TO HEAR SOMEONE SAY, "How extremely shocking!" Some people would probably be surprised to know that the Bible says anything about children playing. This verse not only speaks of them playing, but surprises our prejudices by declaring that *boys and girls* are to play together, and even startles us further by saying that boys and girls are to play together *in the streets!* If not inclined to say, "How shocking this is!" I can quite believe that many would say, "Well, it certainly is marvelous." The prophet, inspired of the Spirit of God, knew perfectly well that people would say it was a marvelous thing, so he immediately continued, "Thus saith the Lord of hosts: If it be marvelous in the eyes of the remnant of this people in those days, should it also be marvelous in Mine eyes? saith the Lord of hosts"—which being put into other words simply means, The thing which surprises you, that you look upon as marvelous, that almost shocks you, is the very thing upon which the heart of God is set. God believes in children playing, He believes in boys and girls playing together, and He believes in them playing in the streets.

This is a picture of the coming age. I do not mind at all what you call it. Call it, if you will, "the golden age." Call it, if you so please, "the millennial age," or if you prefer to drop back into the language of your childhood, speak of it as "the good time coming." It is a picture of the ultimate victory toward which men perpetually looked in the midst of the battle, of the final triumph which was a constant inspiration of earnest and consecrated service. Ever and anon these ancient Hebrew seers saw glimpses of the coming glory, heard notes of the coming harmonies. These men were not near-sighted. They were far-sighted in a far finer sense of that word than that in which we mostly use it today. They saw so far ahead that the things they saw have not yet come to pass. They saw a Kingdom established over which a King should rule in righteousness and in equity. They saw a Kingdom established in which a King should rule, and—mark well the language—not by the sight of His eyes or by the hearing of His ears: these are the bases of all judgment at the present moment. They very often lead us into error. This coming King is to rule in righteousness and equity, as one who knows perfectly and absolutely all the facts of the case. As these men looked on they saw nature at peace, and in the midst of it a little child at play. Let us notice the picture which my text suggests. Zechariah speaks of Jerusalem, Zion, the Mountain of the Lord of hosts. This is not a picture of heaven. It is a picture of earth. This is not the picture of a land and conditions beyond the clouds to which men will escape from peril and strife. It is the picture of conditions which are to obtain here in the world where today sinning and sighing and sorrow abound. This is the picture of conditions which will obtain when the prayer which Jesus taught us to pray, and which, alas, we too often pray carelessly, is realized. "Our Father Who art in heaven. Hallowed be Thy name. Thy Kingdom come. Thy will be done, as in heaven, so on earth." Therefore I say to you that for a glimpse of the Kingdom that is to come, I do not come to a Sunday service, but to a Saturday afternoon in a park. When I want to form some true conception of what God's Kingdom will be like, I do not go to a prayer meeting but to a playground. I think I have exercised my ministry here long enough for no one to charge me with undervaluing either the prayer meeting or the Sunday service. They are but means to the end, however, which end is the playground for the children. The establishment of the Kingdom of God, the building of His city, the healing of all wounds, the realization of all the forces that lie in human life, at their most perfect condition; all that, and more, is by suggestion within my text. I know there are discrepancies in both, but in the park and the playground you are nearer the Divine ideal for child life, and I come there, not because that exhausts the meaning of the coming Kingdom, but because it is the only thing like it today. If I come into commercial life, I find there very little like the Kingdom of God. In the commercial world "in that day shall there be upon the bells of the horses, HOLY UNTO THE LORD." That is a poetic figure of a great philosophy. If I come into the law courts today I find very little like the Kingdom of God. They are doing their best, but it is a very poor best. If I come into the political arena I think I see there men striving after the ideals of the Kingdom, yet we are in prison still, and hampered by the god of mammon. If I want a glimpse of the Kingdom upon which I can base all my interpretation, I haste me to the playground. Be patient with me if I make that personal. If I want my own heart to understand God's coming Kingdom I turn my back upon my study and get to that other room, which is as far from the study as I can put it, where all the noise is, and get amongst my bairns. There I am nearer to the Kingdom than ever I am in my study. Zechariah was a stern prophet, who had no soft things to say in the presence of iniquities; Zechariah was a poet who saw the coming glories. Reading his writings up to this point, you can hardly think of him as having time for a child, and yet suddenly, out of his deep heart, illumined by the glory of the coming days, there sings into the ear of all the centuries the most poetic description of the Kingdom that I find in the whole of the Old Testament. "The streets of the city shall be full of boys and girls playing in the streets thereof."

I draw your attention, first of all, to what this text reveals as the thought of God for the children. Let us imagine for a moment that we are not in London. We will transport ourselves to that Kingdom which is to be, and to that city which the prophet saw. In that city we see, first, that God's ideal for the child is that the child shall play. It is a very significant fact that all the millennial references to the child are references to the child at play. "The sucking child shall play on the hole of the asp, and the weaned child shall put his hand on the basilisk's den." That wonderful day when "the lion shall eat straw like the ox," and the wolf and the lamb shall lie down together in perfect peace, will be the child's playtime. Have you ever taken a child to the zoological gardens, and have you ever been strangely perturbed by the child's deep anxiety to climb over the rails and get in amongst the polar bears? It is a Divine instinct. The child wants to be where God intended it should be, and where God means it to be presently, at play with all the lower animals. "A little child shall lead them." It is the child at play, the child in the midst of nature, set there to play. I charge you that you do not whittle down this word "play" until you have spoiled it. Ruskin says, "Play is an exertion of body or mind made to please ourselves." I think that is a perfectly accurate definition, but I do not think it takes in all the facts of the case. May I suggest that play is work. If you do not believe me and you have a boy four years old, stay at home from business one day, and from morning till night do everything that boy does. I very distinctly remember about a year ago, when one of my boys was four years old, he requested me to play horses with him. I agreed to do so on condition that he be the horse and I the driver. My garden at Norwood runs down in terraces, and I let him go wherever he liked; it is good to let young horses do that. He went to the bottom by one path, turned round and came up again. I had already had enough, but I let him go on. He went down and up that garden six times, and then I said I must go into the house for a few minutes—and I was there an hour. What is play? Play is work which is not a task set. Play is work, not for profit, but out of pure delight in the exercise of strength. I wish all the young manhood would remember that. Whenever you put gain or profit at the end of play you demoralize the play. The child has no thought of profit in play. It is work, not as a task and not for profit. God's ideal for the child is that it shall play, and the characteristics of a little child at play are merriment, earnestness, pity, defense of the weak. Watch natural and healthy children at play and you will find that all these things are manifest in the midst of the play.

If I may carry this a little further I would say that God's ideal for the child is that it should play itself into its work. We talk about the kindergarten system as though it were something we had recently discovered, as though we owed it wholly to Froebel. Here it is in Zechariah. He was a long way ahead. We are getting there perhaps sooner than he thought, but there it is—the children at play. If you watch children by careful, loving, tender watching, they will play themselves into the work for which God made them. In this age of collectivist thinking it is good sometimes to reassert the law of the individual, and every individual ought to be able to say concerning his or her life work, "To this end have I been born, and to this end am I come into the world." That is true, not merely of the poets, dreamers and statesmen, but also of the men and women whom we sometimes insult by saying they do mean things. There are no mean things if they come out of the capacity of the man who is doing them. If a little child learns its work through its play, all through the strenuous years you will find the man playing at his work. I do not mean playing with his work or doing it indifferently, but that it will be a delight to him. When work is what it ought to be in human life it is not a task set, not something done for profit merely, but something done for the sake of the thing done. I have been in a carpenter's shop and seen a man at the bench making some plain piece of furniture, and looking at it and touching it with love as he saw it developing under his hand. That is the real carpenter, brother to Jesus of Nazareth. If you find a man who loves his work he will have as secondary motive under it all the two things for which Paul says we are to work, the support of himself and his family, and to have something to give to him that is in need. Beyond that, work is done for the sake of the work, but children never come to that unless you give them their chance to play. You must begin with playtime for the children. That is God's ideal.

Then notice, further, that there is in the text a revelation of the fact that it is God's purpose that boys and girls shall play together. I can quite imagine that some very good people out of this age, if they could be preserved until that day dawns, and came to this city and saw boys and girls playing together, would think everything had gone wrong, that some catastrophe had happened. I walk round among our schools today and I see over one door "Boys," a little further on I find another door marked "Girls." Presently I come to the "Young Men's Christian Association," and a little farther on I see the "Young Women's Christian Association." We have been doing all we can to keep them apart. We are all wrong. God said boys and girls are to play together. Wherever you find that they do so, naturally, purely, perfectly, you will find that the strength of manhood strengthens womanhood, and the refinement of womanhood refines manhood. That is the perfect family in which brothers and sisters grow up and play together. That is God's ideal. The streets of God's city shall be full of boys and girls playing in the streets thereof.

If that be so, we may go yet a step further, and upon this foundation truth of God's purpose for the child and God's ideal for the child build the conditions of public life. This text is an index to the conditions of public life in the coming Kingdom. If in God's city boys and girls are to play in the streets of the city, then the streets of the city will be fit for the boys and girls to play in. Think what that means in the very simplest way. As Christ makes the child the type of character in His Kingdom, so the child comes to be the test of public life in the city of God. Everything in the life of the coming city will depend upon the little child. Everything will be carried forward in the interests of the little child. Among other things, the streets will be fit for children to play in. Said Isaiah, another of these prophets, "They shall not hurt nor destroy in all My holy mountain." What a city that will be where there will be nothing in the streets to harm little children, physically, mentally, or spiritually! When you have a city with streets fit for children you have a city with streets fit for adults. If the child is safe everyone is safe. Let us walk in imagination through some of the streets of the city of the King. I shall find nothing that can harm the child physically. In that city the drainage will be perfect, and the traffic and everything else will be watched by vigilant eyes for the sake of the children. You can dream your dreams around that. You tell me this is not the Gospel. Then what in the name of God is it? These children whom God loves and speaks of in the terms of playtime in His coming city are to be safe, and the measure in which children are safe in our streets today is the measure in which we have seen this ideal, and are working toward it.

As we walk through the streets of the city of the King, I notice in the next place that in no single shop window can I find any impure literature. On no placard station can I see a bill announcing an amusement, the very bill suggestive of evil and calculated to inflame the passion of a child or youth. No unholy picture can be found. The love of the child will be greater than love of gain. That is the truth about the city of God.

As I go through these streets of the city I find no man ready to pollute young life, no man standing in the shadow of the sanctuary or of the public house watching for his chance to lead a boy who is hardly a youth into the ways of betting and gambling. By no means. In the city of the King the dictum of Jesus will be in operation and the man who is found causing a little child to offend will have a millstone hung about his neck, and be drowned in the depth of the sea, while angels rejoice. There will be nothing anemic and sickly in the city of the King. Righteous wrath will be manifested if anything is done to offend, or cause to stumble, one little child. The streets of the city are to be fit for the children.

Let us go one step further. It seems to me that my text not only reveals to me the purpose and thought of God for children, not only reveals to me what the conditions of public life are to be in the city, but it casts its light upon the home life in the coming Kingdom. It is not only true that the streets are to be fit for the children, but equally true that the children are to be fit for the streets. There are children who come from very respectable houses who pollute the streets by their presence. There are children, proud, despotic, selfish, and, alas, too often impure, to turn whom out to play in the streets would be to defile the other children. I am not blaming the children, for wherever you find such children the blame must be put back on the home from which they come. A child always reflects the home from which it has come. That legend which you hang up in your homes, "Christ is the Head of this house, the unseen Guest at every meal, the silent Listener to every conversation," will be a living reality in that Kingdom. In homes where these things are believed and acted upon from break of day until the sun has gone westering you will have children that you may turn out into the streets who will not harm the streets or pollute them. In the city of the King the home life will be what it ought to be, and out of the homes will come children whose obedience has been won, whose trust has been inspired, to whom high ideals have been presented, not so much by precept as by the practice of those who have had charge of them, children who know God because they have seen Him in the fatherhood and motherhood which has been round about them. Coming out into the streets they will live and walk in the power of all that home has meant to them—children fit for the streets.

If there is one thing tragic in this city it is the picture of the children who have no playtime. What you call their playtime is for some of them opportunity for deeper debasement. Why? Because our streets are not fit for the children, because we have never yet put a little child in the midst of us in our civic affairs and set everything else round the necessity of the little child. I am perfectly well aware that we are struggling toward it, but it is so slow because we have never seen it clearly. Sometimes one's heart is gladdened spiritually, religiously, by things that seem to be very far away, and yet are near to the heart of God. I remember seeing a while ago what came to me as a vision of God's coming glory. I was at the very end of Cheapside, close to the Bank and the Exchange, and suddenly I saw a policeman, a great, strong, muscular representative of the force of the law, raise his hand and hold up all the beating, surging traffic to take a wee bit bairnie by the hand and lead it safely across the street. By so much as we have learned to do that we are coming nearer to the Kingdom. But, oh, my masters, how much there is still to harm the life of the child in our streets. You who listen to me tonight dare not turn your children into the streets to play, but there are children playing in the streets who have no other place to play in, and in the hearts of all children there is capacity for good and the love of the beautiful just as much as in the hearts of your children, if you will find it.

I will tell you a story at second hand. A month or two ago the first Minister of Works of the present Government was walking in St. James's Park. Two or three children were playing there, one of them a girl with tousled hair, dirty and unkempt. The minister of works looked down at this child and said, "Why do you stay here? Why don't you go over there into the Green Park, where you can play on the grass?" The bright eyes looked up into his, and she said, "There are no flowers there." Oh, if we could hear these things! I am not arguing for flowers over there, or if I do argue for them it is that they may gladden the children.

Let us see deeply into this thing. You and I have a responsibility about our streets for the sake of the children. You care nothing for political parties? So much the better. You care nothing about Moderates or Progressives or Municipal Reform? So much the better; but do you care for the bairns? I have figures and statistics which we have been gathering, for we are trying to find out what we ought to do. Do you know such things as this? Right here under the shadow of this church—I begin there for this is our responsibility—there are at least 132 houses in which, on an average, three or four families are crowded together. These bairns must come out into the streets to play, and the streets are not fit for them, and the homes from which they come are not homes that make it likely that their coming will be a blessing to the streets. Are you content to say you have nothing to do with all these things? Say at once you have nothing to do with the Kingdom of God. Say at once you have no interest in the bringing in of that great and glad golden age toward which seers have been looking, and of which psalmists have been singing. You like to look on to that great day and to sing of it, but I think that the men and women who have not shared the travail that makes His Kingdom come are very likely to be shut out of the Kingdom when it does come. I want to lay upon you the burden of this great and terrible responsibility.

I am told there is nothing we can do, or that what we can do is so little. You are not responsible for all that has to be done. You are responsible for the thing that lies next to your hand. You are responsible, first of all, to see to it that whatever you have of influence, whatever you may have of influence, whatever lies at your disposal by way of influence, you ought to take hold of and use in the interest of, I will not say the Kingdom of God as a far distant thing, but of the little child in the streets. What about the children who are not orphans but are worse than orphans? What about the children who are in sorrow and sore need round about us in our own parish? In our parish there are thirty-four public houses, every last one of them a center of death, an instrument for spoiling childhood. There are portions of these streets of Westminster close to us which are nameless as to their condition. You put the blame upon the police. I put the blame finally upon the Church of Jesus Christ.

These men of old, these prophets, how they toiled and strove, how they entered into every department of human life with their messages and their fire, and inspiration, and daring and suffering and blood. What matters it that they never saw the city, if they saw it from afar? They set their faces toward it and died in faith, not having received the promises, and yet the promises would be much longer postponed if they had not so suffered and toiled, and had not so striven. So I say we are working, not merely for the present hour, but for all the future. We are working with the little child before our eyes, determined as the moments come and go to strive and toil and suffer to make the streets fit for the children, to see to it that they have homes out of which it is possible for them to come with some suspicion at least of what morality, cleanness, and uprightness really mean. There is no bairn in all this crowded district that is not as near to the heart of God as the little child you laid to rest in its cot at home. There is no boy who is not protected from the rain and hardly dare go home, and who will become a sharper on the street, robbing you on every hand—there is not one such who is not referred to by Jesus when He said, "It is not the will of your Father who is in heaven, that one of these little ones should perish."

I say to you tonight that our responsibility as a church

and as Christian people for this district must begin there. I am not saying all that is in my heart. I am not saying all I know, but I am making an appeal to you for your interest in prayer, and presently in very definite work. Under the shadow of this church close at hand stands a man day after day, a bookmaker. He has been fined again and again, and he pays a fine as I pay a license to keep a dog, and comes back and carries on his nefarious practices. I am told that we must let these things alone. My answer is that the devil said to Jesus, "Let us alone." Christ's answer is our answer to all these things. We will not let it alone. It is our business not to let it alone. A way must be found by which these men shall be removed, and it be made impossible for them to stand around luring our children to destruction. It is very little we can do. In a few years at least the majority of us will have gone out to the great Beyond, but let us do something. Let us, at any rate, come to close grips with the devil. Let us leave the impresss of our fingers somewhere on him, or else let us be ashamed to look into the face of Jesus Christ when the day breaks and the shadows flee away.

Our city is not the city Zechariah saw. The streets of our city are not ready for the boys and girls to play in. It is our business as we take our way through this life of probation and toil and discipline to see the ultimate, and to consecrate ourselves to that great and holy conflict which at last is to issue in victory. I pray that we may make what application of the study of this verse is necessary for our own new inspiration to new consecration to the thing that lies very near at hand.

"Where shall I begin?" says some man. In your own home. "How shall I begin?" Set the millennium up in your own home. "How can I do it?" Crown Christ there. I do not mean theoretically, sentimentally. I do not mean by singing about Him or praying to Him, or reading the things He said; but by the realization of His ideal there for your own children, and by realization of His ideal in your home as Master and Lord and King. Every home so consecrated, and so realizing His ideal, is a contribution toward the building of God's city. We may begin there, and yet to begin and end there is not to fulfill our responsibility. We must go beyond and what we cannot do singly we must do together. As the host of God we must say to the civic authorities and to all the powers that rule the city's life, "These rulings and governings of yours must be in the interest of the child." If that can be established then I have no further care about the youth and maiden, man and woman, about the aged and infirm. We will begin with the child. God help us to hear His call to us about this district through the plaintive need of the child as it expresses itself to all who have eyes to see, and ears to hear, and hearts to feel.

CHAPTER XXI

A PROFOUND QUESTION

What think ye of the Christ?
MATTHEW 22:42.

THIS IS IN SOME WAYS ONE OF THE MOST INTERESTING CHAPters in the Gospel according to Matthew. It tells the story of a day of questions, of criticism, of opposition, of unbelief. Of the questions the unifying principle was an attempt to entangle Him in His talk: mean and dastardly questions when the spirit of them is recognized. There were questions political, theological, and religious. The political was asked by a coalition of Pharisees and Herodians, two opposing parties, one of them believing that the Hebrew people ought to pay tribute to Cæsar, the other believing that they ought not so to do. The theological question was asked by the Sadducees, and had to do with the resurrection. Finally, the religious question was asked by the Pharisees, and inquired as to which among the commandments was the greatest. Jesus answered these questions one after the other with that surpassing and surprising wisdom which was always characteristic of Him. Then quite suddenly, and I think I may say startlingly, He turned upon His questioners and asked them a question. "What think ye of the Christ?" We must understand this question. He did not ask it just as we may ask it today. We may still take this question and without any violence to its context make use of it, but we must understand how He asked it. Let me remind you that the word "Christ" is but the Greek form of the Hebrew word "Messiah," and apparently to the group of men who stood about Jesus this was not a question concerning Himself. He did not say to them, at least they would not so understand Him, "What do you think of me?" That is not the point of His question. It was a question about their own Scriptures, about their own religion, about their own hope and outlook. It was to all appearance a purely speculative question. He said to them, in effect, "Now, what is your opinion of your Messiah? Whose Son is He?" And in a moment, without any hesitation, and showing their perfect familiarity with their own Scriptures, and that central hope of their religious thinking, they said, "The son of David." Then immediately He said to them, "How then doth David in the Spirit call Him Lord, saying, The Lord said unto my Lord, Sit Thou on My right hand till I put Thine enemies underneath Thy feet? If David then calleth Him Lord, how is He his son?" They had been bringing problems to Him, this was one for them. It is as though He had said, "You have been questioning Me concerning the payment of tribute. You have brought Me a problem concerning the resurrection. You have attempted to make Me minimize the value of the commandments by overestimating the value of one. Now here is a problem for you out of your own law, about your Messiah. "Whose son is He to be?" "David's," was their reply, and they were perfectly correct so far. "But if He be David's son, how can He be David's Lord?" Yet I should be very sorry to make you feel that Jesus was simply attempting to do with these men what they had been attempting to do with Him. He was not attempting to entrap them. He never played mean tricks with men. He left that wholly and exclusively to His enemies. What, then, is the significance of His question? Here again, as on former occasions, He intended to show them that they did not understand their own Scriptures, that according to them there were wonders concerning the Messiah which they had never comprehended. One thing these men did not understand about their Messiah was that He was to be, not merely man, but God. Because the Messiah was to be after the flesh born of David's line He was son of David, but because He was to be immediately and by the mystery of unfathomable miracle begotten of God, He was also to be David's Lord.

But I have not selected this text that we may follow it in its first application. We are no longer asking a question that has to do with a hope, with an ideal, with an anticipation, with a prophecy. We still ask the question, but it has to do with an achievement, with a history, with a Person. When He said, "What do you think about the Messiah?" they were looking on; but we, as we take our New Testament and read the question which is still a living question—every question He asked has an abiding import in its deepest meaning—we are not looking on, we are looking back. We ask the question tonight, and to us the word "Christ" is not the title of One for Whom the world is waiting. To us the word "Christ" has become the name of One Who has come, and abides, and still is to come! To these men the word "Christ" was the title of some person never seen though long hoped for. To us the word "Christ" is the name and title of a Person seen and known, and with Whose story we are all perfectly familiar.

My business tonight is to ask you quietly, not so much as a congregation as in your individual and personal capacity, to answer this question. Here, everything depends, as everywhere else, upon what a man thinks. "As a man thinketh

A PROFOUND QUESTION

in his heart, so is he," so said the Preacher of old. Your attitude toward Jesus Christ and your relationship to Him are alike based upon what you think of Him. You may turn that round if you will and state it thus, your attitude toward Christ results from what you think of Christ, and therefore reveals what you think of Christ. Consequently, the answer to this question is not an answer that can be made by the recitation of a creed. The answer to this question is not an answer that can be made by an affirmation or declaration of the lips. The answer to this question you are giving every day. There is a sense in which you can answer this question conclusively tonight, but you are answering it every day and every hour. If I stand in this pulpit tonight and say to you what I think of Christ, I may do it with perfect sincerity, but I cannot convince you that what I say I think is the thing I think. How will you find out what I think of Christ? You can find out only if you know me in my everyday life, in my everyday activity, in what is my constant relation to Christ. A man's thought of Christ creates a man's attitude toward Christ, therefore I repeat, a man's attitude toward Christ reveals what the man's thought of Christ really is. Herein is the importance of this question. In the asking of it we pass beyond the externalities to the internal things of life. In asking this question we come into the very deepest of us. As I ask this question of my own heart, or let me put it in this way, as I let Christ Himself ask me, "What do you think of me?" it is not a mere question of speculation. It is in the last analysis a question that gets deeper down than the things which are upon the surface, to the very springs and fountains of my being. It does matter supremely for today and tomorrow, and the great forever of God, what I think of Him, because all my relation to Him depends upon that, and because what I am going to be in my own life depends entirely upon what I think of Christ. I stay here because if only I can fix your thought upon the importance of the question the battle is half won and the work is half done. All activity is the result of thought. A conception always underlies a deed. Everything you do in any relationship of life is the direct outcome of some underlying thought, some conception. To put it in another way, at the back of all activity is reason, behind every choice that a man makes there is an impelling cause, and that impelling cause is a thought, a conception in the particular realm in which the activity is manifest. I watch what you do. I cannot watch what you think, but I can know what you think from what you do. We may be helped to an understanding of this question by a trivial illustration. It is this: I stand upon the great highway and I watch the men and women passing up and down, and I see one man cross over from one side to the other. It is a manifest action, but before he crossed over he thought of crossing, and I know his prior thought by that simple action. It is a trivial illustration as I said, but lift it as high as you will, watch it in all the realms of human activity, from the lowest to the highest the same principle applies. What you think is manifest in what you do.

Christ makes demands upon every man in that inner realm of his thinking. He comes into my inner life and presents Himself. I look at Him and I think something of Him. I cannot tell you what I think, and you cannot read that inner thought, but if you will watch me through the next hour, day, week, month, year, you will know what I think of Him by what you see me do with Him.

Mark this mystery of human personality as it is taken into account in this question of Jesus. The final glory of a human being is that of volition, that of choice. I can choose.

I can elect. I can decide. Or, to put it back into the simplest word of all, I can will. This is the dignity of human life.

What lies behind the will impelling it? The emotion. What lies behind the emotion? The intelligence. When I face a fact, whatever that fact may be, I face it first with my mind. I know it, and upon my conception of it in my mind, depends my attitude, my emotional attitude toward it. I like or dislike it; I love or hate it; I admire or reject it. That is emotion. Then I will, and what I will depends upon the attitude of emotion after the intelligence has looked and seen and understood. The thinking is the deepest thing. The emotion is moved by the thinking, the will is impulsed by the emotion. What do you think of Christ? If you have answered that question in your deepest heart I will tell you what happens. You will say either, "Because I think this of Him I love Him," or "Because I think this of Him I hate Him." Then the will will act in yielding to Him or refusing Him, in putting a crown upon His brow or sending Him to the cross out of the way. While the business of the messenger of the cross of Christ is that of appealing to your will, behind your will will be your emotional attitude toward Christ, and at the back of that, the deepest foundation of all, will be your thinking concerning Him.

Here, then, is the supreme question of this hour for us. "What think ye of the Christ?" I am going to attempt to form your thinking by bringing to you certain witness concerning Him. It may be very old, and I am sure it is, yet I desire to put this witness before you once again, and ask you very honestly to weigh the evidence, because upon the basis of your thinking your emotion will act, and upon the basis of that movement of the emotion your will ought to act.

Remember this, it is possible for a man to think one

thing and to be moved emotionally by that conception, and yet, finally, by act of will to refuse to obey the emotion and intelligence. That is the greatest disaster of human life. That is the tragedy which is happening all around us in such congregations as this. You think of Christ the true thing and your heart goes out in admiration and adoration, and then because of the siren voices which are sounding in your ears, because of some fancied advantage of the moment, you contradict your emotion, and belie your intellect, and refuse Him. All that is your own matter. I cannot help you there, no preacher can. I can take the New Testament in my hand tonight and ask you at least to postpone for a few moments the volition and bring your emotional nature once again to the light of your reason.

Let me stop a moment. You are not afraid of your emotional nature, are you? This prevalent idea that the emotional nature and the intellectual nature are in opposition is absurd. This idea that a man's intellect has nothing to do with his fears is to be laughed out of court by high intelligences.

Bring your emotional nature, that godliest wonder of you if you did but know it, to the light of your thinking. For two or three minutes I am going to take you back to three opinions about Christ. I bring these opinions to you hoping and praying that they may help you in your thinking of Him. I bring them to you in the deeper hope that by true thinking, emotional nature may be moved again toward approbation, admiration, and adoration. I bring them to you in the final hope that you will be honest enough to exercise your will in answer to such enlightened emotion when your thinking has been trained by the witness of Scripture.

I bring you, then, three testimonies concerning Jesus, the testimony of God, the testimony of a demon, and the testimony of a man—a voice from the upper world, a voice from the under world, and a voice from the world about us. The voice of God breaking the silence, "Thou art my beloved Son, in Thee I am well pleased." The voice of the underworld, "I know Thee Who Thou art, the Holy One of God." The voice of man, sinner as I am a sinner, "Thou art the Christ."

Think of the setting of these testimonies. The voice of God. Jesus was here emerging from seclusion into publicity. For eighteen years I have no record of His doings or sayings but the briefest. At twelve years of age He passes out of sight with these wonderful words written concerning Him, "He went down with them, and He was subject unto them." I see no more of Him until He is about thirty years of age. No human eye has been watching Him carefully enough to be able to give any record of Him. God had been watching Him during the hidden years. God had been watching, not merely the activity of the man in the carpenter's shop, but watching deeper, as God ever watches deeper, the methods, the motives, and then the work and the words. All these have been in the light of heaven's unsullied standard, and as He stood there, so much one of the multitude that men did not recognize Him as separate from them in any sense—"In the midst of you standeth One whom ye know not"—God broke the silence and declared, "Thou art My beloved Son, in Thee I am well pleased." He sees there is no fault in this Man. There has been no failure in all those hidden years of commonplace life. There has been no flaw in the absolute perfection of His humanity. At last, God has found a Man Who has realized the divine ideal and perfected the divine conception. What do you think of Christ? God thinks Him perfect.

Next I have the testimony of a demon from the underworld. It is a very remarkable testimony. "I know Thee Who

Thou art, the Holy One of God." Remember that evil is not indigenous to the human race, it came from without. When next you quote glibly, "To err is human," remember it is not human to err. Erring humanity is outside the original intention and purpose of God, and outside its own fairest capacity. Do not forget, I pray you, that evil came from without, and do not forget that the whole story of the Bible is the story of attack upon humanity by forces external to itself. For the moment, I am not arguing for an original fall involving all the race, though in some senses I profoundly believe that. I take individual cases, and down through the centuries I see man after man tempted and falling, seduced and sinning. But here is a Man standing on the earth about thirty years of age, and an evil spirit looks into His face and speaks through another human voice and says, "I know Thee Who Thou art, the Holy One of God." "Thou art the Man Who having been tempted has never yielded. Thou hast been tempted as other men have at every vulnerable point, but Thou hast resisted." This is the devil's testimony, that this Man has beaten him. Once in the history of the race the underworld of seducing evil has been foiled, beaten, and all unexpectedly, even from the lips of an unclean fallen spirit, comes the confession of the unsullied purity of Jesus. What do you think of Christ? The devils reckon Him holy.

Pass to the last of these three words of testimony. This time it is the voice of a man, a sinning man, a hoping man, a man such as thou art, oh, my brother, consciously mastered by the forces of evil yet still aspiring after the unattainable good. This man might have said as truthfully as his co-Apostle Paul, "To me who would do good, evil is present." This man, like every other man, was a strange mixture, Dr. Jekyll and Mr. Hyde. That is not a lonely story. There is no man who does not know something of the duality of his consciousness, the beast and the angel, the downward pull and the upward attraction. This man is a man as we are men, and this man is a man who has been looking forward with hope, for we can perfectly understand this confession only as we interpret it from the Hebrew standpoint. In all probability his mother had lulled him to sleep in the days of his infancy with the songs of Zion, and the songs of Zion were the songs of a coming Redeemer. I can quite imagine that she had sung to him Zephaniah's infinite music, "The Lord thy God is in the midst of thee, a mighty One Who will save: He will rejoice over thee with joy, He will rest in His love, He will joy over thee with singing." That is the great lullaby of the mother heart of God. As he passed from infancy to boyhood, he had begun to read the Scriptures and then to recite them in the synagogue. He had watched the light which burned amid the darkness of the age in which he lived, the light of the coming Deliverer, Emmanuel, "Wonderful, Counsellor, Mighty God, Everlasting Father, Prince of Peace," titles never perfectly understood but constituting the song of the coming Deliverer. Standing amid the rocky fastnesses of Cæsarea Philippi, this man looked into the face of Jesus and said, "Thou art the Christ, the Hope of the centuries, the Deliverer for Whom we have been waiting, the One in Whom there merge the majestic might and the meek mercy of the covenant God of Israel." What do you think of Christ? Looking into His face, one of the men who knew Him most intimately, and had followed Him through those three years of discipleship, made this great confession, upon which everything else was based in the coming years, this great conviction which created all subsequent duty: "Thou art the Christ—the One for Whom men have been sighing and longing and waiting, the Opener of the prison, the Setter at liberty of such as are bound, the One for Whom I wait and for Whom I long." "Thou art the Christ." What do you think of Christ?

You may say to me that the testimony I have deduced is old. You may ask, "How may I depend upon the accuracy of the records from which you have read this testimony?" We are being told today that this is all mythical, that God's silence was never broken by Jordan's banks, that the unutterable, deadly silence of the underworld was never broken by a demon, that this man never said these words with any such rich and spacious meaning as I have indicated. Very well, I am not here tonight to argue with you. At this hour the testimony of God and the testimony of Satan, and of man concerning Christ, is the same, and it has accumulated weight, for nineteen centuries have passed on their way, and there is no century in which one voice has ever been lifted to question the testimony of God and the testimony of the devil. I draw my line there for a moment. A great many have doubted Peter's testimony. The whole Hebrew nation, with the exception of such as have turned to Jesus, would deny Peter's testimony. The testimony which says He is the Christ has been denied, is being denied. No voice has been daring enough yet to deny the testimony which is said to be the testimony of heaven, the testimony which is said to be the testimony of hell. What is that testimony? It is absolutely the same. The man standing upon the earth said another thing which included this thing, but the voice of heaven and that of hell merge into one great anthem which is a declaration of the sinless perfection of Jesus. No one has denied it. Men are denying today the accuracy of the records, but who is there can deny the sinlessness of the ideal presented. Here are four little fragments called Gospels, forgeries, if you will have it so, untrue if you will have it so; but forgeries and untrue if they be, they have given the world a portrait of an absolute perfection which no man has dared to call in question. You must not ask me to believe, however, that a few unknown men have given us a portrait of a Person Whose sinlessness no century has been able to question, and that their writing was fraudulent or untrue. It is an unthinkable proposition, and we are driven to the conclusion that this is an actual Man, a sinless Person, a perfect Person. The testimony of God as recorded here is the testimony of God at this hour through the common consciousness of all upright and sincere and honest souls. Once again, the testimony of the devil as recorded here is the testimony of the devil today through all debauched and degraded and depraved souls. God's speech to men today is speech through humanity, and on the highest, noblest, purest level attests the perfection of this One. The speech of evil comes to men also through humanity today, and evil is still saying, "Let us alone, Thou Jesus of Nazareth. Do not interfere with us." Why? Because evil recognizes the perfection of this ideal. The one thing evil does not want is that those who bear His name should interfere with it. Evil is saying to the Church of Jesus Christ, "Let us alone," because it recognizes that wherever the Christ Spirit obtains that spirit lays hands on evil and drags it into the light for its destruction in order that man may be delivered.

The testimony of the New Testament is in perfect harmony with the testimony of this hour. What, then, do you think of Christ? His absolute Deity is the conviction of the children of God. That is the foundation upon which they build. I am quite willing, however, to take you at first upon what seems to be a lower level. The incarnation is flesh which man might touch, and handle, and find the infinite Word. The purpose of incarnation is that man should begin on the level possible to him, the level of his own nature, and through that gate pass to the divine. What do you think of Christ?

In conclusion, I press upon you this word. If in your heart, in the deepest of you, in that inner holy of holies of your inner life, you say what God said and what evil said, "He is the perfect One," then, I pray you, what is your emotional attitude toward that perfect One? Now, will you follow me closely. Do you hate the perfection? Then it is because at this hour you are following courses of sin as was the devil, who said "Let us alone." Do you love the perfect One in the deepest of you? Then it is because already the constraint of the Spirit of God is upon you, leading you toward the thing that is high and noble and true. Never mind for a moment, man, woman, brother, sister, never mind whether you have ever confessed Him or not. What do you think of Him now, at this moment, in your deepest heart? Are you saying, "He is the perfect One"? As you say it, is your whole love drawn out to Him in admiration and approbation? Now, I pray you in the name of God, for your own soul's sake, exercise that majestic function of your personality, your will, and answer the moving of your heart and the conviction of your mind.

There is another question. It was asked a few weeks later by a man who was attempting to juggle with time and eternity in order to save both. In the strenuous hours of his battle between obedience and expedience, Pilate asked, "What then shall I do unto Jesus which is called Christ?" That is my final question for you. What do you think of Him? I cannot invade the shrine of your thinking, but now I ask you, What will you do with Him? I plead with you tonight to answer your deepest conviction. For your own soul's sake, and for the sake of other people about you, stand out and let us see where you are. If you believe He is a fraud fight Him in the name of God and of humanity. If you believe this story is a lie, it is so persistent a lie, so persuasive a lie, so powerful a lie that you have no right to sit idly by. But if in your heart you believe this is true, crown Him, man, dare to crown Him. Oh, for five minutes of honesty and courage to place the crown upon His brow! If this is the truth, the truth is so persistent, so persuasive, so powerful, that you ought to help spread it, and you cannot until you yourself have crowned this Christ.

I beseech you, then, tonight, be definite. The claims of this Christ are such that every man ought to be busy fighting Him, or fighting for Him. I love Paul for this reason, he knew there was no middle course. It must either be haling to prison and death the men who professed the heresy, or pressing on forever toward the regions beyond to tell the story of the Christ. There is no middle place for Jesus in heaven, or earth, or hell, or your heart. It must be either the cross or the throne. Which shall it be? I pray God tonight that those of you who know Him to be true may crown Him.

CHAPTER XXII

ABILITY FOR DISABILITY

Stretch forth thy hand. And he stretched it forth; and his hand was restored.

MARK 3:5.

THE THEME IN THE SERMON IS CHRIST'S ABILITY IN THE PRESence of inability. Every miracle which Jesus wrought was a teaching, and that because the life of our Lord was unified. His was not a life separated into compartments independent of each other. Upon one occasion He said, "I am the truth," a very significant and remarkable statement made by no other teacher: not "I teach the truth," or "I declare the truth," or "I believe the truth," or even "I hold the truth"; but "I am the truth." In the life of Jesus, in His teaching, in His thinking, in His doing, there were none of the divisions which we are so apt to make. We divide between the secular and the sacred, but you cannot find any such division in the teaching of Jesus. To Him all life was sacred. Everything called by us secular when He touched it was revealed to be sacred. He did not divide His life or His thinking into business, recreation and rest. His whole life was effort homed in the will of God—essential truth. Therefore, whatever He touched, He touched from the same central conviction, and whatever He did, He did under the impulse of the same ageabiding principles. If He dealt with a man on the physical side of His being, He acted in exactly the same way as He would when dealing with a man on the mental or spiritual side. He lived and taught in the power of the fact of spiritual law in the natural world. I do not say, "natural law in the spiritual world"—that is an inversion of order—but "spiritual law in the natural world." All natural things were touched by Him from high altitudes of spiritual perception and spiritual power, and, consequently, whenever I take up the story of His dealing with a man on the physical side of his nature I see flaming through it His method in dealing with men in spiritual need, and therefore all the stories of Christ's dealing with physical disability have been used, and rightly, as illustrations of His method with spiritual need. In that way I take this old and familiar story tonight.

My message is to one particular condition of mind or, I might say, to one particular class of persons. I want to speak tonight to those who are fearful and afraid of committing themselves wholly to Christ because of their profound consciousness of some disability within their own life, and there are hundreds of such. I want to speak to the people who, if one should have to deal with them personally about spiritual things, would say, "Yes," to every declaration concerning the glory of Christ, to every affirmation of His perfect example and His gracious tenderness, and yet when urged to yield themselves to Him would utter some word telling of heartbreaking consciousness, of personal disability, and, consequently, of fear. My message is to the fearful. I do not mean at this moment that particular class of people who are afraid to follow Christ with the fear of cowardice. There are such.

It is with another kind and quality of fear that I desire to deal, the fear of the man who says, "Yes, I would like to be a Christian, but I am afraid that I would fail." It is a fear wholly wholesome and to be respected. I say that, not to encourage the fear, for, as God may help me, I want tonight to show you that there is no reason for it, although I respect it. The young man who looks me in the face and says, "I would like to be a Christian, but I am afraid I would dishonor His name in the business house where I am," I respect. "Happy is the man that feareth alway," said the preacher long ago; and he was right. It is the man of caution and of fear, conscious of his own disability, who, if we may but lead him into the true and simple relationship to Jesus Christ, which this little story reveals, will be true to Him, loyal to Him, and will stand against all the storms of opposition. That man is worth helping, worth saving. I want to help him if I can.

Let us try to see this thing as it happened, that we may deduce the spiritual values which lie hidden beneath it. The scene is the synagogue, and, as so often in the life of Jesus, His enemies unconsciously complimented Him. "He entered into the synagogue; and there was a man there which had his hand withered. And they watched Him." Why did they watch Him? "Whether He would heal him on the sabbath day; that they might accuse Him." I am not now interested in the ultimate purpose of these men, the mean and dastardly watching that they might catch Him and accuse Him. Mark this fact, Jesus came into the synagogue, and there was a man who most likely had been there again and again through weeks and months, perhaps years, at all the Sabbath services —a man whose right hand was withered, and immediately the enemies of Christ linked Him with the most needy man in the crowd. It is wonderful what an accurate sense of Jesus Christ His enemies had. They did not at all expect that He would be interested in the chief seat of the synagogue; but they did expect He would be interested in the one man there who was in direst need—the man whose hand was withered.

They linked Him in their thinking with need, and they were perfectly right. Of all the men in the synagogue that this Christ of ours would seek out and attempt to help, that was the one man. If the story is a parable, let us apply it as we go. The one man He wants in this house tonight is the man who is in the direst, sorest need. I do not know where he sits or what his name is, but, my brother, if you are in the grip of some dastardly habit that is paralyzing you, you are the man He is after. He is not half so interested in me just now as He is in you. Blessed be His name—His hand is on me, His ordaining hand, or I dare not speak for Him. But I hear Him saying, *"The Son of Man came to seek and to save that which was lost."* We cannot sift this great congregation. Thank God, we cannot! It is not our work. Hear this, my brother, hidden away in the crowd, as you say that your neighbor does not know how evil you are in your heart, how tight a hold habit has upon you—the Master sees you, and you are the man He is after. They linked Him with need. That is the first thing that flashes out of this story.

He knew their thoughts, and was angry with their attempt to entrap Him and the hardening of heart which was manifest, but He did not allow their criticism and opposition to interfere with His blessing. I hear Him saying, "Stand forth," and when the man stands in the midst He challenges them as to their attitude. Then I hear Him say to the man, "Stretch forth thy hand," and as I watch in wonder and amazement, "he stretched it forth," and as I look to see the result, "his hand was restored." Three things, then, demand our close attention. First, the command of Jesus, "Stretch forth thy hand." Secondly, obedience of the man, "He stretched it forth." Thirdly, the result, "His hand was restored."

Now hear the command, and I want to ask you to do

something which is a little difficult. Imaginatively, will you come into this synagogue with me? Let us forget this building and the people who are about us and transport ourselves in imagination overseas and back through centuries. We are in the synagogue watching. Here is the man with the hand withered. I need not attempt to enter into any explanation. I will take the word as it stands, "withered," devoid of power. Paralyzed, if you will; palsied, if you will; but "withered," nerveless, devoid of feeling, unable to work. That is the picture. As you are looking at the man with the withered hand, I want you to keep looking at him; the one thing you must not do is look at the One who speaks to him. I want you, if you will, to turn your back upon Jesus Christ in contemplating this scene. We are back in the synagogue among all the people who were there, without all the accumulated testimony of the centuries to the power of Jesus Christ which is our heritage and inheritance. There is the man with the withered hand. The one thing he cannot do is to use that hand. It is powerless, nerveless, "withered." As I look at him with my back to Christ, I hear Christ say, "Stretch forth thy hand," and in a moment my mind is in revolt against Christ. I say to Him, "What do You mean by telling this man to stretch forth his hand? It is the one thing he cannot do. Are You mocking his impotence? Are You asking him in the presence of these people to attempt the thing which, if he could do, he would have done long ago? This is the man's disability. Why ask him to do the thing he cannot do?" I say to Christ as He stands there, "This thing is impossible, and therefore it is unreasonable."

I cannot say that save as I keep my eye fixed upon the man with the withered hand. Change your viewpoint. Once again let your imagination have play. Stand with me in the synagogue, and, being perfectly familiar with the disability of the man with the withered hand, for you have known him for years, look into the face of the One Who said, "Stretch forth thy hand." There is always a quality in these stories not present in the cold letter on the page. You must always bring into your thinking the fact of the Person of Christ. This is not imagination. It is proved by all the context and all that happened. If you will follow me, let me try to lead you in an attempt to do, not what the critics did, but what the man did. Put yourself in the place of the man for a moment, and look back straight into the eyes of the One Who has said, "Stretch forth thy hand." I dare venture to affirm that if you can do it, if you can imagine the man doing it, if you will forget the spiritual application and see merely the story, you will at once see what I am trying to bring you to. On that day I think I know the things which passed, flash after flash, through this man's mind. The first thing was this, "He says, 'Stretch forth thy hand.' I cannot do it." Then he looked straight back into those eyes, and I think he said in his heart, "He would not tell me to do it if He did not mean something that I cannot comprehend. I cannot do it, but I will do it because He says it. I shall *will* to do it." I think it is very likely that doubt lurked at the back of his mind while his will prompted obedience, but the will did prompt obedience. That is the important truth. Looking into the face of Jesus, that face which carried its own argument perpetually as all the stories reveal if you read them carefully, the man said in his heart, "I cannot, but I will." It is a strange contradiction, but that is what he said that day in his heart. The moment he said, "I will," to the command of Christ, he began to find the forces that he had lacked pulsating through the nerves that had made no response, and all strength was his, and he stretched out his hand.

Surely the picture carries its own teaching. First of all,

it teaches me that when Jesus begins to touch any man's disability his perpetual method is that of bringing the man face to face with the one impossible thing in his life. He does not undertake a case, and undertaking it say, "Now we will not notice the evil thing, we will begin outside it." He goes right to the heart of the paralysis, as it is manifest in the case of the man He is dealing with. I do not know what Christ is saying to you particularly, specifically; but I do know this, He is bringing you face to face with the one thing which has mastered you and kept you away from Him for so long. He does not stay to admire the hand you can use. That is not His business. He draws your attention and concentrates your thought immediately upon the power that is paralyzed.

You say to me, "In this great scheme of salvation is it not true that the whole man is paralyzed?" It may be so, but this is also true, that every man coming to Christ comes at first in his supreme weakness, in one point of supreme difficulty. If I may put the thing from another standpoint, men are kept away from Christ by some one thing, some pride of the eye, or some lust of the flesh, some habit of the life, some desire of the carnal nature, some one thing. If it were possible for all the mists to melt about us tonight, and we who have never yielded to Christ could be seen in the clear light of the absolute truth, it would be found that in every case there is one thing hindering. When Jesus said to the young ruler, "One thing thou lackest," He was not dealing with one case only, but with a case which stands forevermore as the type of those who need Him and yet refuse Him. His method is always that of bringing men face to face with the master paralysis of the life. "Stretch forth thy hand." The one thing you cannot do, do! The one thing you are unable to do at this moment, do that!

So far, all this appears to be not calculated to help, but

to affright, the soul. Yet we must begin where Christ begins. Is it some habit which masters you? Christ says, "Abandon it now and forever." Is it some one power that is paralyzed in your life? Christ says, "Use it." You tell me your difficulty is right in the center of your being, with your will. You have no will power. Christ says, "Exercise your will and abandon yourself to Me by an act of will." Is your hand withered? Stretch it out. That is His perpetual method.

Now notice the obedience. "He stretched it forth." Let us try to see how this happened. I think there are three of the simplest things to be noticed. First of all, there was a deep conviction in the heart of the man that his hand was withered. In the second place, there was created in his mind, somehow, a profound conviction that Christ was not there to mock him, that Christ was there in some way to draw attention to his disability in order to turn it into ability. In the third place, by confession of faith, the man attempted the thing commanded, in obedience to the One commanding, and in the moment when he made that confession of faith by an act of will, he made contact with all the infinite resources of Christ, and there came, like a new dynamic, healing, helping life, and he did the thing he could not do. Again the picture is a parable.

There is no man here who will stretch out his hand in obedience to Christ save upon the basis of a profound conviction of need. If you do not know the withering of your power, if you have never yet felt the grip of habit upon you, if you are still unconscious of paralysis, I do not think I can persuade you to this Christ, at least, not by this address. It is to the man who knows his need that this story appeals. You must begin where this man began.

You have begun there; you are so far toward Christ. You know your need. I am quite willing to drop out of account all the rest of the congregation if I can talk to one man hidden away. You know your need. You say, "One power paralyzed? Why, all my high essential powers are paralyzed. In the grip of one habit? I am in the grip of more than I care to name. Incompetent in one power? My whole life is paralyzed." You know your need. Now I pray you look into the face of Christ and think well of what He has proved Himself equal to do in all the centuries that have passed, and remember this, that what He has been doing He still is doing, and what He is doing for others He waits to do for you. In your heart is a great confidence in His ability to save certain men. Honestly and logically apply that confidence to your own need first. Say, if you will, that you cannot think how He can help you, but remember that He Who has helped scores of cases, hundreds, thousands of cases such as yours, is surely not limited in your lonely case among all the sons of need that the centuries have produced. May there come back to you confidence in His ability.

But neither conviction of need nor confidence in Christ's ability will bring healing. Healing can come only when a man, convinced of need, sure of His ability, obeys His command, and by an act of will surrenders to Him. Obedience determined upon by act of will, then contact is made with Him in His power, and the hand willed to be stretched forth because He commands it becomes the hand made whole as the other.

What was the last thing in the story? The result: "his hand was restored." Matthew tells us that his hand "was restored whole as the other." Here was a change from disease to health, from weakness to power, from uselessness to usefulness. All was wrought in the moment when in obedience to Christ, he did the impossible thing and found the power to do it communicated in the act of his surrender.

Here again the picture is a parable. In the moment in which a man, by obedience to Jesus Christ, abandons himself to Him, and then wills to do the thing he has never been able to do, in that moment, because Christ commands it, he makes contact with Christ's power, and there comes into his life a change more wonderful, more marvelous, spiritually, than was the change wrought in the hand of this man physically, and yet the same in essence. In the moment of your surrender and your obedience you will be changed from spiritual disease to spiritual health, from spiritual disability to spiritual ability, from spiritual uselessness to spiritual usefulness, for in all the withered powers there lie dormant possibilities which can be quickened only by the touch of the life and resources of Christ. Christ's life and resources can touch these powers only as man's will yields to Christ's will and he begins to use the activity of obedience. The moment that surrender is made, power is communicated, and the whole spiritual life is changed. That is the Gospel. It is not an explanation of all the mystery of the process or of the mystery of the communication of life, but that is practically exactly what Christ does for men. How many people there are here tonight who are conscious of spiritual disability, seeing the vision occasionally, but never able to realize it; feeling a passionate desire for communion, for purity, for holiness and spiritual power, yet always mastered by evil things! Before you leave this building tonight Jesus Christ can change your death into life, your disease into health, your blindness into vision, your incompetence into competence, your disability into ability, your "I cannot" into your "I can."

Unless Jesus Christ can do that, He cannot help me, and He cannot help hundreds and thousands of men. What Jesus Christ is waiting to do, and is able to do, and has been doing for men through all the ages, is not to present an ideal to them which they are to imitate, but to communicate life which enables them to realize the ideal they have seen. What Jesus has done is not to give men directions how to use the withered hand, but to communicate power to the withered hand that they may be able to use it under the impulse of indwelling life.

Is there anything else here? It is not written, but I think we may follow the story. What happened to the man afterward? What happened to his withered hand afterward, the hand no longer withered but whole, restored like the other? How can he maintain that hand in strength? I think I see him going away from Jesus that day saying, "Well, this is wonderful. See here, this withered hand is healed. I have not been able to lift anything, and now I can lift things easily. I have not positively felt life in it, and now it thrills with life." Then I can imagine him saying to himself, "I have obtained a great blessing today. I must take care of it." Then I can imagine that he takes that hand—healed, restored, made whole as the other—and carefully wraps it in bandages to preserve it, and places it somewhere in his bosom to take care of it, and keeps it there lest it should be harmed again. You see the folly of the whole supposition. You see the tragedy of the folly if you carry it out far enough. Let a man do that, and the hand will wither again, for life is maintained in strength by use. When Christ gives a man back his power it is not that the man may guard it, but that he may use it. That man will retain the life in its fullness by using it, by taking hold of weights and lifting them; if he is a mechanic, by taking up his tools, by going back to work. That is the meaning of the healing of the withered hand. Man is not to take care of his withered hand by bandaging it, but to preserve it in strength by using it for the thing for which it was first created.

That which we have ventured to add to the picture is

also a parable. You say, "There was a time when I saw His face. There was a moment when I came back with my withered powers to the Christ, and in obedience to Him I commenced to use them, and He gave me back those powers; but I have lost them. My hand is withered again. Instead of power there is paralysis, which seems more deadly than of old." How have you lost your power? There may be many ways with which I am not dealing. One way of losing power is that of perpetually attempting to take care of it instead of using it. There are hundreds of people who lose their spiritual power by the very attempt they make to conserve it. I am not at all sure that the churches are not in danger of being filled with weak, nerveless, anemic men and women because they are so forever anxious to deepen their own spiritual life. I am not sure that the perpetual restless hurrying to and fro in the attempt to conserve personal spirituality is not a prolific source of spiritual paralysis. In the physical realm you have known some people who are forevermore carrying round a thermometer and taking their temperature. They have always got their hand on their pulse, and are wondering whether they are quite so well as they used to be. You know these are the people who are never in robust health. If you can make them break their thermometer and get their hand off their pulse and turn out and work, they will be better. What is true in the physical is true also in the spiritual. I want to warn you with all my heart against perpetual spiritual introspection. As Christ gives you new power use it in the world's wide field for Him. Think more of the need of the man who is down than of your own personal need. Think more of the enterprises of your Lord than of your own strength or weakness. Look less in, and more out, and up into the face of Jesus, and take every power He gave you when you trusted Him, and get out on to the field in ceaseless, hard toil for Him and His Kingdom. Then your spiritual life is likely to be deepened and strengthened and broadened, and instead of anemic and sentimental religion, we shall have full-blooded, robust, strenuous Christianity, which will lift the world and help and bless it. Do not put your restored hand into a sling. Use it. That is the meaning of this story.

In conclusion, I go back from that added word, that carrying out of the picture, a little beyond the actual happenings in the synagogue, and bring you to the central thought, for I want to help the man who is afraid. Are you afraid because you know your own weakness? Your fear is wholesome. But now, I beseech you, for one moment take your eyes off your own weakness and fix them upon Christ. If you will do that, then hear Him say, "Stretch forth thy hand," and know this, when He tells a man to do the impossible thing, He does it knowing that He has in His gift all that is needed to help the man do it. The moment you obey He makes over to you the resources of His power.

I may fine down this whole message and bring it to this final word. Take your eyes off your own disability and fix them upon His ability. Doing that, obey Him, and by obeying Him make contact with His power, and you will feel the thrill and force of it and know its result in restoration of lost and paralyzed powers. Do not think of this as a sermon, but as a message to you. There are some here tonight who crossed this threshold with a reverent and absolutely sincere desire to sit in the quiet of the sanctuary and hear some message from on high, yet you know that in your life is the thing that spoils. You hate it as much as any other man hates it—and more; but you feel that it is your master, that it is useless trying. So it is, in your own strength! If you have got as far as that, you are not far from the Kingdom of God.

But now, I beseech you, from your weakness look to Jesus' power; from your inability turn to all that He is able to do, and begin again, not to try in your own strength, but to trust and to obey. Though you make no sign of your surrender, if you will do so, in the moment of crisis that waits for you just over the threshold of the sanctuary at the close of the first day of the week, in the moment of crisis that waits for you tonight, you will find His strength made perfect in weakness, and the thing you could not do you will be able to do through Him Who strengtheneth you.

CHAPTER XXIII

THE PURPOSE OF THE ADVENT

1. To Destroy the Works of the Devil

To this end was the Son of God manifested, that He might destroy the works of the devil.

I JOHN 3:8.

WE ARE APPROACHING THE FESTIVAL OF CHRISTMAS. IN THE calendar of the Christian year this is the first Sunday in Advent. I am proposing to speak for four successive Sunday evenings on the purposes of the Advent. The importance of the subject cannot be overstated. The whole teaching of Holy Scripture places the Advent at the center of the methods of God with a sinning race. Toward that Advent everything moved until its accomplishment, finding therein fulfillment and explanation. The messages of the prophets, seers, and the songs of psalmists trembled with more or less certainty toward the final music which announced Jesus' coming. All the results of these partial and broken messages of the past led toward the Advent. It is equally true that from that Advent all subsequent movements have proceeded, depending upon it for direction and dynamic. The writings which we have in the Gospel stories are all concerned with the coming of Christ, with His mission and His message. The last book of the Bible is a book the true title of which is The Unveiling of the Christ. Not only the actual messages which have been bound up in this one Divine Library, but all the results issuing from them are finally results issuing from this selfsame coming of Christ. It is surely important therefore that we should understand its purposes in the economy of God.

There is a fourfold statement of purpose which I propose to make. The purpose to destroy the works of the devil, the purpose to put away sin, the purpose to reveal the Father, the purpose to establish by another Advent the Kingdom of God in the world.

In dealing first with the purpose to destroy the works of the devil I am attempting to follow the order of historic appreciation. There is a sense in which these purposes go forward concurrently, the destruction of the works of the devil, the taking away of sin, the unveiling of the face of the Father and the administration of the Kingship of God toward consummation. In yet another sense we may state the order of these things differently. We may say that He came first to reveal the Father, then to deal with sin, presently by way of the second Advent to set up the Kingdom in the world, and ultimately and finally to destroy the works of the devil. I think, as I have already intimated, that so far as historic appreciation of the purposes of God is concerned, I have suggested to you the true order. To the men of Christ's own age, both those who yielded to Him and those who rebelled against Him, He was first of all a reformer—and I pray you do not interpret the meaning of that word "reformer" by those who have followed in His wake or those who preceded Him, but gather all your thought of it from what He was in Himself—a soul in conflict with all that was contrary to the purposes of God in individual, social, national, racial life.

Such was Christ, and there is a sense in which when we have said this we have stated the whole meaning of His coming. His revelation of the Father was toward this end; His putting away of sin was a part of this very process, and His second Advent will be for the complete and final overthrow of all the works of the devil.

Confining ourselves, however, to the simplest meaning of this particular passage, let us notice, first of all, John's description of the Advent. He does not say, "For this purpose, or to this end, was Jesus of Nazareth born." That would be true, but only part of the truth.

Remember, there can be no question as to Whom John referred when he said "the Son of God." We all know that he was writing of the One of Whom he always wrote. We are taken back irresistibly, however, to words at the beginning of John's Gospel and Epistle. "In the beginning was the Word, and the Word was with God, and the Word was God . . . and the Word became flesh, and tabernacled among us." "That which we have seen with our eyes, that which we beheld, and our hands handled." It is impossible to read these words and imagine they are wholly or exclusively spiritual statements. John is most carefully defining the Person. In all the writings of John it is evident that his eyes are fixed upon the man Jesus. Occasionally he does not even name Jesus, does not even refer to Him by a personal pronoun, but indicates Him by a word you can use only when you are looking at an object or a person. For instance, "*That* which we have seen with our eyes, *that* which we beheld, and our hands handled." Upon another occasion John said, "He that saith he abideth in Him, ought himself also to walk even as *that One* walked." It is always the method of expression of a man who is looking at a Person. Forevermore the actual human Person of Christ was present to the mind of

John as he wrote of Him. How intimate he had been with Him we all know. One of the most tender and beautiful things in all the story of the life of Jesus is the story of John's love for Him, pure human affection for Him. The other disciples loved Him in a sense, and I do not undervalue their love, but it was of a different tone and quality from that of John. You cannot imagine Peter getting very intimately near to Christ. There was something of distance, of breeze and bluster, and of beauty, about the love of Peter. He would be quite content to talk to Jesus across the table, but John must get close to Him and lay his head upon His bosom. There was none of the disciples so intimately associated with the actual human personality of Jesus as John. When John refers to Him it is always in words that thrill and throb with the warm tenderness of human consciousness, of human friendship. Yet there is not one of you here who does not know that if I said no more I would not have uttered half the truth. If John the mystic, the lover, laid his head upon the human bosom of the Man of Nazareth, he heard the beating of the heart of God. If he laid his hand upon Jesus when he talked to Him he knew that beneath the warm touch of the human flesh there beat the mystic majesty of Deity. "That which our hands handled, concerning the Word of life." Mark the contradiction of it in this materialistic age of ours. Can you handle a word? Can you handle life? Yet John says, "This is what we have done." He is perfectly conscious of the flesh, but supremely conscious of the mystic Word veiled in flesh and shining through it. He is perfectly conscious of the human and gets thereby to Deity. So that when John comes to write of this One he speaks of Him as "the Son of God." He remembers the warmth of His bosom, the gentleness of His touch, the love-lit glory of His eyes, but He is "the Son of God."

The word "manifested" presupposes existence prior to manifestation. In the Man of Nazareth there was manifestation of One Who had existed long before the Man of Nazareth.

The incarnation was not an act by which God began to be in any single sense. It was not an act by which God came into nearness to human life. It was an act by which God manifested His nearness to human life, and by which manifestation He was able to do in human life and in human history things He could not have done apart from that selfsame method of manifestation. "To this end was the Son of God manifested."

Now we come to the statement of purpose. The person referred to, the devil. The things to be destroyed, the works of the devil. The purpose declared, to destroy the works of the devil.

The enemy is described here as the devil. I want to take other passages from the writings of John and let their light fall upon this name. In the eighth chapter of John's Gospel it is recorded that Jesus, using this very name, declares of the devil that "he was a murderer from the beginning . . . he is a liar." A little further on in the Gospel it is declared it was he who put it into the heart of Judas to betray Christ. I read in the context of my text that he is the fountainhead of sin, the lawless one. Gather up these thoughts concerning this personality—murderer, liar, betrayer, the fountainhead of sin, himself missing the mark because of lawlessness—and it will immediately be manifest what his works are. The work of the murderer is destruction of life. The work of the liar is the extinguishing of light. The work of the betrayer is the violation of love. The work of the archsinner is the breaking of the law. These are the works of the devil.

First, as to the destruction of life, for he is a murderer.

This consists fundamentally in the destruction of life on its highest level, which is the spiritual. Alienation from God is the devil's work. It is also death on the level of the mental. Vision which fails to include God is practical blindness. On the physical plane, all disease and all pain are ultimately results of sin and are among the works of the devil. These things all lie within the realm of his work as a murderer, destroyer of human life. The Greek word might perhaps be translated more forcefully "man-slayer." He is the slayer of man, in the spiritual, which is supreme; in the mental which marks consciousness, whether spiritual or material; in the body, which is the instrument of the spirit, whether for good or evil. The man-slayer is one who comes in to spoil humanity, to rob it of its life, to blind it spiritually toward God, to limit it mentally because of the blindness of the spiritual, and to bring into it all manner of disease and death in the physical realm.

He is more. He is the liar and to him is due the extinguishing of light, so that men blunder along the way. All ignorance, all despair, all wandering over the trackless deserts of life, are due to the extinction of spiritual light in the mind of man. I can quite imagine someone saying, "You are going outside the realm of what is true when you declare that all ignorance is the devil's work." I abide by that statement, perhaps for reasons which are not ordinarily advanced or held. I will make one contrast in your mind tonight. I claim that in this Man of Nazareth as pure man there was an utter absence of ignorance. His thinking was perfectly clear. He as man saw right through to the heart of mystery, and that because He was never brought under the dominion of sin, never brought under the dominion of the evil one, was able in His life perpetually to rebut every advance of the prince of darkness, who is a liar from the beginning. I am not merely speaking of Him as One infallible in spiritual things. I believe He was also absolutely infallible in other things. I am asked today if I imagine that Jesus knew the laws of nature by the discovery of which in recent years men have made such rapid progress. Yes, absolutely. He knew every one. I am asked if I believe that He understood the mystery of electricity. Yes. Then you say, "Why did He not tell the race?" The race was not ready for the knowledge. What is true in the spiritual realm is true also in the scientific. He had many things to say which men were then not able to bear. I for one have no part or lot in the view of Christ that He was scientifically half ignorant, while spiritually infallible. You say, "Then He was not upon our level." He was not upon our level. No perfect man was ever upon our level. There was in Him no sin, no darkness, no limitation, and you have one gleam of this fact in the impression He produced upon the men of His own age. He went up to Jerusalem and was talking in the midst of men of culture and men of light and leading, in the midst of the school men. What did they say of Him? "How knoweth this Man letters, having never learned?" "Whence hath this Man the accent of the school, never having been to school? How is it that this Man in His teaching is most evidently familiar with the things we have obtained through strife and difficulty?" They did not answer their question. Men today cannot answer their question, save as they recognize that here was a Man never having learned yet knowing, and seeing clearly to the heart of things. I go back from that illustration, which is in some sense a digression, and yet I think you see its purpose. All ignorance is the result of the clouding of man's vision of God. "This is life eternal," age-abiding life, high life, deep life, broad life, long life, comprehensive life, "that they should know Thee the only true God, and Him Whom Thou didst send, even Jesus Christ." The proportion in which man knows God is the proportion in which he sees clearly to the heart of things. You say, "How is it that Christian people have not been able to see these things? How is it that the great discoveries of science have not been made by Christian people?" I would have you remember first that the discoveries of science have always been made in a Christian atmosphere. In the second place, the redemptive work of Christ will not be perfected in humanity until that mysterious morning of His second Advent, when we shall have our new bodily powers as well as our new spiritual powers, and when man is wholly restored to God. Let me say this as superlatively as I believe it. In that day manhood will laugh at the foolish pride of this day, which thinks it understands this world. Sinning man has but scratched upon the surface of the infinite mysteries of this world. By and by, when the redemptive work of Christ has been perfected in man, and in the world, we shall find that all ignorance is banished and man has found his way into light. But the liar, the one who brings darkness, has made his works far spread o'er all the face of humanity, and all ignorance and resultant despair and all wandering aimlessly in every realm of life are due to the work of the one whom Jesus designated a liar from the beginning. Again, the violation of love, as a work of the devil, is seen supremely in the way he entered into the heart of Judas and made him the betrayer. All the avarice you find in the world today and all the jealousy and all the cruelty are the works of the devil.

Finally, He is the supreme sinner. Sin is lawlessness, which does not mean the condition of being without law, but the condition of being against law, breaking law. So that all wrong done to God in His world, all wrong done by man to man, all wrong done by man to himself, are works of the devil.

To summarize them, death, darkness, hatred, find them where you will, are works of the devil.

The Son of God was manifested that He might destroy the works of the devil. If at the beginning we saw Him as a soul in conflict with all these things, remember that was an indication of the program and a prophecy of the purpose. The Advent which we celebrate was not merely the birth of a little child in whom we were to learn the secret of childhood and in whom presently we were to see the glories of manhood. All that is true; but it was the happening in the course of human events of that one thing through which God Himself is able to destroy the works of the devil.

"To destroy." What is this word? It is a word which means to dissolve, to loosen. It is the very same word that is used in the Apocalypse about loosing us from our sins; or, if you will be more graphic, it is the word used in the Acts of the Apostles when you read that the ship was broken to pieces; loosed, dissolved, that which had been a consistent whole was broken up and scattered and wrecked. The word "destroyed" may be perfectly correct, but let us understand it. He was manifested for what? to do a work in human history the result of which should be that the works of the devil would lose their consistency. The cohesive force that makes them appear stable until this moment He came to loosen and dissolve. He was manifested to destroy hatred by the gift of love. He was manifested to destroy lawlessness by the gift of law. He was manifested to loosen, to break up, to destroy the negatives which spoil, by bringing the positive that remakes and uplifts.

He was manifested to destroy the works of the devil

as to death by the gift of life. This means first spiritual life, which is fellowship with God. It means also mental life, the vision of the open secret. Not yet perfectly do we understand, but already the trusting soul in this house, utterly devoid of education, hears more in the wind at eventide, and sees more in the blossoming of the flowers than any scientific man. Was it not Huxley who said that if our ears were but acute enough we would hear the flowers grow. You say that is a purely scientific statement. I know it is, and science, in the last analysis, is spiritual. Christ has so far invaded the world that the men who do not name His name are beginning to spell out this great truth. The merely physical scientist of a generation ago has passed never to return. I hear of whitening dawns of psychological investigation, but what does it mean? That men are gradually beginning to hear the singing. There is no simple-hearted child of God in this house but that looking into a flower sees the face of God. I think, perchance, I have told you here before of something that happened in my boyhood's days which I have never forgotten. There came to my father's house a young fellow who had been led to Christ but recently in one of my father's meetings. One day he took me down the garden—I was but eight years old—and he plucked a nasturtium leaf, and putting it in his hand he said, "Look at this." Boylike, I thought he had found a great curiosity, and hurried to see it. I did not see what he saw. The day came when, by the grace of God, I saw it also. He said, "See, is not God beautiful?" For me, you may take all your botanists if you will give me that man with the leaf in his hand. That is not imagination. It is the open secret. It is what Carlyle called the great significance shining through. Mrs. Barrett Browning was right—

> Earth's crammed with heaven,
> And every common bush afire with God;
> But only he who sees, takes off his shoes—
> The rest sit round it and pluck blackberries.

How many there are in the "rest"!

He who sees has the true intellectual vision, which Christ has bestowed in His gift of life. "This is life eternal, that they should know Thee the only true God." The gift of life was to destroy death, and the man who has His gift of life laughs in the face of death, laughs triumphantly, and—yes, I will say it—makes fun of death! Do not misunderstand me—I mean for himself, never of the sorrow which comes to the bereaved. I still believe, say what you will, that there was laughter in the Apostle's tone when he said, "O death, where is thy sting?" As though he had said, "What hast thou done with thy sting, death? What hast thou done with thy victory? I trembled in thy presence once, O rider upon the pale horse, but now I laugh in thy face, for thy paleness has become the glistening white of an angel of light." So He destroys the works of the devil by giving the gift of life which destroys death.

As for darkness, this is intimately associated with the thing already said, the gift of light; but remember light always comes out of life. If there be death then there is no vision. If there be life there is light. Light means knowledge and hope and guidance, so that there is no more wandering aimlessly. By bringing light into human life and into the world Christ has destroyed the works of the devil.

As for hatred, He destroys hatred by His gift of love, benevolence—and I am not using the word idly as we often do; I am using it in all its rich, spacious, gracious meaning—benevolence, well-willing, self-abnegation, kindness in the Apostle's sense of the word who, when writing to the Galatians, gives kindness as one of the qualities of love, the specific doing of small things out of pure love. All these things are things by which the works of the devil are being destroyed. Hatred, avarice, jealousy, selfishness, how are these things destroyed? By shedding abroad love which is the warmth of life, as light is its illumination. By these things He destroys the works of the devil.

As for lawlessness, this Jesus destroys by the gift of law, passion for the rights of God, service to my fellow men, the finding of self in the great abnegation, and the finding of self in perfect freedom because I have become the bond-slave of the infinite Lord of Love. The works of the devil, what are they? Death working within us, the spirit that is against truth and light, the darkness of ignorance. The spirit of hatred and malice, avarice and jealousy and the whole unholy brood of things which are unlike God, lawlessness lying at the base of all, the refusal to submit, these are the works of the devil. Nineteen centuries ago the Son of God was manifested, and during those centuries in the lives of hundreds, thousands, He has destroyed the works of the devil, mastered death by the gift of life, cast darkness out by the incoming of light, turned the selfishness of avarice and jealousy into love, joy, peace, longsuffering, kindness, goodness. He has taken hold of lawless men and made them into the willing, glad bond-servants of God. So has He destroyed the works of the devil.

Do not forget the meaning of the Advent historically. It was the invasion of human history by One who snatched the scepter from the usurper. It was the intrusion of forces into human history which dissolved the consistency of the works of the devil, and causes them to break and fail. "How long, O Lord, how long?" is the cry of the heart of the saint today. Yet take heart as you look back and know that force has operated for nineteen centuries and always toward consummation. Still, the works of the devil are manifest, the works of the flesh are manifest. Yes, but the fruit of the Spirit of life which has come through the Advent of Christ is also manifest. All over the world today on many a branch of the vine of the Father's planting the rich clusters of fruit are to be found. All, so far, is but preliminary. It is twilight only. High noon has not yet arrived; but it *is* twilight, and noon must come. What the Advent has wrought it will still work. That which it has accomplished in the face of opposition it will accomplish. That which has dissolved the vested and established evils proves to my heart the certainty of the ultimate victory. I tell you that if we have but eyes anointed to see we shall discover the fact that all the works of the devil in the world are wrapped about by the slow burning fires that came when the Son of God was manifested that He might loosen, dissolve, destroy the works of the devil.

The last word is to be personal. The Advent personally was the coming of the Stronger than the strong men armed. It was the coming of One to destroy the works of the devil in my own life. Are they not destroyed? Are they not shaken to their foundations? Are they still established in the fiber of your being? Do you know as you sit in this house tonight that the works of the devil, death, darkness, hatred and rebellion are the master forces of your being? Then I bring you the Evangel. I tell you of One manifested to destroy all such works. I tell you not merely as a theory, but as having the testimony of history attesting the truth of the announcement of my text. I do not move you by that! Suffer me, then, to tell you as a word of personal and actual experience: not that in me the victory is perfectly won, not that the Master's work is accomplished, but that in me, solemnly, I bear the testimony, the forces of this Christ have operated and are operating, and the things that were formerly established are loosened and are falling to decay. He was manifested to destroy the works of the devil. If tonight you are in the grip of forces of evil, if you realize that in your life his works are the things of strength, then I pray you turn with full purpose of heart to the One manifested long ago, Who is here now, Who, in all the power of His gracious victory, will destroy in you all the works of the devil and set you free.

CHAPTER XXIV

THE PURPOSE OF THE ADVENT

2. To Take Away Sins

Ye know that He was manifested to take away sins; and in Him is no sin.

I JOHN 3:5.

LAST SUNDAY EVENING WE SPOKE ON A VERSE IN THIS SAME chapter, "To this end was the Son of God manifested, that He might destroy the works of the devil." If the works of the devil are death, darkness, hatred and lawlessness, the one word "sin" expresses all these things for us. Sin is due to death and issues in death, that is, death as separation from the life of God. Sin is due to darkness—the carnal mind which cannot see the things of God—issues in yet denser darkness. Sin is due to hatred—the man continuing in sin continues a carnal man, not knowing God, is at enmity with God—and issues in yet profounder hatred. Or, comprehensively, it may be stated that sin is due to lawlessness as a principle expressing itself in lawlessness as an activity. Thus in our text we get nearer to an understanding of the purpose of the Advent as it touches our human need.

The simple and all inclusive theme which the text suggests is, first, that the purpose of the Advent was the taking

THE PURPOSE OF THE ADVENT

away of sins, and secondly, that the process of accomplishment is that of the Advent.

Let us first, then, take the purpose as declared. "He was manifested to take away sins." In order to understand it we must take the terms in all their simplicity, and be very careful to find what they really mean. "To take away sins." What is intended by this word "sins"? The sum total of all lawless acts—the thought is incomprehensible as to numbers. I think I shall carry you with me when I say that there is no human being here who would care to have the task allotted to him of counting up his own lawless acts. If the thought is indeed incomprehensible as to numbers let us remember that in the midst of that which overwhelms us in our thinking are our own actual sins. The actual sins which we cannot enumerate are nevertheless included in this declaration of purpose. For a moment postpone the activity of your mind which suggests difficulties as to how anyone can do such a thing as this; leave out of the question the whole thought of process and simply face the avowed declaration of purpose "manifested to take away sins." "Sins," missings of the mark, whether willful missings of the mark or missings of the mark through ignorance, does not at present matter. The word includes all those thoughts and words and deeds in which we have missed the mark of the Divine purpose and the Divine ideal: those things which stand between man and God, so that man becomes afraid of God because he recognizes that in his sins he has violated the Divine purpose and broken the Divine law; those things which stand between man and his fellow man, so that man becomes afraid of his fellow man, knowing that he has wronged him in some direction; those things which stand between man and his own success. Call them failures if you will, call them by any name you please, so that you understand the intention of the word.

When John the Baptist looked upon Jesus, he said, "Behold the Lamb of God, which taketh away the sin of the world." There he used the same word but in the singular. There he referred to the principle manifesting itself in lawless acts. He used a word which includes all sins, and therefore is, in some senses, the profounder word, and yet in our text we understand the writer to mean that the Advent was in order to the taking away of all acts of lawlessness springing out of the attitude of lawlessness, of all practice of wrong-doing issuing from the principle of wrong life.

Let us now examine the phrase "to take away." This is a statement of result, not a declaration of process. There is a marginal reading which says "to bear sins," and in the Gospel of John there is also a marginal reading, "Behold the Lamb of God, which taketh away," or "beareth the sin of the world." These words are not incorrect if we are very careful to understand what they really mean. The Hebrew equivalent of the word "taketh away" is found in that familiar story of the scapegoat. It was provided that this animal should be driven away to the wilderness, "unto a solitary land." This suggested that sins should be lifted from one and placed upon another, and by that one carried away out of experience, out of consciousness. That is the simple signification of this declaration, "He was manifested to bear sins." If you take this word and track it back—not always a safe process, but here, I think, a helpful one—to its root meaning, it is, "He was manifested to *list* sins." He was manifested in order that He might come into relationship with human life, and passing underneath the load of human sins lift them, take them away.

Either this is the most glorious Gospel that man has ever heard, or the greatest delusion to which man has ever listened. I care nothing, for the moment, about your theological tendencies, or convictions, or prejudices—you may choose your own word! What I do care about is that there is in the heart of every man and woman in this house a consciousness of sin. No one of us would be prepared to say, "I have never deliberately done the thing I knew I ought not to do." That is consciousness of sin. You may attempt to excuse it. You may even say that it does not much matter, that the sin was the result of some infirmity of the flesh. You may even go so far as to say that the fact that you have repeatedly done the thing you knew was not the right thing was simply part of a process in which you were learning not to do it. So ingenious is the human heart that it will attempt to excuse itself by all kinds of fallacies. I do not believe there is a single person here who will deny the charge—if you deny the arguments I care nothing.

I will go one step further, and declare that in the deepest of you, in the best of you—again notwithstanding theological opinions, or prejudices, or convictions, as you choose—the one thing you hate most of all in your past is your own sin. You may affect to excuse it. You may be ready to argue with me as to the reason for it and the issue of it, but, if you could, you would undo it. If you could make it not to be, there are some here tonight who would be ready to sacrifice right hand or right eye. You may profess to have turned your back upon these evangelical truths which we declare, and yet you know you have sinned, and you wish you had not.

Passing for a moment from that outer fringe of men and women, who are somewhat careless about the matter, to the souls who are in agony concerning it—to the men and women who know their sin and loathe it, to the men and women who carry the consciousness of wrongs done in past years as a perpetual burden upon their souls—and there are many of them who have never confessed it, who have never spoken to another soul about it, but nevertheless hate the memory of their own sins—I say that to such, a declaration like this is the cruelest word or the kindest that can be uttered. Cruel if it be false, kind indeed with the kindness of the heart of God if it be true. If somewhere, and somewhen, and somehow, in human history One was manifested to lift sins and bear them away; if by some means I can find some just and honorable peace of conscience notwithstanding sins and sin, then have I found blessing greater than any man can give me. I dismiss for the moment for the sake of my argument not only the outer fringe but also the inner circle of burdened souls, and I speak as a witness. Turning aside from advocacy, I bear testimony that if it be true, that He was manifested somehow, in some deep mystery that I shall never perfectly understand, in order to get beneath my sins, *my* sins, my thought of impurity, my words of bitterness, my unholy deeds, and lift them and bear them away—that is the one Evangel I long for more than all. More valuable to me, a sinner, than anything else that He can do for me is this.

In order that this great purpose of the Advent, as declared, may be more powerfully and better understood, let us reverently turn to the indication of the process which we have in this particular text, for while the supreme value of the text last week was its unveiling of the purpose of the Advent in victory gained over the enemy of the race, I am inclined to think that the supreme value of this declaration of purpose is its indication of process. "He was manifested to take away sins." Notice the Person referred to. "*He* was manifested." Who was the Person? "Ye know," says John, "that He was manifested." The reference certainly is to some One. If you go back over this chapter you come presently to the statement, "Beloved, now are we children of God, and it is not yet made manifest what we shall be. We know that, if He shall be manifested, we shall be like Him." Whom? The same Person is being referred to as in my text. I go back a little further and read, "Behold what manner of love the Father hath bestowed upon us, that we should be called children of God: and such we are. For this cause the world knoweth us not, because it knew Him not." Whom? I go yet further back, into the preceding chapter, and trace my way until I come to the twenty-third verse, "Whosoever denieth the Son, the same hath not the Father: he that confesseth the Son hath the Father also." You cannot read the context of this text without seeing that, in the thinking of the man who wrote it, there is identity between God and the Son. It is perfectly evident that John here, as always, has his eye fixed upon the Man of Nazareth, and yet it is equally evident that he is looking through Jesus of Nazareth to God. That is the meaning of his word "manifested" here. It is the Word made flesh. It is flesh, but it is the Word. It is something that John had appreciated by the senses, and yet it is Someone Whom John knew pre-eminently by the Spirit. When he says in this same letter, "Everyone that hath this hope set on Him purifieth himself, even as He is pure," he means hope set on God finally, on the Son by manifestation. So that the Person who is presented to our view here is that One Who in human life was the manifestation of God Himself. "He was manifested." He was before manifestation. Who was He before manifestation? Because Whosoever He was before manifestation, He was in manifestation; and Whosoever He was before manifestation and in manifestation, He was in the taking away of sins.

Notice that after John makes the affirmation, "He was manifested to take away sins," he adds this great word, "In Him is no sin." Will you let me put that into another form? Let me render the actual word of John in slightly different terms, "Missing of the mark was not in Him." The One in Whom there was no missing of the mark was manifested for the express purpose of lifting, bearing away, making not to be, the missings of the mark of others. Mark that declaration of the eternal and essential sinlessness of the One Who came. We can interpret the language of John only by the teaching of John; so without apology I take you back again to the introductory word in his Gospel, "In the beginning was the Word, and the Word was with God, and the Word was God." No missing of the mark was in Him. He was sinless through all the unmeasured and immeasurable ages. "In Him was life; and the life was the light of men"—all created things springing from the energy of that mysterious One in Whom was no sin, in Whom was no missing of the mark in the mystery of creation. "All things have been made by Him"; that is continuity of activity in creation. In Him, the Upholder as well as the Creator, there was no missing of the mark. Presently "The Word became flesh, and tabernacled among us, and we beheld His glory, glory as of the Only Begotten from the Father, full of grace and truth." In Him was no missing of the mark. Presently we see Him yielding Himself to death, and even there, in the hour of His death, there was no missing of the mark. Through resurrection, by way of ascension at this moment at the center of the universe of God, the same Person, and in Him is no missing of the mark.

"He was manifested"—and in the name of God I charge you do not read into the "He" anything small or narrow. If you do you will at once be driven into the place of having to deny the declaration that He can take away sins. If He was man as I am man merely, then though He be perfect and sinless He cannot take away sins. If into the "He" you will read all that John evidently meant according to the testimony of his own writing, from which alone I have been making my quotations—if you will read into it all John meant, "He," the Word made flesh, in Whom was no missing of the mark before or after He was manifested to take away sins, you begin to see something of the stupendous idea, and something of the possibility at least of believing the declaration that "He was manifested to take away sins."

Consider the manifestation and sins, as to man. The terms of the promise of the Advent were, "Thou shalt call His name Jesus; for it is He that shall save His people from their sins." From hell? Certainly, but I pray you remember, only by saving them from their sins. From the punishment of sin, because from sin itself. That was the great word, "He shall save His people from their sins." When the songs to which the shepherds listened were heard, what said they? "There is born to you this day . . . a Saviour, which is Christ the Lord." The promise of the Advent was that of the coming of One to lift sins.

During the probation of the long years this Person was meeting all the forces of human temptation and overcoming them. I think we may accurately and reverently speak of the long years of probation as testing years, years in which there was being wrought out into human visibility the fact of the sinlessness of the Son of God.

During His life and ministry what were the words of Jesus? Words revealing the meaning of sin. Words calculated to rebuke sin and to bring men away from sin. What were the works of Jesus? By works I mean miracles and signs and wonders. They were chiefly works overtaking the results of sin. You tell me that the miracles of Jesus were supernatural. I tell you they were always restorations of the unnatural to natural positions. When He cured disease it was not a supernatural thing, but the restoration of man to the normal physical condition. He was taking away the results of sin. So all along the line of His miracles of healing and His calling back out of death He manifested His power. I see Him forevermore in grips with sin, showing men tentatively, not yet finally, how He had power to lift sins. Once, in the course of a miraculous revelation of that wonderful power, He said to a man, "Thy sins are forgiven thee," and He was immediately criticized. What was His answer to the criticism? "What reason ye in your hearts? Whether is easier, to say, Thy sins are forgiven thee; or to say, Arise and walk? But that ye may know that the Son of Man hath power on earth to forgive sins, I say unto thee, Arise, and take up thy couch." You will sadly misread that story if you think He did some piece of jugglery in the physical to convince them of His power in the moral. There was most intimate connection between the man's palsy and his sin, and Jesus demonstrated His power to lift sin by setting the man free from the result of sin and sending him on his way in sight of the men who had heard Him. These men who criticized had no more to say. They criticized Him for pretending to forgive sins, but when they saw the man raised they had enough simple mental intelligence to see the connection between the thing said and the thing done.

I come now to the final thing in this manifestation, the process of the death, for in that solemn and lonely and unapproachable hour of the cross I come to the final fulfillment of the word of the herald on the banks of the Jordan, "Behold the Lamb of God, which taketh away the sin of the world." It is not open for us in these days to attempt to interpret that word of John by the day in which we live, or by the conditions in which we live. We can interpret that word of John only by the simple facts in the midst of which he stood when he uttered it. Remember that phrase, "the Lamb of God," could have but one significance in the ears of the men who heard it. This was the voice of a Hebrew prophet speaking to Hebrews, and when he spoke of the Lamb taking away sins, they had no alternative other than to think of the long line of symbolical sacrifices which had been offered, and which they had been taught shadowed forth some great mystery of Divine purpose whereby sin might be dealt with. When John stood there in the midst of the great ethical revival which came under his preaching, and said, "Behold the Lamb of God, which taketh away the sin of the world," we must explain his language, not by any poetical license of this age, but by the deep religious intention of the man who uttered it, and by the religious understanding of the people who listened to it. In all probability, when John uttered that word there were men from all parts crowding up to the Passover Feast, taking with them lambs of sacrifice in great numbers. In the midst of all the ritual, these men were arrested by the voice of John crying, "Behold the Lamb of God, which taketh away the sin of the world." So in the hour of death you have the ultimate meaning of that great word. Whereas by manifestation, from first to last, He is forevermore dealing with sins and with sin, lifting, correcting, arresting, by gleams of light suggesting to men the deepest meaning of His mission, it is when I come to the hour of His unutterable loneliness and deep darkness and passion baptism that I have that part of the manifestation in which I see as nowhere else and as never before the meaning of my text, "He was manifested to take away sins."

Reverently let us take one step further. The manifestation and sins—as to God. Let me take you back simply to this affirmation that the manifested One was God. If that be once seen then we shall forevermore look back upon that Man of Nazareth in His birth, His life, His cross, as but a manifestation. The whole fact cannot be seen, but the whole fact is brought to the point of visibility by the way of incarnation. If indeed this One be very God manifested, then remember this, the whole measure of humanity is in Him and infinitely more than the whole measure of humanity. Do not forget the last part of my assertion. If you take the first part only—that the whole measure of humanity is in Him, you may imagine that humanity is the measure of Deity. I did not say so. But the whole measure of humanity is in Him. It is true of the whole race, from its beginning to its last, that "in Him we live and move and have our being"; that we are as to first creation and essential meaning of life, "the offspring of God." The whole race is from God and of God, and I repeat, the measure of humanity is in Him, but He is infinitely more; it is also true that the measure of all created things is in Him—and infinitely more. Beyond the utmost bound of creation, God is. All creation, heaven and earth, suns and stars and systems, angels and archangels, principalities and powers, the hierarchies of whom we hear but cannot perfectly explain their nature or their order, all these are in Him; but He is infinitely beyond them all. They are but the dust in the balances which His right hand holds, and it is an arrogant and ignorant assumption to declare that humanity is the sum of God. All humanity is within the compass of His upholding might. No man can escape from God. In some deep sense of the word, no man can live a Godless life. "If I make my bed in Sheol, behold, Thou art there. If I take the wings of the morning, and dwell in the uttermost parts of the sea; even there shall Thy hand lead me, and Thy right hand shall hold me." Humanity is not the measure of Deity; but the measure of humanity is in Deity. "He," the immeasurable, "was manifested to take away sins."

I begin to wonder. In amazement I begin to believe in the possibility of lifting the burden of my sin. The cross, like everything else, was manifestation. In the cross of Jesus there was the working out into visibility of eternal things. Love and light were wrought out into visibility by the cross. Love and light in the presence of the conditions of sin became sorrow —and became joy! In the cross I see the sorrow of God, and in the cross I see the joy of God, for "it pleased the Lord to bruise Him." In the cross I see the love of God working out through passion and power for the redemption of man. In the cross I see the light of God refusing to make any terms with iniquity and sin and evil. The cross is the historic revelation of the abiding facts within the heart of God. The measure of the cross is God. If all the measure of humanity is in God and He is more, and the measure of the cross is God, then the measure of the cross wraps humanity about so that no one individual is outside its meaning and its power. When next you ask, or hear anyone else ask, "How can one man bear the sin of the race?" say, "He cannot, and he never did." One man cannot bear the sin of another man, to say nothing of the sin of the race. He Who was manifested is God. He can gather into His eternal life all the race as to its sorrow and its sin, and bear them.

Yet remember this—I would state this with great carefulness—it was not by the eternal facts that sins were taken away, but by the manifestation of those facts. My text does not affirm, and there is no text that begins to affirm, that He Who was manifested takes away sins. There is a sense in which that is true; but this is the truth, "He was manifested to take away sins." It required the "He," the Person manifested, but it required His manifestation. Most reverently do I declare that the passion revealed in the cross was indeed the passion of God; but the passion of God became dynamic in human life when it became manifest through human form in the perfection of a life and the mystery of a death.

Man's will is the factor always to be dealt with, and whereas the sin of man was gathered into the consciousness of God and created the sorrow of God from the very beginning, it is only when that fact of the sorrow of Godhead is wrought out into visibility by manifestation that the will of man can ever be captured—or ever constrained to the position of trust and obedience which is necessary for his practical and effectual restoration to righteousness. Wherever man thus yields himself, trusting—that is the condition—his sins are taken away—lifted.

If it be declared that God might have wrought this selfsame deliverance without suffering, our answer is that the man who says so knows nothing about sin. Sin and suffering are coexistent. The moment there is sin there is suffering. The moment there are sin and suffering in a human being it is in God multiplied. "The Lamb was slain from the foundation of the world." From the moment when man in his sin became a child of sorrow, the sorrow was most keenly felt in heaven.

Yet I would that my last word should be a word specifically and especially to the man who is burdened with a sense of sin. I ask you to contemplate the Person manifested. There is not one of us here of whom it is not true that we live and move and have our being in God. God is infinitely more than I am, infinitely more than this whole congregation, infinitely more than the whole human race, from its beginning to its last. If infinitely more, then all my life is in Him. If in the mystery of incarnation there became manifest the truth that He, God, lifted sin, then I can trust. If that be the cleaving of the rock, then I can say as never before,

> "Rock of ages, cleft for me,
> Let me hide myself in Thee."

He was manifested and by that manifestation I see wrought out the infinite truth of the passion of God, what we speak of—and whether our language be the best or not, who shall tell?—as the Atonement. All the mystery of Deity was rendered visible by the Advent, the Incarnation, the Manifestation, so I know that here and now, as nineteen centuries ago on the rough Roman gibbet, as surely as God is God, here and now are the living values of the thing of which men sang and of which we still sing. Here and now I trust, and here and now I know that my sins are lifted, carried, borne away.

CHAPTER XXV

THE PURPOSE OF THE ADVENT

3. To Reveal the Father

He that hath seen Me hath seen the Father.
JOHN 14:9.

THIS IS NOW THE THIRD STUDY ON THE GENERAL SUBJECT OF the purposes of the Advent. Having spoken of the fact that Jesus was manifested to destroy the works of the devil, and of the fact that He was manifested to take away sins, we now turn to that wonderful fact that He was manifested to reveal the Father. I have chosen to take this, His own statement of truth, in this regard because of its simplicity and its sublimity. In our translation of the passage, so simple is it that no word of two syllables is employed save the word "Father." "He that hath seen Me hath seen the Father"; and yet so sublime is it that among all the things Jesus said concerning His relationship to the Father none is more comprehensive, inclusive, exhaustive than this. Its very simplicity leaves us no room for doubt as to the meaning of our Lord.

The last hours of Jesus with His disciples were passing away. He was talking to the disciples, and four times over they interrupted Him. Peter first, "Lord, whither goest Thou?" While He was yet answering Peter, Thomas said, "Lord, we know not whither Thou goest; how know we the

THE PURPOSE OF THE ADVENT

way?" While He was yet dealing with Thomas, Philip said, "Lord, show us the Father, and it sufficeth us." Ere He had done with Philip, Jude said, "What is come to pass that Thou wilt manifest Thyself unto us, and not unto the world?" The lonely Christ, recognizing the fact that the nearest friends of His life, His own followers, did not perfectly understand Him, could not walk with Him along the *via dolorosa*, were afraid of the gathering shadows, yet taught them, patiently and gently answering objections, clearing away difficulties, storing their minds with truth.

Philip's interruption was due, in the first place, to a conviction of Christ's relation in some way to the Father. He had been so long with Jesus as to become familiar in some senses with His line of thought. He had heard over and over again strange things fall from the lips of the Master. He had listened to the wonderful familiarity with which Jesus had spoken of God as "My Father." In all probability, moreover, Philip was asking that there should be repeated to him and the little group of disciples some such wonderful thing as they had read of in the past of their people's history. He would have read therein of the great and glorious theophanies of days gone by, of how the elders once ascended the mountain and saw God; of how the prophet had declared that "in the year that King Uzziah died I saw the Lord sitting upon a throne, high and lifted up, and His train filled the temple"; of how Ezekiel had declared that when he was by the river Chebar he had seen God in fire, and wheels; in majesty and glory.

It was to that request, based upon a vision of Christ's relationship to the Father, based upon the memory of how God had manifested Himself to the men of olden days, that Jesus replied. I cannot read this answer of Jesus without feeling that He divested Himself of set purpose of anything that approached stateliness of diction, and dropped into the common speech of friend to friend, as looking back into the face of Philip He said, "Have I been so long time with you, and dost thou not know Me, Philip? he that hath seen Me hath seen the Father." Mark the simplicity of it. They were most familiar with Him. I think you will agree with me that it requires no stretch of the imagination to believe that they had looked upon His face more often than upon the face of any other during the three years. They had listened with greater interest to the tones of His voice than to any other sounds that had come to them during that period.

The very simplicity of it is its audacity. The word may not be well chosen, and yet I take it of set purpose. If you want to know how audacious and daring a thing it is, put it into the lips of any other teacher the world has ever produced. Looking into the face of one man, who was voicing, though he little knew it, the great anguish of the human heart, the great hunger of the human soul, Christ said, "He that hath seen Me hath seen the Father," and in that declaration He claimed absolute identity with God. So much for the setting of my text and the claim thereof.

That claim has been vindicated in the passing of the centuries. The conception of God which is triumphant, intellectually capturing the mind, emotionally capturing the heart, volitionally capturing the will, came to the world through that One Who, standing Man before man, yet said to Him, "He that hath seen Me hath seen the Father."

My purpose this evening is not to argue but to consider. I shall ask you therefore to consider with me, first, what this revelation of God has meant to the race; and, secondly, what it has meant to the individual.

First, consider the highest knowledge of God which man

had before the Advent, and the new values consequent upon the manifestation in Jesus.

What conception of God had man before Christ came? Taking the Hebrew thought of God, let me put the whole truth as I see it into one comprehensive statement. Prior to the Advent there had been a growing intellectual apprehension of God, accompanied by a diminishing moral result. There had been a growing intellectual apprehension of truth concerning God. That is the first half of my statement. It is impossible to study the Old Testament without seeing that gradually there broke through the mists a clearer light concerning God: the fact of unity of God, the fact of the might of God, the fact of the holiness of God, the fact of the beneficence of God. These things men had come to see through the process of the ages. There had been progressive understanding of the fact of God's might. There had been progressive understanding of the fact of His holiness. There had been progressive understanding of the truth of His beneficence. Yet, side by side with this growing intellectual apprehension of God, there was diminishing moral result, for it is impossible to read the story of the ancient Hebrew people without seeing how they waxed worse and worse in all matters moral until the last. The moral life of Abraham was far purer than life in the time of the kings. Life in the early time of the kings was far purer than the conditions which the prophets ultimately described. This diminishing moral result is not to be wondered at. In proportion as men grew in their intellectual conception of God, it seemed increasingly unthinkable that He could be interested in their everyday life. Morality became something not of intimate relationship to Him and therefore something that mattered far less. In some senses that has been repeated during the last half century. The discoveries of the scientists have created an ever-increasing sense of the greatness of the universe. Every decade has given man a larger grasp upon the truth of the universe. With the progress of man's intellectual apprehension of the greatness of the universe, there has been an increase necessarily in his conception of the God of the universe, until at last God has grown out of knowledge and men have declared that He is unknowable, and have defined Him as force, as intelligence—or as the operation of force and intelligence combined. The greater the universe, the greater the God, and the greater the God, the less man has been able to appreciate his relation to Him.

Think of the great Gentile world as it then was, and as it still is, save where the message of the Evangel has reached it—for the things of the Gentile world prior to the Advent are the things of the Gentile world until this hour, save where the Gospel of the grace of God has reached it.

In Gentile thought there is always a substratum of accurate consciousness. Go where you will, get down deeply enough, and you will find in the common consciousness of humanity a substratum of truth. When it begins to express itself it does so falsely. When it begins to take that deep underlying conviction, and put it into form or expression it breaks down; but there is universally a sense of God.

Occasional flashes of light have broken out of this underlying subconsciousness. We have had such remarkable teachers as Zoroaster, Buddha, Confucius, men speaking true things flashing with a new light.

Notwithstanding these things, a perpetual failure in morals and a uniform degradation of religion have been universal. No voice which has spoken some message of truth out of the subconsciousness in the passing of the centuries has been able to lift those to whom it has been addressed in the moral scale. The history of the Hindu religion is, perhaps, the most conspicuous illustration of this fact. Buddhism as it is practiced today and Buddhism as Buddha lived and taught are at the poles asunder.

Wherever you find Gentile nations you find these things true—a substratum of accurate consciousness, occasional flashes of clear light, but perpetual failure in morals and uniform degradation of religion. The failure has ever been due to lack of final knowledge concerning God.

At last there came the song of the angels and the birth of a child. At the close of one swiftly passing generation of teaching and of working, of gathering a few souls together, there stood One in the midst of a little group of disciples, and at the same moment in the midst of all humanity, and He looked into the face of one man and said, "He that hath seen Me hath seen the Father."

Through that Advent and ministry there came to men a new consciousness of God.

I turn to the centuries that have passed since His coming. What effect has that coming had in the realm of revelation? By that I mean among those who had received revelation from God. First, the inclusion in His teaching and manifestation of all the essential things which men had learned in the long ages of the past. He did not deny the truth of the unity of God. He re-emphasized it. He did not deny the might of God. He declared it and manifested it in many a gentle touch of infinite power. He did not deny the holiness of God. He insisted upon it in teaching and life, and at last by the mystery of dying. He did not deny the beneficence of God. He changed the cold word "beneficence" into the word throbbing with the infinite heart of Deity, "love"! He did more. He brought to men the new, that toward which they had been groping but had never found. That which men had imperfectly expressed in song and prophecy He came to state. "He that hath seen Me hath seen the Father." Not Elohim, not Jehovah, not Adonahy, none of the great names of the past, all of them suggestive, but "He that hath seen Me, hath seen *the Father*." In and through Him that truth of fatherhood was revealed. When I say that I beseech you remember that fatherhood means a great deal more than we sometimes imagine it means. It is not merely a term of tenderness. It is also a term of law and discipline. But Fatherhood means supremely that if the child have wandered away the Father will suffer everything to save and bring it home again. Within the realm of revealed religion this truth emerged, that the one God, mighty, holy, beneficent, is the Father Who will sacrifice Himself to save the child. There man found the point of contact in infinite love which never abandons him, never leaves him. That is the truth which, coming into revealed religion, saved it from being intellectual apprehension minus moral dynamic, and sent running through all human life rivers of cleansing, renewal, regeneration.

Wherever Christ comes to people who have never had direct revelation, He comes first of all as fulfillment of all that in their thought and scheme is true. He comes, moreover, for the correction of all that in their thought and scheme is false. All the underlying consciousness of humanity concerning God is touched and answered, and lifted into the supreme consciousness whenever God is seen in Christ. All the gleams of light which have been flashing across the consciousness of humanity merge into the essential light when He is presented. I will take the illustration which is the lowest and the simplest, and therefore perhaps the profoundest at this point. It is an old story, I have often used it before. In Africa are found men of whom we speak as superstitious, perhaps the lowest in all the scale intellectually. The only form of religion they have is that of which we speak as fetish worship, which means nothing less and nothing more than that the uninstructed mind of the savage connects with some charm—a little piece of stick, a little piece of leather—certain values that are beyond his ken, supernatural values. He does not think it possible to be fortunate in business, in pleasure, in home or in marriage or anything else save as he is accompanied by his fetish. That is a low form of religion. You smile at it—and yet I know of people in England who carry charms about with them. In Africa, if you are about to trade with one of these men after he has driven his cattle hundreds of miles, and discovers that in his unutterable folly he has not brought his fetish with him, you cannot persuade him to trade with you. He will tramp all the weary miles back again, and postpone his traffic for days, weeks, months, because he cannot trade unless that fetish is with him. You smile at him. When Jesus meets that man he does not destroy that belief. He fulfills it. Christ comes to him and says in effect, "You are perfectly right in your underlying consciousness that you cannot be fortunate in business or home or marriage or pleasure unless you have dealing with the thing that is more than you are, the supernatural. You must have God with you." Jesus takes out of the black hand the fetish, the little piece of leather or stick, and flings it away and puts back into the hand His own pierced hand, saying, "Lo, I am with you all the days—business days, pleasure days, home days, all the days. Never do business without God." Before you mock the African who will not traffic without his fetish learn this, that if you do business without God you are far more heathen than he is. Christ comes not to contradict the essential truth of Buddhism but to fulfill it. He comes not to rob the Chinaman of his regard for parents, as taught by Confucius, but to fulfill it, and to lift him upon that regard into regard for the One great Father, God. He comes always to fulfill. Wherever He has come, wherever He has been presented, wherever men, low or high in the intellectual scale, have seen God in Christ, their hands have opened and they have dropped the fetishes and the idols and have yielded themselves to Him. If the world has not come to God through Him it is because the world has not yet seen Him; and if the world has not yet seen Him the blame is upon the Christian Church.

The wide issues of the manifestation of God in Christ are the union of intellectual apprehension and moral improvement, and the relation of religion to life. When you are tempted to admire Buddhism, or to admire Confucianism, and to think that in these God has spoken to men, never forget that in no system of religion in the world has there come to men the idea of God which unites religion with morals save in this revelation of God in Jesus Christ. There is through all India today divorce between religion and morals. There a man may be the most immoral of all men and yet be religiously a saint. But wherever this manifestation of God comes, and the heart of God and the sacrifice of God, behind His unity and His might, His holiness and beneficence, emerge into view, there men have found that religion means morality.

I pass, in the second place, to say some few words concerning the effect of the manifestation in relation to the individual. Here I propose to see one man as illustration. I think we cannot be truer to the text than by taking Philip, the man to whom Christ spoke. Mark the words of Jesus to him, "Have I been so long time with you, and dost thou not know Me, Philip?" The evident sense of the question is, "You have seen enough of Me, Philip, if you have really seen Me, to have found what you are asking for, a vision of God." There is no other interpretation of Christ's question possible. "Show us the Father and it sufficeth us," was Philip's request. "Have I been so long time with you, and dost thou not know Me, Philip? he that hath seen Me hath seen the Father." He surely meant that Philip had seen enough of Him to have found the Father. What, then, had Philip seen? What revelations of Deity had come to this man who thought he had not seen and did not understand? Christ evidently intended to say he might have seen and might have understood. What were the things to which Christ referred? I am not going to indulge in speculation. I might gather up the general facts of His teaching and His doing, but I think we shall be safer if we adhere to what Scripture tells of what Philip had seen.

All the story is in John. Philip is referred to by Matthew, Mark, and Luke as being among the number of the Apostles, but in no other way. John tells me of four occasions when Philip is seen in union with Christ. I will take the first three, for the last is the one in which our text occurs. Philip was the first man Jesus called to follow him. I do not say the first man to follow Him. There were other two who preceded Philip, going after Christ in consequence of the teaching of John. Philip did not go to inquire. It is distinctly stated in the first chapter of John's Gospel that Jesus found him and said, "Follow Me." That was the first man to whom Christ used that great formula of calling men which has become so precious in the passing of the centuries. "Follow Me." What happened? "Philip findeth Nathaniel, and saith unto Him, We have found Him, of whom Moses in the law, and the prophets, did write." That was the first thing that Philip had seen in Christ, according to his own confession, One Who embodied all the ideals of Moses and the prophets. When he said, "We have found Him, of Whom Moses in the law, and the prophets, did write," he did not refer to any particular word of Moses. The word he used covers the whole of the Old Testament teaching. What he meant was, "We have found Him Who embodies the ideal of Moses, and the ideal of the prophets, all the teaching of Moses, all the messages of the prophets. We have found Him." It was the cry of a soul inviting another soul. It was the cry of a soul who had this conviction borne in upon it— Here is One Who fulfills all the ideals and suggestions and intentions of the whole religious economy of the past! That was the first thought.

I find Philip next in the sixth chapter, when the multitudes were about Christ and they were hungry. Jesus singled out Philip and said to him, "Whence are we to buy bread, that these may eat?" John is very careful to state that Jesus did not ask that question because He needed advice, "for He Himself knew what He would do." He asked it to prove Philip. Philip answered, "Two hundred pennyworth of bread is not sufficient, that everyone may take a little." That is the background. What happened next? Philip, who considered it impossible to feed the hungry multitude, is next seen with the other disciples seating them ready to be fed, incredulously, perhaps; I do not know. Then he watched this selfsame Jesus take the loaves and fishes of the lad and break them. Then with the others he carried the food to rank after rank until all the assembled multitude were fed. So that Philip had now seen Someone Who in a mysterious way had resource enough to satisfy human hunger. That is not all. Philip then listened while in matchless discourse Jesus lifted the thought from material hunger to spiritual need and declared, "I am the Bread of Life." So that the second vision Philip had of Jesus, according to the record, was a vision of Him full of resource and able to satisfy hunger both material and spiritual. I see Philip next in the twelfth chapter. The Greeks coming to him said, "Sir, we would see Jesus." Philip found his way with Andrew to Jesus, and asked Him to see the Greeks. Mark the relation with the Father, and that there was perfect harmony between them, no conflict, no controversy. He saw, moreover, that upon the basis of that communion with His Father and that perfect harmony, His voice changed from the tones of sorrow to those of triumph, "Now is the judgment of this world: now shall the prince of this world be cast out. And I, if I be lifted up from the earth, will draw all men unto Myself." That was Philip's third vision of Jesus. It was the vision of One acting in perfect accord with God, bending to the sorrow that surged upon His soul in order that through it He might accomplish human redemption.

We now come back to the last scene. Philip said, "Show us the Father and it sufficeth us." Gathering up all the things of the past, Christ looked into the face of Philip and replied, "Have I been so long time with you, and dost thou not know Me, Philip? When thou didst first see Me did there not come to thee the conviction that in Me there was the embodiment of law and righteousness? When thou didst watch Me feed men didst thou not understand that I am the One Who can satisfy all the hunger of the human heart? In the mystery of that strange hour when thou didst bring the Greeks to Me didst thou not understand that in union with God I am moving toward unutterable pain in order that men may be set free?" No, Philip had not seen these things. We are not to blame him. They were there to be seen, and by and by, the infinite work of Christ being accomplished and the glory of Pentecost having dawned upon the world, Philip saw it all. Then Philip saw the meaning of the things he had seen and had never seen, the things he had looked upon and had never understood. Then Philip found that having seen Jesus he had actually seen the Father. When he looked upon One Who embodied in His own personality all the facts of the law and righteousness, he had seen God. When he had looked upon One Who could touch the loaves of a lad until they fed a multitude, and One Who could deal with the spiritual needs of restless hearts until they were rested, he had seen God. When he had seen a Man Who shrank from sorrow yet pressed into it because through it in co-operation with God He could ransom humanity, he had seen God.

This manifestation wins the submission of the reason. This manifestation appeals to the love of the heart. This manifestation demands the surrender of the will. Here is the value of the Advent as revelation of God.

Let my last word be one in which I ask you solemnly to see what this means in your case. Call back your thoughts from the wider application of the earlier part of my sermon. Call back your thoughts for a moment from the particular application in the case of Philip, and think what this means to you. Is it true that this manifestation wins the submission of your reason, appeals to the love of your heart, asks the surrender of your will? Then to refuse God in Christ is to violate at some essential point your own manhood. To refuse, you must violate reason which is captured by the revelation, or you must crush the emotion which springs in your heart in the presence of the revelation, or you must decline to submit your will to the demands which the manifestation makes.

May God grant that we shall rather look into His face and say, "My Lord and my God"! So shall we find our rest and our hearts be satisfied. It shall suffice as we see the Father in the Christ.

CHAPTER XXVI

THE PURPOSE OF THE ADVENT

4. To Prepare for a Second Advent

Christ also, having been once offered to bear the sins of many, shall appear a second time, apart from sin, to them that wait for Him, unto salvation.
HEBREWS 9:28.

WE COME THIS EVENING TO CONSIDER THE LAST OF THE FOUR great values of the first Advent. We have spoken together of the fact that He was manifested to take away sins, that He was manifested to reveal the Father; and now we come finally to this great truth that He was manifested to prepare for another manifestation, that He came once in order that He might be able to come again. All the things of which we have spoken as constituting the values of the first Advent were necessary in order that there should be another Advent.

Our thoughts are turning with gladness to the first coming of Jesus. The light that shone o'er the plains is shining around us; the songs which the shepherds heard we also hear; and the new hope that filled the hearts of shepherds and Wise Men in that Eastern land at the Advent of Jesus is in our hearts at this time.

Yet we are all conscious that nothing is perfect, that the

things which He came to do are not yet done, that the works of the devil are not yet finally destroyed, that sins are not yet experimentally taken away, that in the spiritual consciousness of the race God is not yet perfectly known. As the writer of this said in another connection, "Now we see not yet all things subjected to Him." The victory seems not to be won. There seems to be very, very much still to do. Or, if I may put this into another form, it is impossible to read the story of the first Advent and to believe in it, and to follow the history of the centuries that have followed upon that Advent, without feeling in one's deepest heart that something more is needed. The first Advent demands something else.

Therefore, we turn with relief to the declaration of the New Testament which formed the very hope and song of the Early Church, the declaration which states that He Who has come will come, that the first Advent was indeed preparatory, and that the consummation of its meaning can be brought about only by another coming, as personal, as definite, as positive, as real in human history as was the first.

Think of the fact stated in my text: "Christ . . . shall appear a second time." There is no escape, other than by casuistry, from the simple meaning of these words. The first idea conveyed by them is that of an actual personal advent of Jesus yet to be. To spiritualize a statement like this and to attempt to make application of it in any other than the way in which a little child would understand it is to be driven, one is almost inclined to say, to dishonesty with the simplicity of the Scriptural declaration.

This statement is not peculiar to the letter from which it is taken. It is the teaching of the whole of the New Testament. To the man who has given up the New Testament as final, authoritative, and infallible, I have no appeal. We have

THE PURPOSE OF THE ADVENT 341

no common ground. If you are attempting to erect a Christian structure upon your philosophizing I have no time to argue with you. I respect your conviction, I believe in your honesty, but I part company with you. To me the New Testament is the living, final, absolutely infallible Word of God.

I find a great many Christian people, however, who believe that as surely as I do, who yet seem not to be perfectly sure of a second personal Advent of the same Jesus. I repeat, and again I would say it carefully, with no desire to offend or hurt the convictions of any, that you cannot take your New Testament and read it simply and honestly without coming to the conclusion that the Christ Who came is still to come. There may be diversities of interpretations as to how He will come and when He will come. I am not discussing these tonight. We may part company as to whether He will come to usher in a millennium or to crown it. I think that is important, but I am not careful now to argue it. When the risen Christ had passed out of the sight of the men who waited upon the mountain side and in astonishment looked at the clouds which had received Him, angels appeared to them who said, "This Jesus, which was received up from you into heaven, shall so come in like manner as ye beheld Him going into heaven." He is coming or the angels were wrong.

Paul in all his writings is conscious of this truth of the second Advent. In some of them he does not dwell upon it at such great length or with such clearness as in others, for the simple reason that it is not the specific subject with which he is dealing. In the Thessalonian letters you have most clearly set forth Paul's teaching concerning this matter. In the very center of the first letter we have a passage which declares in unmistakable language that "the Lord Himself shall descend from heaven, with a shout, with the voice of the archangel, and with the trump of God: and the dead in Christ shall rise first: then we that are alive, that are left, shall together be caught up in the clouds to meet the Lord in the air, and so shall we ever be with the Lord." "It was this hope which more than anything gave its color to the primitive Christianity, its unworldliness, its moral intensity, its command of the future even in this life." The latter sentence is a quotation from the book of a man who does not hold the position I hold, who does not believe as I believe in the actual second personal Advent of Jesus, who, nevertheless, recognizes that this view gave the bloom to primitive Christianity and constituted the power of the early Christians to laugh in the face of death, and to overcome all forces which were against them.

That is not peculiarly Pauline. Writing to those who were in affliction, James said, "Be ye also patient; stablish your hearts; for the coming of the Lord is at hand."

With equal clearness, Peter said to the early disciples, "Be sober and set your hope perfectly on the grace that is to be brought unto you at the revelation of Jesus Christ."

John, who leaned upon his Master's bosom, and who wrote the most wonderful of all mystic words concerning Him, said, "We know that, if He shall be manifested, we shall be like Him; for we shall see Him even as He is. And everyone that hath this hope set on Him purifieth himself, even as He is pure."

Jude said to those to whom he wrote, "Ye, beloved, building up yourselves on your most holy faith, praying in the Holy Spirit, keep yourselves in the love of God, looking for the mercy of our Lord Jesus Christ unto eternal life."

That is but a rapid passing over of the great field of New Testament teaching. To summarize yet more briefly the things to which I have already referred, I would declare that every New Testament writer presents this truth as a part of the common Christian faith. I believe there is nothing more needed in our day than a new declaration of this vital fact of Christian faith. Think what it would mean if the whole Church still lifted her face toward the East and waited for the morning, waited as the Lord would have her wait—not star-gazing and almanac examining, but, with loins girt for service and lamps burning, waiting as she serves. If the whole Christian Church were so waiting she would cast off her worldliness and infidelity and all other things which hinder her march to conquest. It is because we have lost the bloom of hope that our songs are so poor. If we may but hear again the promises of the New Testament, the assurances of the Word that He Who came is coming, then there will be strength in service and new fortitude for suffering, and new hope for all the world in its sin and its sorrow and its sighing.

Our text does more than affirm the fact of the second Advent. In a somewhat remarkable way, it declares the meaning thereof, "Christ . . . shall appear a second time, *apart from sin*."

To understand this rightly we must look upon it as putting the second Advent into contrast with the first. That is what the writer most evidently means, for the context declares that Jesus was manifested in the consummation of the ages, to bear sins. That we have considered. He now says that "Christ . . . shall appear a second time, apart from sin." Consequently, I repeat, to understand this rightly we must look upon it as putting the second Advent in contrast with the first. All the things of the first Advent were necessary to the second, but all the things of the second will be different from the things of the first. The whole of the first Advent was conditioned within the fact of sin. Jesus came to deal with sin. By His first Advent sin was revealed. Men never truly understood the meaning thereof until He came, and by the light of His presence in human history flung it into clear relief. From the slaughter of the innocents which accompanied His birth to His own death upon the cross His presence in the world flung hatred into view. The slaughter of the innocents was the action of a false king who feared a new king coming to snatch his scepter, and hatred manifested itself in devilish cruelty to little children. Our Lord's own cross was the place where all the deep hatred of the human heart expressed itself most diabolically in view of heaven and earth and hell.

There was also revelation of darkness as contrary to light. "Men loved the darkness rather than the light," was the supreme wail of the heart of Jesus. His presence in the world was, moreover, revelation of spiritual death as contrary to life. In the perpetual attempt of men to materialize His work, the attempt of His own disciples as well as all the rest, and their absolute failure to appreciate the spiritual teaching He gave, we see what spiritual death really is.

In His first Advent He not only revealed sin but bore it. In the words, "Christ also, having been once offered to bear the sins of many," the reference is not merely to the final movement of the cross. The word "offered" is used in reference to God's action in giving Him. It would be perfectly correct interpretation to supply the word "offered" by the word "gave," the word which you have in John's Gospel, "For God so loved the world, that He *gave* His only begotten Son." Let us put that word here, "Christ also, having been once *given* to bear the sins of many, shall appear a second time." All through His life He bore sin. All through the long, long days, He was putting Himself underneath sin in order to take it away. He bore its limitations throughout

THE PURPOSE OF THE ADVENT

the whole of His life. In poverty, in sorrow, in loneliness He lived, and all these things are limitations resulting from sin. All poverty is the issue of sin. It is well we should remember that. The problem of poverty has a deeper problem lying at its heart which is the problem of sin. I do not mean that the poor man is the sinner always. Far from it. It is very easy for people who live in comparative ease and comfort, or in affluence, to write about the blessings of poverty. There are no blessings of poverty save as God does overrule all the grinding and crushing of human life for some essential good. All poverty is the result of sin, either of the man who is poor or of some other who is robbing him. When Jesus Christ entered into flesh He entered into the limitations which follow upon sin and He bore sin in His own consciousness through all the years. Not poverty only, but sorrow in all forms. Sorrow is lack. The sorrow of bereavement is the lack of the friend. Every sorrow is a sense of lack, something wanting, something gone, and Jesus lived through all the years "a man of sorrows, and acquainted with grief." And in His long loneliness He lived in the midst of limitations resulting from sin. Finally gathering all these things to a crisis, He reached the ultimate issue of sin, bearing it, carrying it, lifting it, placing Himself, very God as well as very man, underneath it until all its weight was upon Him—the weight of its poverty, for "though He was rich, yet for your sakes He became poor"; the weight of its sorrow, for all the sorrows of the human heart were upon His heart until He uttered that unspeakable cry, "My God, My God, why hast Thou forsaken Me?" Such was the story of the first Advent.

Now hear my text. Having finally dealt with sin and destroyed it at its very root in His first Advent, Jesus' next coming, His second Advent, is to be that of victory. He will come again, not to poverty but to wealth. He will come again, not to sorrow but with all joy. He will come again, not in loneliness, but to gather about Him all trusting souls who have looked and served and waited. We are celebrating the Advent when there was no room for Him in the inn. When He comes again the whole world and the universe will make haste to make room for Him. At the close of the first Advent we saw Him holding the reed of mockery, robed in the purple of contempt, crowned with thorns, surrounded by a mob. When He comes again He will hold the scepter of the universe in His right hand; upon His brow there will be many diadems; He will be panoplied with all the splendor of God, and ten thousand times ten thousand angels will be the cohorts that accompany Him. All in His first Advent of sorrow and loneliness, of poverty and of sin, will be absent from the second. The first Advent was for atonement, the second will be for administration. He came, entering into human nature and taking hold of it, to deal with sin and put it away. He has taken sin away, and He will come again to set up that Kingdom, the foundations of which He laid in His first coming.

I pause for one moment to say I am not dealing with the different phases of the Advent, with the fact that He will first gather His Church to Himself and then establish the Kingdom on earth. I am viewing the whole in general outline, recognizing the different phases, but insisting now only upon the glorious and gracious fact that this One Who came is yet to come.

Let us go one step further, and we shall find that my text declares the purpose of the Advent. "It is appointed unto men once to die, and after this cometh judgment; so Christ also, having been once offered to bear the sins of many, shall appear a second time, apart from sin, to them that wait for

Him, unto salvation." A similarity is suggested. "It is appointed unto men once to die, and after this cometh judgment." Over against that dual appointment stands "So Christ also, having been once offered to bear the sins of many, shall appear a second time, apart from sin, to them that wait for Him, unto salvation." As His first Advent was parallel to the appointment of death, His second Advent is parallel to the appointment of judgment. "It is appointed unto men once to die . . . Christ also, having been once offered to bear the sins of many." It is appointed that after death there shall be judgment—He "shall appear a second time, apart from sin . . ." But the contrast seems to break down. The similarity is not carried out. There is a strange differentiation in the ending of the two declarations, and we must notice it. We expected that it would have been written to complete the comparison, thus, "It is appointed unto men once to die, and after this cometh judgment; so Christ also, having been once offered to bear the sins of many, shall appear a second time, apart from sin, unto *judgment*." That would seem to be a balanced comparison, but the writer does not so write. Notice how this very difference unfolds the meaning of the first and second Advents. It is appointed to men to die—He was offered to bear the sins of many. After death judgment—He is coming again unto salvation. As the first Advent negatived the death appointed unto men, the second Advent will turn the judgment into salvation.

"It is appointed unto men once to die." It is often somewhat carelessly affirmed that men must die. While admitting the truth of this statement, we inquire *why* must they die? Ask the scientist. Science can no more account for death than it can account for life. It has never been able to explain the mystery of the beginning of life. It has never yet been able to say why men die. *How* they die, yes; *why* they die, no!

We are all reconstructed on the physical side every seven years. The essential personality is not reconstructed, but maintains its individuality through all the processes of reconstruction. I am the man I was seven years ago, and yet there is not a particle of this tabernacle, through the medium of which I speak to you tonight, that would have been here had I been here seven years ago. Waste of tissue and breakdown of the physical is a constant process of remaking. The mental in man gains breadth and strength and beauty as years pass on. The man who has run out the allotted three score years and ten, or for whom God has lengthened the lease a few years, mentally and spiritually is greater than he has ever been before, but the reconstruction of the physical is not quite so perfect as it used to be, the elasticity is missing, the vision is becoming dim, the new-made temple is not quite so fibrous and tough as the old one. Why? I wait for scientific answer, but I wait in vain. No man without revelation has ever been able to tell me why the physical ceases at maturity to reconstruct itself with ever-increasing strength. I will tell you why. Death is the wage of sin. Science will admit that death comes by the breaking of certain laws. Science will use some other word than the word "sin." Sir Oliver Lodge tells us that sensible men do not use the word "sin." I am a little tired of the Church's worship of Sir Oliver Lodge. I am surprised at the way Christian ministers have welcomed his creed. I have every respect for him as an honest scientist, but he does not understand Christianity. His creed is not the Christian creed. If there is no place for "sin" and "blood," there is no room for Jesus Christ. "It is appointed unto men once to die" by the fiat of God Almighty because they are sinners, and no man can escape that fiat.

But Jesus Christ was offered by God to bear the sins of

many—that was the answer of the first Advent to man's appointment to death.

Beyond death there is another appointment, that of judgment.

Who shall appeal against the absolute justice of that appointment? He "shall appear a second time, apart from sin . . . unto salvation." To those who have heard the message of the first Advent and have believed it, and trusted in His great work, and have found shelter in the mystery of His manifestation and bearing of sin, to such, salvation takes the place of judgment. But to the man who will not shelter beneath that first Advent and its atoning value judgment abides. All the things begun by His first Advent will be consummated by the second.

At His second Advent there will be complete salvation for the individual—Righteousness, Sanctification, Redemption. We believed, and were saved. We believe, and are being saved. We believe, and we shall be saved. The last movment will come when Our Lord comes.

What of those who have fallen on sleep? They are safe with God and He will bring them with Him when He comes. They are not yet perfected, "God having provided some better thing concerning us, that apart from us they should not be perfected." They are at rest and consciously at rest. They are "absent from the body . . . at home with the Lord," but they are not yet perfected, they are waiting. We are waiting in the midst of earth's struggle, they in heaven's light and joy, for the second Advent. Heaven is waiting for it. Earth is waiting for it. Hell is waiting for it. The universe is waiting for it.

That coming will be to those who wait for Him. Who are those who wait for Him? Let Scripture interpret this. In the Thessalonian Epistle I find Paul's description of the early Christians, "Ye turned unto God from idols, to serve a living and true God, and to wait for His Son from heaven." The first thing is the turning from idols. Have you done that? The second thing is serving the living God. Are you doing that? Then because you have turned from idols and are serving Him you are waiting. That is the waiting the New Testament enjoins, and to those who wait, His second Advent will mean salvation. There is waiting other than that, but we have no share in it. That is our waiting, because we have heard the Evangel of the first Advent and know it. The whole creation waiteth, "groaneth and travaileth in pain together until now." I hear the sob of the waiting myriads in China and Africa and India. They are waiting. They have never yet heard of the first Advent. They are waiting. They know not for what. They cry as a child in the night, with no language but a cry. Oh the pathos and the tragedy of it!

"Christ shall appear." Glorious Gospel! He shall appear, to heal the wounds of all creation. "He comes to break oppression and set the captives free." He is coming to rule with a rod of iron, which means absolute and inflexible equity. Ofttimes there is more love in justice than in mercy. When He Who came in meek mercy long ago comes again, He will come in majestic might, and also in love. He will come to gather out His trusting souls and then to establish His own rule and set up His own government. What a day of burning it will be for some! What terror will come to the hearts of those who have lived and fattened upon devilism!

He is coming! That is my hope and confidence. That is my hope and my song for the world this Christmastime. He came to commence, to initiate. He will come to complete. "Christ . . . shall appear a second time, apart from sin . . .

unto salvation." Salvation means judgment wrought out in the impulse and power of love.

We stand tonight between the Advents. Our relation to the first creates our relation to the second. To receive Him as rejected is to be received by Him at His coronation. To accept His estimate of sin and share in the value of His atoning work is to enter into His coming administration of righteousness. To trust in the first is to wait for the second.

How stands it between my soul and the Advents, first and second? I am not trying to cast a cloud over the merriment of Christmastime. But have a reason for your merriment, and in God's name cease your merriment if the Child Who was born, and of Whom you sing, is excluded from your heart and hearth and home. The blasphemy of it! The tragedy of it! The shame of it! People who by persistent sin are crucifying this Christ afresh every day yet make merry this Christmastime. If you have admitted Him and found room for Him for Whom there was no room in the inn, if you have handed Him the kingdom of your life though the world still rejects Him as in the days of old, then make merry. Let your songs abound. Let your hearts be glad. Give the children a good time. But I warn you against all merriment if you have shut Him out, for He comes again, and if, in spite of the light of the first Advent you have rejected Him, He must, on the basis of eternal justice, reject you. He is coming. May we so trust Him as to the meaning and merit of His first Advent as not to be ashamed of Him when He comes again!

www.ingramcontent.com/pod-product-compliance
Lightning Source LLC
Chambersburg PA
CBHW052142300426
44115CB00011B/1491